PLOU

Fall 2005

GUEST EDITOR
Antonya Nelson

EDITOR
Don Lee

MANAGING EDITOR
Robert Arnold

POETRY EDITOR
David Daniel

ASSOCIATE FICTION EDITOR
Maryanne O'Hara

FOUNDING EDITOR
DeWitt Henry

FOUNDING PUBLISHER
Peter O'Malley

PLOUGHSHARES, a journal of new writing, is guest-edited serially by prominent writers who explore different and personal visions, aesthetics, and literary circles. PLOUGHSHARES is published in April, August, and December at Emerson College, 120 Boylston Street, Boston, MA 02116-4624. Telephone: (617) 824-8753. Web address: www.pshares.org.

SUBSCRIPTIONS (ISSN 0048-4474): $24 for one year (3 issues), $46 for two years (6 issues); $27 a year for institutions. Add $12 a year for international ($10 for Canada).

UPCOMING: Winter 2005–06, a poetry and fiction issue edited by David St. John, will appear in December 2005. Spring 2006, a poetry and fiction issue edited by Kevin Young, will appear in April 2006.

SUBMISSIONS: Reading period is from August 1 to March 31 (postmark dates). All submissions sent from April to July are returned unread. Please see page 234 for editorial and submission policies.

Back-issue, classroom-adoption, and bulk orders may be placed directly through PLOUGHSHARES. Microfilms of back issues may be obtained from University Microfilms. PLOUGHSHARES is also available as CD-ROM and full-text products from EBSCO, H.W. Wilson, ProQuest, and the Gale Group. Indexed in M.L.A. Bibliography, American Humanities Index, Index of American Periodical Verse, Book Review Index. Full publisher's index is online at www.pshares.org. The views and opinions expressed in this journal are solely those of the authors. All rights for individual works revert to the authors upon publication.

PLOUGHSHARES receives support from the National Endowment for the Arts and the Massachusetts Cultural Council.

Retail distribution by Ingram Periodicals and Bernhard DeBoer. Printed in the U.S.A. on recycled paper by Capital City Press.

 ISBN 1-933058-01-3

CONTENTS

Fall 2005

Cover art: *Dangerous Words* by Maysey Craddock
Mixed media on paper, 12″ x 8″, 2000
Note: The cover image was digitally extended.
Courtesy of Francine Seders Gallery

Ploughshares Patrons

This nonprofit publication would not be possible without the support of our readers and the generosity of the following individuals and organizations.

COUNCIL

William H. Berman
Denise and Mel Cohen
Robert E. Courtemanche
Jeff and Jan Greenhawt
Jacqueline Liebergott
Turow Foundation
Eugenia Gladstone Vogel
Marillyn Zacharis

PATRON

Linda C. Wisnewski
William Collatos Family Foundation

FRIENDS

Robert Hildreth
Tom Jenks and Carol Edgarian
Howard M. Liberman
Patrick O'Brien
Christopher and Colleen Palermo

ORGANIZATIONS

Emerson College
Houghton Mifflin
Lannan Foundation
Massachusetts Cultural Council
National Endowment for the Arts

COUNCIL: $3,000 for two lifetime subscriptions and acknowledgement in the journal for three years.
PATRON: $1,000 for a lifetime subscription and acknowledgement in the journal for two years.
FRIEND: $500 for a lifetime subscription and acknowledgement in the journal for one year.

ANTONYA NELSON

Introduction

In Story v. Novel, the story nearly always wins. In my opinion. I've written in both genres, and these days, when asked which I prefer, I say story. I like the precision of the language, the focus of the angle, the intensity placed on the moment. I like spending just that length of time, and no more, with that person and his or her mess. I have a short attention span. I grow impatient.

I've heard that's true of our national nature, in general, that we're in a hurry, *USA Today* far outsells *The New York Times*, and that immediate gratification still far outranks that other sort. We want our food fast and our weight loss even faster. We absorb information best delivered via bumper sticker. If this is so, I wonder why the short story isn't preferred by the Average Reader, that army of ADD-afflicted people who must make up the general and book-buying public. Take a poll, and you'll find that most people in the Story v. Novel conflict favor the novel. Just this spring *The Atlantic Monthly* joined many of its slick magazine peers by announcing that it would be cutting back on its offerings of short stories.

As for being a fiction writer, neither your agent nor anyone affiliated with New York publishing houses want to hear that the three hundred pages of prose you're prepared to send to them is a collection of stories. Their latest strategy in addressing this dilemma is to ask that you at least attempt to wrest a "Story Cycle" out of your collection, find some way or other to make the book resemble a novel. That, and the promise that, next time, you'll get your act together and produce something they can sink their teeth into, something they can take to the bank, a real live novel.

So okay, if we're so vapid and busy and distractible, this country of book buyers and readers, why do New York and John Q. Public desire the *longer* form? I'll take a stab at addressing this seeming paradox: short stories are depressing. Ask any undergraduate member of a class reading them exclusively. Short stories tell the tale of a single suffering soul—the man who's wakened to find himself transformed into a giant bug; the woman set loose in a landscape where the killer Misfit is afoot; the guy fixated on mending, replacing, adoring, and then losing his *overcoat;* or poor Nick Adams, who is sent relentlessly by his author to learn lessons he'd rather not know; or those Chekhovian mopes whose humanity is only restored after an intimate brush with humiliation. Short stories are about individuals, these mentioned above and many others. They are generally in the process of losing something (idealism, innocence, health, virginity, friends, a spouse, a child, a parent, their very life) with only the consolation of spiritual enlightenment to compensate. And said compensation, btw, is oftentimes a moot point, since, in many instances, the character has died and it's actually the reader who stands to benefit.

As I see it, that's the problem with rooting for the short story: it's usually about an individual. And the shape of an individual's life is fixed: beginning, middle, end, which is to say: birth, life, death. The organic trajectory of a short story seems to reflect that basic, inevitable shape. In general, it declines.

But novels are usually about communities. There are whole groups of people for the reader to follow around, whether it's a small community like a family, or a big one like czarist Russia or turn-of-the-century New York City. And communities, unlike individuals, mostly survive. They carry on, even in the face of losing individual members; their trajectory, in other words, is not about decline but about sustenance, growth even. And I think that the reading public would rather take home that message, that one about enduring rather than expiring. There are many ways to reconcile death, to make peace with it, and I think the human animal instinctively gravitates toward reassurance that there's some point to its existence. Our children and grandchildren provide similar comfort: we won't be here, but they will. Sometimes that allows the panic-stricken mortal to breathe deeply and keep going.

The short story is a truncated exposure to a moment—protracted or brief—in an individual's existence. This character is generally in crisis, and the crisis reveals his or her true personality, the sum total of humanity available to him or her, and it's oftentimes insufficient. Woefully so. As a reader, you might identify with that sense of feeling inadequate to the task before you, and you might take some solace from the story, might deeply embrace some essential truth about the human condition and its puny, pathetic, highly limited frailty. Maybe. But maybe it just kills your buzz to read those depressing short stories that reiterate what you've no doubt already intuited: one sad day you're going to die. Many people don't like short stories—don't like them, don't understand them, won't read them, won't buy books of them.

Wouldn't take the care and time to write them well, wouldn't know where to send them when they were ready, couldn't enjoy the fruits of those labors in the form of the contents of this journal.

But there's "you," communal, and then there's "you," individual.

That's right, *you.*

BETH ALVARADO

Just Family

Rachel was the one who delivered the message. In the middle of dinner, she remembered the phone call, stood up, tossed her braid over her shoulder, and dug in her pocket for a scrap of paper. "Mom," then she looked warily at her father, "Dad, the prison called again today." She squinted at her eight-year-old scrawl. "They said Uncle Tony gets out tomorrow afternoon. He can be picked up at the a-n-n-e-x."

Ellen sighed. "You remember your uncle Tony," she said, keeping her voice light, wanting to reassure her daughter. She knew she should be feeling, if not elated, then at least relieved, as if the long ordeal were finally over and Tony could rejoin the living. After all, in the cosmic scheme of things, his crimes were like the buzzing of a gnat. She knew this. Still. She knew what prison could do to a man, remembered all the guys they'd known in the old days, how they came out jumpy as hell. Mean. Just like when guys got home from Nam. No telling what would set them off. And, like them, Tony was being released to nothing: no home, no wife, no friends, a daughter he didn't even know. Nothing. *Nada.*

But Rachel just shrugged. What was there to remember? She was only three when he got sent up. Five years ago. They'd only been to visit him once.

"It'll be okay, *mi'ja,*" Richard said. "You'll see." Then, to Ellen, "My mom has already asked if he can work with me." He raised his eyebrows. What could he do? Tony was his little brother. He got up and opened the refrigerator. Popped open a beer. Surveyed his garden out the back window. The corn was just coming up. His nana had always had a garden when he was a child, tomatoes climbing rickety stakes. *Yerba buena* beneath the faucet. Chard and *chiles* and hollyhocks. He and Tony had often hidden between the rows. He couldn't remember a time before Tony was born.

Daniel looked up from his spaghetti. "What?" he asked, his mouth full, sauce smeared on the corners of his lips.

"Your uncle Tony is getting out."

"Oh, oh," he said, "better hide the checks." He was kidding; he liked Tony. At eleven, he remembered his uncle, how he took him to see *Star Wars,* over and over, no matter how many times Daniel asked.

"What if we don't *want* him to get out?" Rachel's shoulders were still hunched in a shrug.

Richard said, "Guess I'd better fix the lock on that door."

"Put bars on the windows," Daniel laughed.

"Warn the neighbors," Ellen went along. But what would she tell them if there were suddenly a series of break-ins? Oh, don't worry. It's just my brother-in-law. He only takes what he can carry. He doesn't have a car.

Richard killed his beer. "It'll be all right," he said again. He threw the can in the trash and then walked out the front door, stood in the yard. The neighbor kids were riding their bikes on the sidewalk, zooming in and out of the street to pass one another. To Richard, suddenly, the place seemed foreign. Not like the barrio he'd grown up in where everyone had known everyone for generations. Here, people moved in for a few years. Until their kids were grown. He guessed it was like any working-class neighborhood in America: narrow streets lined with trees, small houses constructed of red brick or burnt adobe or siding. In the evenings, men parked their work trucks along the sidewalk; women still hung clothes on the line; children whooped and hollered until dusk. The last few years, though, you could see things going downhill. Broken windows got boarded up instead of replaced. People were keeping their trucks until the wheels fell off. Hell, it was hard for him to find enough work—for an ex-con, like Tony, it would be impossible, and, Richard figured, with a guy like Reagan in office, things would get worse before they got better. He didn't have any choice but to help Tony out. Otherwise. *¿Quien sabe?*

When Richard walked back into the kitchen, he put his hands on Ellen's shoulders and then kissed the top of her head before sitting back down at the table. She traced the knobby bone on his wrist. His fingers were absently tapping the smooth wood of the table. A few petals from the bouquet of bougainvillea next to him drifted down to the table and scattered, the thin petals veined like leaves, curling brown on the edges. She'd bunched them into a vase, the clusters spilling over, magenta against the white wall. Behind him, the glass doors and fawn haze of twilight. His dark hair, Daniel's, Rachel's, the reddish tints the light made. All of it could be so easily disturbed, a stone tossed into a pool, but she knew they couldn't lock Tony out of their lives any more than they could stop the flooding back of memory. And that was the intrusion she feared, the intrusion of the past. She and Richard had done many of the same things Tony had done, only they quit and he got caught—and now he'd spent five of the past eight years in prison.

She had this weird feeling—it wasn't *déjà vu,* exactly, it was more like she could suddenly see her life as a time-traveler might see it. She could see Richard as he was, a man in his early thirties, lines at the corners of his eyes. His hair was short. And there she was, no longer rail-thin. She was someone's mother. Two someones. How did we get here, she wondered, in this house, parents of two children?

It was almost as if time had no continuum, it wasn't a line but a dimension, and it had cracked and let Richard and Ellen walk into the room—Richard and Ellen when they were *young.* Long hair, confusion in their eyes. Those ghosts of themselves wandered around the house, from room to room, dazed. Shit, they said, can you believe it?

The next day Ellen called in sick and kept the kids out of school. They packed some fruit, nuts, and water in a daypack and drove up to the state park. It was a perfect day, a clear sky, cool air even though the sun was already warm. They walked slowly up the paved road that took them into the canyon. Every now and then they stopped and looked at the saguaros. Soon, Ellen told them, the flowers would bloom, crown them. She pointed out the new buds on the thin branches of the ocotillo. The grass was a tender green, the poppies and yellow paper flowers in bloom.

After a while, they decided to climb up a large ravine. They had to hop on the rocks to cross the stream. Daniel climbed well, but Rachel needed a little help up the huge granite slabs. "Lean into the mountain," he told her. A few times, he stood on the top of the boulder and held his hand out to Ellen. He picked out a trail, holding back branches of acacia and creosote as Ellen and Rachel followed.

After about fifteen minutes, they rested on a large slab of rock. Daniel said he thought they were the only ones who had ever climbed that far. Rachel started collecting small pieces of quartz that were imbedded with mica. She wanted to know if she'd found silver. Ellen wondered when children got used to the world. When did they stop seeing? She told them she wanted them to notice everything around them. "Even the way the light is," she said. She said she wanted them to think about important things. "Not just who you like or who likes you. Or what clothes to wear." She told them to look at the mesquite trees, how they were a velvety color of green you saw only in early spring.

Rachel stuffed her rocks into a pocket of the daypack. "But I *do* wonder who likes me," she said.

Daniel threw a small stone. It arced out and just missed the stream below. "What Mom means is she wants us to think about the world and the ecosystem and things like that."

"I know." Rachel gave him a dark look. "One time I even asked her who made it so a tree is called a tree and a cat a cat and not the other way around."

Ellen wanted to laugh—Rachel was competitive about everything—but, instead, she put her hand on her arm. "Sshh. A cardinal." They watched the bright red as it flashed through the green of the canyon, and then Daniel went back to throwing stones and Rachel to collecting them.

"I don't like Uncle Tony," Rachel said suddenly, plopping down next to Ellen. "I don't like people who hurt my nana."

"Maybe you don't remember any good things about him," Ellen said.

"Like what?"

"Oh, like he likes ketchup on his bologna sandwiches. Instead of mayonnaise."

"That's a *good* thing?"

"He can do card tricks," Daniel said.

"He likes those shows about animals on TV," Ellen said.

Rachel scrunched up her face.

"Once he took Steph and me to the zoo," Daniel said.

"He has a sickness," Ellen said. "He never should have gone to jail."

"Oh." Rachel was quiet for a while. "It's because he's Mexican, huh? That's why they sent him."

Ellen laughed. "Now you sound like your father." She pulled out some oranges and began to peel them. It was so quiet she felt as if they were alone in the canyon, as if time were suspended, and she wanted to hold on to that moment of peace, of simply being with them. To memorize it. She knew they would grow too fast. Away from her. She would have to let them go out into the world. She wouldn't be able to keep them safe. Not even from themselves. Not even from their own dangerous inclinations.

They were already, each of them, so separate from her, different from both her and Richard. And it bothered Richard a little, she knew, that they were not like him, not Mexican enough—really, she supposed, that was the way to put it. That was what bothered him. Especially about Daniel. Daniel with his haircut skater-style, and his long colorful shorts and big T-shirts. He looked like a kid from one of those big houses in the foothills. Ellen could see him through Richard's eyes, almost as someone else's child, a child who had never been deprived of anything—who had never been hungry or without suitable clothing, who had never been discriminated against. He had never known any of the pain that still colored Richard's childhood, and while that was exactly what Richard wanted, what he had worked so hard to provide, she knew it also worried him. He was afraid Daniel would grow up weak, that he would become just the kind of man Richard scorned. You should see them, he'd say of the college kids who worked for him in the summers, they've had everything handed to them. They don't know what it means to work. And you should hear them put us down. They're not going to be in construction all their lives.

Look, she'd tell him, the kids I work with at the store are the same way. Give them time. At eighteen I'd always had everything I needed. Suffering doesn't necessarily make you a good person.

But she knew he imagined her childhood as always smooth, like the water of the pool in her parents' backyard. She had her own bedroom, a car at sixteen. A gasoline credit card. You were spoiled, he always told her.

When he and Tony were young, their family lived in the back of an old Chinese grocery. The grocery had been boarded up years before when one of the grocers was murdered with a cleaver. Richard said that at night the lights in the grocery would suddenly go on, even though there was no longer any electricity in that half of the building. On some nights, they could hear the cleaver clacking on wood. Another time they lived in an old house with wooden floors and a fireplace. The fireplace turned out to be fortunate because, more often than not, the electricity, water, and gas were turned off. Their mother cooked in the fireplace. He remembered her leaning over and lifting the lid to check on the beans. He remembered walking next door with a bucket to get water from their neighbors' faucet. At dusk, he used to run down the alley to the store for milk, and the *winitos* who hid in the bushes reached out and grabbed at him. In the morning, a *winito* or two, maybe the same ones, knocked at their back door, and his mother gave them cups of coffee and pieces of tortilla or bread. When his father came home late at night from the cantinas, he told them stories about *la llorona,* the coyote, the girl who danced with the devil. Richard remembered only parts of those stories, but they all remembered the hole in the wooden floor and the cat that came up one night and sat on their father's chest as he slept, trying to suck the breath out of him. They all remembered being hungry.

Ellen sometimes wondered if she had married Richard because his childhood was more interesting than hers. Exotic. Not only that, but it had a certain clarity hers lacked. His memories were definite and hard-edged, they had the quality of stories, while hers were impressionistic, dark colors. In his, there was good and evil personified: cats who might be the devil. In hers, everything was blurry, shapes suggested by color or shadow, and underneath, always, her father's drinking, her mother's bitterness. An angry silence. There was no story. Everything remained unspoken. When they finally broke up and sent her to boarding school, she'd been relieved, not lonely. Even her mother's threat of disinheritance, when she eloped with Richard, was no obstacle. Ellen had seen it as a final rupture, a declaration of independence neither she nor her mother could ever go back on. Richard's family was her family now, her chosen family, his brother and sisters substitutes for those she never had.

Not only had he grown up in a different world than she had,

but, in some ways, he still lived in a different world. He always said he knew, by feelings, what would happen and what would not. He knew when his grandmother was going to die because he dreamed that some neighbor women came and stood outside her fence. They were dressed in black and they were throwing stones at the house and a week later his nana died from an operation. The night Tony's best friend died, Richard dreamed the death, the details of the overdose, the bathroom, the police, all clear in his mind. Before Tony got sent up, Richard dreamed about a painting by Diego Rivera, the one with a white wall, a window that looks out on nothing, a black revolver on the windowsill.

She often thought of these things, past dreams and past events, and told herself they proved nothing, they didn't determine the present or the future. But sometimes, at night, lying in the darkness next to Richard, she'd know they were right. She knew because before she fell in love with him, she had a dream that he came to her and said, Everything will be all right. In the dream, they were flying through darkness, they were lying down, flying among the stars, and he put the palm of his hand against her cheek. He whispered it again: "Everything will be all right."

A few weeks later, when Richard brought Tony by the house, Ellen couldn't help but be surprised by his pale skin, by how much weight he'd gained. Richard was much thinner than Tony now, and much darker, from working out in the sun. Tony's hair was curlier, it had always been curlier, wild sometimes, but now it was short, slicked back.

"Whew," he greeted her with a bear hug. "Looking go–od."

"Gained some weight," she laughed. "But then so have you."

He laughed, and a curl fell down on his forehead; he shook it back in place with one movement. Pachuco style. He had a tattoo on his forearm. She remembered him without it. And when he spoke, he spoke with an accent, something he had never done before. In prison, it was important to be part of *la raza.*

Ellen set out chips and salsa, got them each a beer, and then joined them in the living room. They talked for a while, mostly Richard and Tony talked about work, and then Tony said, "Remember that guy Reid?"

Richard nodded, absently, and picked up the sports section. He didn't want to talk about the old days anymore. All day at work for the past week, it was all Tony had wanted to do, tell him about the guys they'd known who were now in the joint, or tell him about his new *carnales,* his brothers. That was how he talked. Hey, bro. It bothered Richard no end. He hoped it was some kind of reentry phenomenon.

"Reid's dead," Tony said, "they found him in Nogales. In an alley. They just dumped him there. He'd OD'ed, and they didn't even try to revive him. Just took his dope and his money and left him in the alley." He looked at Richard for a reaction. "They didn't find him for days."

"And? What did you expect?"

Tony gave a low whistle. "That's cold, man." He shook his head at Ellen. "Can you believe how cold some people are? He was there for days. Until these dogs started dragging him out."

Richard lifted the newspaper in front of his face again.

"The last time I saw Reid was when we visited you guys up at the Fort," Ellen said. "That picnic we had, remember?" They had brought food and spent the day in the visitors' yard, gathered around the long picnic tables at the minimum-security prison. She had been surprised Tony and Reid could be friends there. Especially after the things she'd heard about the prison in Florence. Tony couldn't talk to whites or blacks at Florence, not even if he'd known them on the outside, but when he got transferred to minimum security, the Fort, he'd said it wasn't as bad.

The funny thing was, Ellen had known Reid long before she ever met Richard and Tony. She always remembered him in a car, driving fast, one hand on the wheel, blond hair messy with wind. Then there was the time they were sitting in the park and he rolled up his girlfriend's sleeve to show Ellen where he'd stabbed her with a syringe, over and over, these dime-sized purple bruises. There were some things she preferred *not* to remember.

Tony was staring out the window at the leafy branches of the mulberry. At the work trucks lined up and down the street and the kids on their bicycles. He sighed, "You guys have lived in this house a long time."

He looked *desorientado,* like he was a foreigner or, more likely, as if the passage of time had just registered. She was about to say something. Maybe about the tree, or living there, maybe simply about the past, it's behind us, everything has changed. Time to move on, Tony.

He said, "I called over at Jenna's mom's house yesterday, and they wouldn't let me talk to her. Hell, even in prison, you get visitors."

He walked around the room. Picked up the picture on the bookcase, the one Ellen had taken of Stephie with Daniel and Rachel for his mother.

"Look, I was understanding. I told her, You do what you've got to do. When I get out, we'll put things back together. But now I'm out, I see how it is." When neither Richard nor Ellen responded, he walked over to the window. "Shit, she could at least let me see Stephie."

Richard was scanning some stats on the sports page; he didn't want to touch this one. Neither did Ellen. They both knew Tony could be explosive on the subject of Jenna. After all, he had taken the fall for her, and she had divorced him almost as soon as he got sent up.

Tony lit a cigarette. "It's like this, when I was in there, I knew it was hard for her. I told myself, Fucking is only fucking, but she'd better not give her love away."

Richard sighed. "Somehow I always thought the two were connected."

"What world do you live in?" Tony blew smoke out in an angry stream.

Richard put the newspaper down. "So what do you have to learn in this life? Patience?"

Tony jerked his head back. "What's that supposed to mean?"

"You know. All the time you've had to sit and wait. Because of all the times you've made other people miserable."

Tony's laugh was quiet. "Well, maybe that's why I'm here, big brother. I'm your punishment. For all those things you did." He narrowed his eyes at Richard. "*Veras?*"

"Right. That makes all kinds of sense."

Ellen stood up and put her hand on Richard's shoulder. "Oh, I don't know," she said, trying to smooth everything over. "I figure it doesn't matter so much where you end up so long as you do something in life."

"My philosophy exactly. Life is like a train. You may as well enjoy the ride." Tony grinned at her and sat back down. "And that's just what I plan on doing."

The sudden shift of perspective, how he turned everything around, that's what bothered her. She sat on the arm of Richard's chair. "I hope things work out for you," she told him. But she knew he heard something else: Don't fuck us over. Ever again.

"Tony could stay clean," Richard said, "if only he had a memory."

He was lying in bed when he said this. Ellen had just slipped in, her skin was cool next to his, and she smelled like rosewater, clean, but not sweet. It was the same soap his family had used when he was a child, and so he didn't know what made him feel calm, Ellen next to him, or the scent not that it mattered. What mattered was that he felt calm, cared for, part of someone else's life. As he had as a child. As he did every night when she slid into bed. That's what he meant about Tony. There were things that provided continuity, scents were one of them, memory another, and continuity gave you a home, not only in the world, but in the larger scheme of things.

Ellen rolled over, facing him. His breathing was so quiet, she thought he had fallen asleep, but he was lying on his back, his eyes open in the dim light from the window.

"But he never remembers anything. Or it's all twisted somehow."

"I know," she said, "the way he was talking about Jenna. He gets out expecting everything to pick up where he left off. All those years, zap, they're gone." For Tony, she thought, there was only the moment. No past, no future. Maybe prison was like dope in that way: you went into another world, time stopped, you came out blinking your eyes.

She ran her fingertips up and down Richard's bare chest. It was sad, all so sad. Tony had taken the rap for Jenna so she could take care of their little girl; then she gave Stephie to her mother and turned her back on him. Like that. His sacrifice meant nothing. Tony, living in that cell for five years, no one to touch him in tenderness. What did that do to a person, she wondered, not only the deprivation of the natural world—sky, sun, wind, plants—but of human touch? A kind word. Someone to confide in.

"What am I afraid of, anyways?" she asked suddenly. "We don't have the kind of things he would steal."

"I don't know about you," Richard whispered, "but I'm afraid he'll start again. And then we'll lose him," he said. "I'm afraid he's going to die."

She wished she could be as good as Richard, but she could foresee a time where Tony's death might seem inevitable. A relief, even. And, yes, she knew why Richard felt guilty. They had done their share of experimentation, but they'd never *hurt* anyone.

"God," he said, "God, I regret those years."

"What does that mean?" she asked him. "That you would go back and change your life if you could? You would *be* somebody else?"

He'd always told her, If my parents had just stayed in the barrio, I'd be a doctor, a lawyer, like all my friends from junior high. But no, they moved us to the east side, to the white schools, to keep us out of trouble, give us opportunities, and what did we do? We started hanging out with guys like Reid. That's what drugs do. When you're an outsider, they give you instant community.

She tried to see herself as someone other than who she was, someone who had made other choices, but she couldn't. She could see herself leaning against a wall at school; she was very thin and very smart. She never had to study. She was wearing black, always black T-shirts and navy bell-bottoms; her hair was long and frizzy. She was lost in an opium dream. The other girls walked by in their villager skirts and button-down blouses and Capezios. They carried their pompoms. They giggled when the boys talked, tilted their heads, gazed up at them. But that had never been Ellen's dream. Ellen had never wanted to be like those girls. No, she had wanted to be different. Daring. A risk-taker. In her dream, a blue car sped down a curved mountain highway, the ocean on one side, cliffs on the other, the car gliding around the corners. She touched the steering wheel ever so slightly, her hand on the wheel, her long fingers light on the leather, she could almost think the car around the corners.

And then, there was another image, this one from memory: she and Jenna are backing out of Reid's driveway. They're loaded, Ellen's driving. Jenna has just lit a cigarette and handed it to her. Tony comes out to say goodbye, and Jenna and Ellen say, high as anything, Don't start, Tony, don't ever start. In the rearview mirror, Ellen sees Richard, tall and thin, hair past his shoulders. He's come over to Reid's house to score. Richard. She knows he's Tony's older brother, but she's never really seen him before. Never seen his eyes, how shy they are. The Garcia brothers are both standing next to her car, and that's what she sees, Richard's eyes.

Tony, Jenna says, don't do it. And yet only a few days later he's sitting in the back seat of a Chevy, and Ellen's kneeling on the front seat, facing him. He's wrapped the belt around his arm and pumped up, and Reid sticks the needle in Tony's vein. Pulls the plunger back, the blood surges in dark red, then Reid pushes the plunger forward. Ellen's watching Tony's face, waiting to see his eyes pin; waiting, impatiently, for her own rush.

Tony, the last to try it, the first to get strung out. Within a year, he had black marks snaking down his arms. This is important, she thought, it explains our guilt. Or why our complicity feels like guilt.

She pressed her face to Richard's neck. He was her drug now. When he held her at night, she settled in, felt her body all along his, the edge of her self melting into him. Osmosis. He made her feel calm. She exhaled. She felt it. The exhale. Relief. She must have been holding her breath ever since they'd heard Tony was getting out.

Richard couldn't sleep. He kept replaying the eruptions of Tony's anger. Everything was a struggle. Twice Tony had taken a swing at him. Richard was beginning to wonder if it had been a mistake to give him a job, but there was no point in telling Ellen any of this. Although, he supposed, if he lost the job, he might *have* to tell her.

Shit, he couldn't *afford* to lose this job. And all because of Tony's temper. But it hadn't been Tony's fault. Not really. The woman had yelled at him first. Actually, she had yelled at this *chapato* landscaper, not even five foot high, looked Guatemalan, probably didn't speak much English. Maybe not much Spanish. Looked Indian. Richard remembered that he had walked over to the edge of the roof as soon as he'd heard her voice, afraid, immediately, that Tony had done something. He'd leaned over the parapet wall to get a clearer view. But it hadn't been Tony. There the woman stood, the homeowner, in her turquoise running suit and gold sandals, towering over the landscaper. She was berating him, pointing first at a trench, then at plants someone had trampled, and then right in his face. The landscaper stood, arms folded across his chest, watching her impassively. His calm expression and lack of response was probably making her blood pressure go up by the second.

The confrontation would have ended soon after. That's what usually happened. The homeowners just liked to blow off steam. Or maybe they thought complaining would get them some extras. They hated to pay for the extras, especially the ones who could afford them. They would yell at you, you'd tell them to take it up with the contractor, then the contractor would yell at you. Thing was, they still had to pay, and the more they had to pay, the more they wanted to make you pay. So you had to fucking take it. You had to stand there and let them know, that yes, you understood the hierarchy. They had more money than you did, which meant they had more power, which meant they got to be rude. Being rude was part of their privilege. Of course, Tony knew all that as well as he did, but Tony had always made it a point not to buy into any system.

"Look," Tony had pointed to the landscaper's truck, "he *plants* plants." He was speaking very slowly and patiently as if the woman had an IQ of about ten. "He doesn't *trample* plants. And he *doesn't* dig trenches."

Even before Richard had seen the woman's face flame up, he'd known it was too late. He wouldn't be able to get off the roof quickly enough. He watched the landscaper make a quick exit. It was just the woman and Tony now, the trench—thank God for the trench—between them.

She'd leaned forward and jabbed her finger at Tony. "Well, then, who did it?"

"Satan," Tony had hissed, narrowing his eyes. "Satan did it."

The woman's face had gone momentarily slack from surprise, but she recovered. "We'll see," she snapped. She stalked back towards her house.

"Satan?" Richard had asked when he finally made it down the ladder. "Satan? Tucson Power dug the trench."

"Oh, really, Richard? You sure?"

"Fuck, Tony, you can't go yelling at the homeowners. Even if they are idiots."

"Did I yell?" he'd yelled. "You call that yelling?"

"Calm down!" Richard had looked over at the woman's house.

"You fucking calm down!" Tony had then stomped off the job.

Richard couldn't believe it. He climbed back up the ladder. He was going to have to try to finish alone. Of course. And, of course, soon after the incident, a truck had pulled up in the driveway. It was Earl, the project supervisor, laconic and weary, made weary by a job Richard would have hated even more than his own.

"So," Richard had said, when Earl came back out of the woman's house, "you the clean-up crew?"

"She swears you got up in her face and threatened her." Earl raised his hand to stop Richard's objections. "I know. I know you. And I know this woman. But she threatened to call the cops. She wants you off the job. Now."

"I'll leave when I'm finished."

"That's what I told her." Earl looked at her house. "Tough shit, lady." He lifted his cap and scratched his head. " 'Course you know I'll hear about this from Tom."

"Sorry. But there isn't a whole hell of a lot I can do about it now."

As Richard walked Earl over to the truck, he'd told him the story. Earl had laughed, "No wonder." Then he climbed in and rolled the window down. "Piece of advice," he'd said, "don't let your brother near the homeowners. Tattoos scare 'em, and they sure don't want to hear about Satan."

Richard couldn't sleep. *Satan?* He got out of bed and walked down to the living room and turned the TV on, no sound. The shadows flickered on the walls. Tony talked about Satan all the time now. He'd become a Jesus junkie. Well, no atheists in foxholes or prisons and all that, but how did he get to be so sanctimonious? *A lie weighs the same as murder.* He actually said things like that. Told Richard he'd done time for him, washed away his sins. Ellen's, too. Not to mention Jenna's. And in some weird way, Richard knew, he bought into it. He'd often had this idea that he should have gone instead.

The Welcome Home party was just family. Ellen was playing the good hostess. She put a pitcher of margaritas on the table. "Anything else?" she asked. "Before I sit down?"

Tony tapped a pack of cigarettes and said, "Come on, Artie boy, push those chips to the center of the table. You're not afraid of losing, are you?"

He and Richard were sitting at the table with the older sister, Grace, and her husband, Art. They were playing five-card draw. Art had a poker face, the gift of being invisible, until he cleaned everybody out. He was one of those guys who was really good with horses because of some mystical affinity, maybe. And Grace, willful and strong, her thick black hair and long legs, coltish even in her late twenties, was—like Richard always said—the horse even Arturo would never be able to tame.

Art tipped back. He took his time, pushing one chip at a time, slowly, into the pot.

In the kitchen, the younger sister, Amelia, was making potato salad, slicing black olives into the bowl. She was as small and thin as she had been as a girl, less than one hundred pounds, and yet she had given birth to two nine-pound babies. Her husband, Victor, said they inflated upon delivery. Her three-year-old son was pulling on her shirt. Patience, Manny, she said, and then put an olive on each of his index fingers.

Once, before Tony got sent up, when he ripped off their mother's house, he had stolen Amelia's favorite things, a sterling-silver dove her *nina* had given her for her first Holy Communion, a pair of jade earrings, and a wooden box her *nino* had brought home from the Philippines. Still, she forgave him without question, as everyone always did, came to the party and made potato salad, and when Tony asked her what she was going to be when she grew up, she just laughed and said, I *am* grown up.

Once, Ellen had told him, with every person you hurt, you hurt yourself. They are what hold you in this world. But he always managed to turn it around: they had never let him into their world, he said.

Tony was saying that he didn't like Salvadorans. "There was this one in jail, cut off a guy's hand with a machete."

"Why'd he do that?" Daniel asked, sitting down.

"When they threw him in the holding tank with us," Tony said, lighting a cigarette, "he was all messed up. They'd beat him up bad. Not the pigs. These guys at a bar. They took him in the john, beat the shit out of him, and ripped him off. It wasn't the first time, either."

"Sounds like a bright guy," Ellen said, looking at Daniel's face. She wondered if she should let him listen to all of this. "Keeps going back for more."

Tony blew out a stream of smoke and said, "You wanna hear what happened?"

Grace made a disgusted sound. "Not really."

She was studying Tony. Now that he and Jenna were seeing each other, she was sure he was going to start using again. They all knew the signs. His eyes changed color, to green, and got all pinned when he was loaded. His voice got husky. And then, there would be the more obvious signs, marks on his arms, money borrowed and never paid back. Eventually, missing items. It was sad, but whenever anything was missing, the assumption was as quick and accurate as a heartbeat: Tony.

"So this Salvadoran decides he's not gonna let them push him around. This dude was maybe five-two, a little sucker, and he goes home and gets his machete. When he comes back, these dudes are still in the bar, drinking up his money, and he goes up to one of them and pulls the machete out. Well, the guy stands up and tries to shield his head, like so," Tony held his arm in front of his face, "and the machete slices the guy's hand in two, like that, man. Clean. All the fingers gone, the thumb cut in half."

Ellen tried not to see the stump or the blood, but her mind worked that way, she could see everything. Not only that, but it brought to her mind all the things he'd seen and heard and told them. How, at Florence, he saw this guy throw kerosene or something in another con's cell, then a match, and the guy's a fireball, locked in, everyone else shouting and banging on the bars, afraid the fire will spread. And another time, how Tony had to shank this guy, a friend on the outside, to prove his loyalty to *la familia.*

Tony, they had said, what happened in there doesn't matter, it's a different world.

But, of course, it did matter. Now that he had been out for a while, it was obvious. What had happened and, especially, what he had done to survive it weighed him down, kept him there, away from the rest of the family.

"You wanna play, you're gonna pay. That it, Tony?" Richard tapped his cards on the table.

"Anyways, they throw this guy in the tank with us, and he

wants to plead self-defense. I tell him, you better cop a plea, man, otherwise, they're gonna bury you."

"So?" Richard asked. "Did he cop a plea?"

"Yeah. He got five years." Tony laughed and ground out his cigarette. "One year for each finger."

Art shook his head. "Sounds heavy," he said. He stretched, cracked his knuckles. "Time for some serious poker."

Tony smiled his slow smile. "Get ready to lose."

"Oooh," Daniel said, "I'm scared."

"So," Tony asked Daniel, "you always wear nail polish?"

Daniel shook his bangs out of his eyes and gave Tony a coy look. He had let Rachel practice on him that afternoon. Dark red on his right hand, blue on the left. Ellen remembered them sitting in a square of light on the living room floor. Daniel was watching cartoons. She thought Rachel had even done his toes.

"What's the matter?" Daniel laughed. "Don't you like the color?"

In one swift movement, Tony was standing. He had whipped Daniel out of his chair and was holding him upside down by his legs.

"You know what they call people like that?"

"The purple is my favorite," he lisped, still laughing.

"Fags."

"Okay, Tony," Richard said.

But Daniel was not scared. "You should see my toes," he howled.

"Enough," Ellen said, frowning at him in warning. Why did he have to be such a clown?

"Give it a rest," Grace said. "The kid's gonna be an actor."

"You know what happens to them in prison?" Tony shook his head as if he were thoroughly disgusted. He deposited Daniel back in his chair and sat down in his own. "All I'm saying's he should know how the world is."

"At *eleven*?" Ellen asked.

Tony shrugged: *Oh, well. I tried.* He picked up Grace's toddler, Annie, and let her hold his cards. Told her which ones to discard, and she slapped them on the table.

Dealer's choice. Daniel called five-card draw, one-eyed jacks wild, and jokers wild in straights and flushes.

Tony leaned back in his chair. "Where are Victor and Amelia? Don't tell me they're keeping their *mota* to themselves."

Grace said, "Amelia is in the kitchen. Pass me the ashtray."

Tony persisted. "Victor and Berto and that guy they brought with them, they're out back toking up, right? Why not spread the wealth around?"

They all looked out the sliding glass door, at Victor, Amelia's husband, and his brothers, Berto and Chito. They were all huddled in a circle around the brick barbeque, drinking beer. They were dressed in Levi's, jean jackets, flannel shirts, and wore their hair long and shaggy or in ponytails with baseball caps. All except Victor, who had style, who wore his hair short on top and long in back. *Que suave, ese,* Richard and Art teased him. Victor passed a joint and then turned his attention back to flipping the steaks.

Grace said, "If you want to smoke, go outside. Nobody's stopping you."

Art said, "Notice the muscles on that landscaper today? Ever seen a chick with pecs like that?"

Tony's voice got this edge. "You trying to tell me that this kid's never seen anyone smoke pot?"

"Como chingas." Richard put his cards down. "I'm sure he has." He looked at Daniel. "Have you?"

Daniel grinned. "Nah, never."

"Okay, Tony?" Richard's voice was soft. *"Bastante."*

Tony stood up, bumping the table against Richard, spilling the beer. He tossed his cards in front of Richard and made his voice just as soft. "Fuck you. We're not at work. Don't tell me what to do."

On his way out, he punched the living room wall, and the drywall gave, a small fist like indentation. The front door slammed. It was quiet except for the sound of the younger children playing in Rachel's bedroom, the fan whirring through the smoky light over the table.

"Temper, temper—huh, Daniel?" Amelia shook her head at him. She was standing in the doorway to the kitchen, wiping her hands on a dishtowel. Richard fished the wet cards out of the beer.

Ellen looked at the dent in the wall. Someday, she thought, we'll have little shelves and pictures in odd places all over our house, just like Richard's mom does, covering all the places where Tony got mad.

Art shook his head. "Hope you guys like knickknacks."

They all sat back down, and Art began the soft shuffling.

Grace looked at Richard. "You and Tony never could get along."

"Sure, Grace, it's my fault."

She waved her hand in the air, forget it. Then said to Daniel, "Did your dad ever tell you how your uncle Tony used to spend a half hour every morning before school combing his hair?"

Daniel shook his head.

"There were six of us—four kids!—and one bathroom, and he took forever. So when he finally did come out, hair just so, your dad used to," she reached over and tousled Daniel's hair, "do that. And then Tony, crying, would chase him all the way to school."

Richard shook his head. "Remember that game we used to play with the rope, where we held it and the other kids ran and jumped over it? But when it was Tony's turn, we'd yank the rope tight and clothesline him?"

Art and Richard both tipped back in their chairs and laughed. Rachel placed a plate of food on the table in front of Ellen and then climbed up in her lap. "You going to share?" Ellen whispered in her ear. Rachel tore a piece of tortilla, wrapped it around a chunk of barbequed steak, and offered her mom a bite.

"Or the time," Richard said, "when he wouldn't help with the yard work and Grace and I got some of the neighbor kids to help us tie him up. We wanted to hang him upside down from the tree so he'd agree to do the raking."

Daniel looked shocked. "You hung him from a tree?"

Grace laughed. "We tried, well. But he was too heavy."

Richard pointed his beer at Daniel. "He asked for it. That was hard work, and he was just sitting there in the shade laughing at us for doing it. One of those palm fronds sliced me a good one, right through my jeans, and that sucker wouldn't help."

Richard sighed, clicked his pop top with his thumb. "Every goddamn thing, no matter how small, Tony's got to tell me I don't know what I'm doing. He knows a better way, a faster way. Finally I told him, Look, I've been doing this for years while you've been sitting on your ass in prison."

Art laughed. "Yeah, he sucks you into saying things like that, and then he says, Fine, fuck you, and walks off the job."

Everyone was quiet, just the shuffling of the cards, a huge moth beating its wings against the glass door. Grace stirred her margarita with her finger, took a sip. "Give him some time."

"Yeah," Amelia said, "he's only been out for a month. He's got to adjust."

Art got up and put his hand on Grace's shoulder. "Time," he said and shook his head, almost as if he were puzzled. "What the hell is more time gonna do?"

"He talks about the joint like it's home. You should hear him, the guys, the guys, the guys." Richard tapped the table for emphasis. "They're his family now."

Grace and Amelia sighed at once.

"He's changed, I'm telling you. Hell, he thinks hot dogs from the 7-Eleven are *good*!"

Art was the only one who laughed. It was the saddest thing he'd heard yet.

"He got paid today. That's why he was so anxious to leave." Richard folded his cards and looked at Grace. "Don't be thinking everything's gonna be different."

"Well," Amelia said, "I'm hiding my checks." She looked around sheepishly. "I can't afford it, well."

"Listen to us," Grace said, "just listen to us."

They all looked at one another.

"It isn't up to *us*," Ellen said.

There was a longer silence, and Richard said, "Yeah, well, that's true."

Victor, with Amelia's and his youngest slung over his shoulder, came in from the back. He wore his T-shirt, a black one that proclaimed *Good but not Cheap!*, stretched tight over his muscles. "Where'd Tony go?" he asked. "What'd you guys do to him this time?"

They all shook their heads and laughed. Art nodded his head at Richard. "Ask him. It's his fault."

Daniel and Rachel had been absolutely quiet during the whole conversation. Ellen guessed they would learn that there were consequences, certain things you should never try or do or say. Maybe. She hoped that's what they would learn. Maybe they would learn that even adults don't have all the answers.

But when Daniel started asking Grace to tell more stories—about the old house, the old neighborhood—Ellen guessed that maybe knowing too much too soon was scary, too. Just as scary as the silence she had struggled to decipher as a child.

"Wasn't Beatrice a witch?" he asked Grace.

"That's what they say," she said. "They found a trunk in her house when she died, and it was full of books about black magic and full of dolls." She looked around at the kids. "You know the kind they stick pins in? When her son found these things, your tata told him to take them to the priest."

"Once Beatrice gave us these little sacks of herbs, remember, Grace?" Amelia said. "And she hung them on strings around our necks. We both got really high fevers. I kept dreaming about these women walking around our bed. Women in white gowns. Chanting. Every now and then, they'd reach their hands out at us like they wanted us to come with them." She shivered. "I knew they were dead." She shivered again. "We were so sick, and my mom didn't know what to do. But when my dad saw the sacks of herbs, he took them and burned them. Right away, our fevers broke. Remember, Grace?"

"That's not all," Grace said. "When I was going over to Beatrice's, the things I said in anger would come true. For instance, once when Richard refused to give me a ride, I said, I hope you get a flat tire. And he got one. And once, when I was mad at Tony, I went over and put my hand, just my fingertips, really, on the windshield of this car he was sitting in, and the windshield cracked. It wasn't cold outside or nothing. It just cracked." She made this face that said: now you tell me.

Rachel was pressing her back against Ellen's chest as if she'd like to disappear inside her. The other children were gathered around the room, their eyes shining, especially Grace's oldest, Andi, who kept saying, Tell us a *story,* Mom, not a *memory.*

"Okay, one," Grace said. The younger children were drifting off to sleep on a quilt she'd spread on the floor in the living room. She looked over at them and then at Andi and Daniel and Rachel, she narrowed her eyes and made her voice low, almost as low as a whisper. "This story is about a girl who wants to go to the dance so badly that she threatens her mother. She says, I don't care what you say, I'm going anyways. And her mother threatens her back. If you go, *mi'jita*, she tells her, I'll lock you out. Don't think I won't. The girl shrugs, she doesn't believe her mother, and she goes to the dance anyways. When she's there, she dances with this very handsome stranger, a man no one has ever seen before, a man no one else will dance with. And they dance all night, twirling around and around, and then, just after the last song, when she turns to say goodbye, he's disappeared. On the way home, she wonders if she'll ever see him again. It's very dark, and it's a long way home, and just as she's passing some bushes, she thinks she feels someone walking behind her. She stops, she hears footsteps. Then she turns, and she thinks she sees these red eyes in the darkness, she feels his hot breath. She begins to run faster and faster. Still he's behind her. Faster and faster, she runs. Finally, she reaches her door, but it's locked. She knocks and knocks at the door, she calls for her mother, but her mother wants to teach her a lesson. She won't open the door. She listens and listens to her daughter's cries, to her scratching at the door, but, still, she won't let her in. Finally, her daughter is silent. And the mother, thinking she's learned to obey her, opens the door. But her daughter is nowhere to be found. There's no trace of her. No blood, no clothing, no tracks. Nothing. Only the door is torn to shreds. The mother calls out to her. There's no answer. She calls to her neighbors for help, and they all call and call for the girl and search for her, but no one ever sees her again.

"You know," Grace said, looking right into their eyes, one by one, "they say the Santa Cruz used to run all year round. They say there used to be a lake there, in Carrillo Gardens, where the dance was held, but after that night, after the girl danced with the devil, the river dried up. So did the lake. That's what your nana told me, anyways. She told me they never had any dances after that."

Rachel had Ellen's hands pressed firmly over her ears. Ellen cupped her palm and whispered beneath it, "I will never lock you out, *mi'ja*."

As Ellen looked at the sleepy faces of the children, at Grace and Amelia as they lifted their sleeping kids and murmured to them, It's all right, sshh, it's all right, she could see what Grace had always seen: there was no way they could give up on Tony. The feeling was, if the fabric of the family held together, they could somehow keep him among the living. But it wasn't just for his sake. Grace wanted the family to stay whole for all of them, for the children. Like her mother, she believed in holding the family together at any cost. One tear, and she was afraid it would all begin to unravel.

GEOFFREY BECKER

Cowboy Honeymoon

Kaufman drove from one fire to another. In Baltimore, there had been a train wreck in the Howard Street tunnel, the northern end of which was not far from the small house he owned, tucked away on a side street behind the hulking wreck of a Victorian hotel, and three doors down from a gay bar with no sign or windows. The train was loaded with toxic chemicals, and stuck in the tunnel as it had been, there was little the authorities could do. The downtown air filled with the smell of melted plastic and electrical wire. Temperatures reached one thousand degrees in the tunnel, so hot that the cars glowed.

In Jackson, it was wood smoke, thick as a campfire when the wind blew from the south. A whole mountainside was burning. Fat insect helicopters traveled back and forth from the airport, huge baskets dangling under them like egg sacs. Around town, signs everywhere read, "Thank you, firefighters!" The air hurt your eyes, and Kaufman had to run his wipers to clear ash from the windshield of his Subaru.

Everything in the hotel bar gleamed, from the hanging racks of stemware to the long, polished mahogany bar itself to the picture windows in the seating area. They were atop a mesa, with views in all directions. Kaufman felt as if he'd been somehow transported to the pages of the kind of magazine he'd never read on purpose.

"See that couple?" said Rhonda. It was cocktail hour at the Rusty Buffalo. After one day working for Irving Straight, Kaufman was already wondering about his decision. The man did huge saccharine oils with titles like *Beddin' 'em Down,* and *Chow Time,* depicting sunburnt Marlboro men, cows, and horses at twilight.

At a table by the window, he observed a woman who looked to be in her mid-thirties, with frizzy dark hair and black plastic-framed glasses. The man with her seemed somewhat older, had a shaved head, and looked bored.

"Yes," he said. "I see them."

"They're here through an Internet auction—one of those travel sites. Only when she got here this morning and saw their room, she pitched a fit and said it was their honeymoon. They had room 11. It's small, and there isn't any view. She starts crying right there, I mean sobbing. What a show."

"You think she's lying?"

"Of course she's lying. She's some spoiled East Coast chick."

"What did you do?"

"I gave her the honeymoon suite." Rhonda applied Chapstick to her lips. Her hair was tinted blond, her skin tanned and creased around the eyes, and yesterday Kaufman had noticed a geometric tattoo barely rising out of the back of her jeans, the same as a lot of his students had back in the city.

"That was nice of you," he said.

"It was available. With the fire, I'm getting cancellations like crazy. But I want to have some fun with them. I really want to push this. There is no way they're married. I don't even think he wants to be here, to tell you the truth."

"How do you know? They're wearing rings."

"That doesn't mean anything—I wear a ring. You get to a certain age, you just do. Hell, he might be married to someone else. Anyway, they've got reservations for dinner here tonight, and I've arranged to have a cake appear. I'm having Paco decorate their table with balloons, and the waitstaff are going to come out and sing. You should have seen her, crying like a six-year-old. Like the world owes her something. Know what I wish you'd do? Hit on her. It'll be good practice for you, and who knows? Maybe you'll get lucky."

Kaufman looked again at the woman, tried to imagine starting some kind of conversation. Jackie, the girlfriend he'd moved in with after college but never married, had died almost ten years ago, and though he'd dated on and off since then, it hadn't been with much success. There was no one in his life right now, although he liked to think he had prospects—the young blonde he'd met in his last painting class, for instance, who liked Elvis Costello. Or the antiques dealer he'd met recently at the Walters on Rhumba Night, who was interested in old maps (there had been an exhibit on). Who was he kidding? The blonde was twenty-three, maybe younger, while Kaufman was forty-two, surely out of her range. The antiques woman seemed to believe that Greek civilization had followed, and indeed improved upon, that of Rome. He had no prospects. "I don't hit on married women."

"Here's what I'm telling you. That woman is in an unhappy relationship. She might sleep with you just to push things with *him*."

"What would that say about me?"

"I'm sorry, Skip. You're right. You need another drink?" She was the one who'd given him the nickname, and he didn't even know why. That was being a younger brother—eight years old, and one day you suddenly had a new name, which no amount of protest was going to change. Even his parents had begun using it.

"Please. I had a hard day on the range." As he said this, he noticed that the man was getting up.

"Go downtown and see what Irving's paintings are selling for. Forty thousand bucks. For that kind of money, maybe you could paint a few Indians."

"It's kitsch."

"Of course it's kitsch. What did you expect? People around here pay a couple of million dollars for a log cabin in the woods that has a Jacuzzi, hot tub, and Sub-Zero, they need something atmospheric for the walls. Irv also happens to be a very fine painter. In the world of Western art, he's very highly thought of."

The woman was now alone, and she did seem sad. "I don't doubt it," he said.

"Ooh." Rhonda poked his arm. "Go over and bring her another margarita. Compliments of the house. Talk to her."

"How?"

"Just ask her how she's enjoying herself."

"Maybe, but on one condition. You go do something else."

"All right. I have to make some calls, anyway. But I want a full report."

Kaufman went to the bar, had Dreadlock Larry mix two margaritas, then brought them to the woman's table.

"On the house," he explained. "I wonder if I could join you. That is, if you're alone."

"I'm alone," she said, eyeing the drink he held out. She motioned with her head toward the opposite chair, and Kaufman slid into it. "My husband has gone to the room to play mandolin."

"A musician."

"I didn't say that." She had high cheekbones, wide-set green eyes. "Are you related to that manager?"

"You're good. Most people don't see the resemblance."

"Well, I see it."

"Can I tell you something?"

"What?"

He leaned forward, and was pleased that she did, too. Their faces were only inches apart. He very much wanted to touch her. "My sister doesn't believe you're married."

"Sure she does," she whispered. "She gave us the honeymoon suite."

"Because you cried."

"I cry all the time. It doesn't mean I'm lying."

Kaufman sat back, and so did the woman. He felt as if they'd known each other a long while, and he couldn't explain it. He'd heard of people having chemistry, but he'd never quite known what the expression meant. Perhaps this. "All the smoke in the air sure makes for a nice sunset."

"You like sunsets?"

"It's in my job description. I'm a painter. I'm working for a famous Western artist right now, finishing his stuff. I can't tell you his name. I had to sign a contract."

"Finishing what parts?"

"Scenery, bodies. He does faces, and he does the underpaintings, but I do a lot of the filling in. Right now, I'm working on a boulder."

"Is that ethical?"

"A boulder?"

"The whole thing."

"I think so."

She was looking out the window again. The shirt she had on was sleeveless, and her long, thin arms were nicely muscled. "Well, I guess it's not surgery," she said. "Anyway, I am."

"Sorry?"

"Married. And this is my cowboy honeymoon."

"My sister's probably jealous. She's older than I am, and neither of us is married."

"You ought to try it. It's everything it's cracked up to be and more."

"Look at that fire," he said.

"You don't think we're in hell, do you?" She took a long swallow from her drink.

He didn't think this was going all that well. "What do you do?"

"I'm in advertising. I dream up amusing scenarios for selling things. You know those milk ads where a cow comes walking through that family's living room while they're watching TV? That's one of mine."

Kaufman pretended to know what she was talking about, even though his TV had died two years ago during a thunderstorm, an electric bleat of protest before falling silent. He had yet to replace it. "Are you from New York?"

She nodded, drew a circle in the frost on the side of her glass with her finger. "Hey, you want to go for a hike tomorrow?"

"Sure. What about your husband?"

"His plantar fasciitis is acting up. I want to do Jenny Lake."

"I'm supposed to work in the morning, but I could go around one."

"Then we'll meet at the front desk," she said, cheerily. "It's a date."

Kaufman did not stick around for the cake. Instead, he got a burrito at a place in town, walked briefly around the square, looking in the windows of the various galleries and souvenir shops. He felt exhilarated, strange. The salt from the margaritas had left him thirsty, the air didn't contain enough oxygen, and his heart seemed to be working overtime. He saw a kid lose three scoops of ice cream in what appeared to be slow motion, watched all the while by a fascinated collie tied to a parking meter a few yards away.

Irving Straight's studio was a separate building behind a modest house five blocks south of the town center. He'd shown Kaufman where he hid the spare key under a cinder block beside the house, and now Kaufman let himself in. He liked the clutter of a studio, the sense of work ongoing, the random splotches of color that accumulated on everything. A big oak desk with a combination TV and VCR on it took up much of one wall, and various videocassette tapes were piled up alongside. Straight believed in keeping old Westerns playing for atmosphere. Already, Kaufman had listened to *Red River* and *El Dorado.*

He went to the painting he'd been working on and took another look at his boulder. There was a rattle of movement behind him as Irving Straight came in. He was in his late fifties, with white hair he combed straight back, and oversized glasses that magnified his eyes out of proportion to the rest of his face. He wore a droopy handlebar mustache.

"A burglar," he said. "I hope you don't have a gun." He went to the boulder and stuck his face right up to the canvas, then backed away.

"What do you think?"

"Try a smaller brush. And try to think a little more cowboy. Think Gary Cooper, Randolph Scott, maybe even Lee Marvin. Henry Fonda, for that matter."

"Those are actors."

"I know they're actors, Art School. That's not the point. It's what they embody, the whole spirit of the thing. I don't know if this is going to work out."

Kaufman looked at his boulder. "I'll try harder," he said.

"I wasn't keen on hiring you, you know, considering the circumstances with Rhonda and me. I thought it might just muddle the waters. But she can push a point when she wants to. I used to fix cars for a living. You were a teacher, right?"

Kaufman thought how odd that use of the past tense sounded. He'd taught his last class less than a month ago. What was he now? Starting over. A colleague of his had dropped dead back in the spring, and he was only forty-five. Two weeks later, Kaufman had submitted his resignation. It didn't make him feel brave, or even particularly nervous. It felt like the only thing he *could* do.

"Circumstances?" he asked.

Irving Straight took a bottle of water out of the small refrigerator under the window, unscrewed the cap, and took a swallow. "She didn't tell you about us?"

"She just said you were friends."

"I've known her five years now, but only for the past two was it romantic. Up until last month, when I called it off."

Rhonda had dated a drug dealer in high school, and Kaufman could still hear the purr and hack of his idling motorcycle outside their house late at night as he'd drop her off. Her subsequent relationships had all seemed influenced by that unfortunate paradigm, and Kaufman didn't ask many questions. "I didn't go to art school," he said. "I just took a few classes."

"She wants to get married," said Straight. "I already did that, thirty years ago, and I wasn't good at it. Ask my ex-wife, ask my two kids. What I'm good at is right here in this room—I paint my pictures, and then I have a girlfriend for my not-painting time. It might sound hard, but it's the facts. I never represented it different, and Rhonda knew that all along. I hired you because I think you can do the work, not because I feel guilty. That's all. But you have to show me that you *can* do the work." He returned the water to the fridge. "That's not getting it," he said. "You want to go have a real drink?"

At the Cowboy Bar, the men wore ball-strangling Wranglers with big belt buckles, Western shirts, and mustaches; the women all had long hair, hip-hugger jeans, midriff-revealing tops, and serious makeup. Everyone had on a hat. Kaufman followed Irving Straight to a table, sat, and ordered the same thing he did—a double Jack Daniel's on the rocks. He could tell the tourists from the locals fairly easily. In Baltimore, there was only one bar he went to regularly, right in his neighborhood, because he liked their grilled chicken sandwiches. Otherwise, he'd become a recluse, moving between his living room, the kitchen, the bedroom upstairs, and the spare room where he painted.

"Rhonda likes this place," said Irving Straight.

Kaufman looked at his watch and wondered if dinner was over back at the hotel. "How does it feel to get forty thousand dollars for a painting?"

"I wouldn't know. The gallery takes fifty percent. But, yeah, I see what you're driving at." He cracked a knuckle. "It's a kick in the ass." He sipped his drink. "So, look, just tell me one thing. She's seeing someone new, right?"

"I don't know," said Kaufman.

"You don't?" His eyes hovered behind his lenses like pond creatures. Kaufman had the impression that Irving Straight was honestly surprised by moments when the world appeared not to be entirely about him.

"Okay, yeah, she is. A mandolin player." The band was playing an old Little Feat song that Kaufman recognized, and could remember Jackie singing along to back in their apartment on Calvert Street. The thrift-shop furniture, the tattered stereo speakers up on cinder blocks. *Put on your sailing shoes.* He'd have called that rock, back in the seventies, but now he saw how it might have been country. On a talk radio show somewhere near Omaha, he'd heard a caller say, "I know hindsight is fifty-fifty, but..." He'd liked that, even repeated it aloud. As he'd driven, Kaufman had stored each brief passing image—an abandoned gas station, a collapsing barn, a gleaming new mall set like a child's toy amid the cornfields—in his mind. These things were unambiguous.

"Being an artist means sacrifice, man," said Straight, poking at an ice cube. "Don't fool yourself. Happiness doesn't have anything to do with it, and neither does getting laid."

Kaufman was awakened by his sister on the phone at a little after seven a.m. His room was similar to the regular guest ones, except that it was located by the service building, which housed gardening equipment and large electric pumps that came on and off all night long. "So, where did you go last night?" she asked.

"Into town. I had drinks with Straight." Kaufman picked sleep out of his eyes and squinted at the bright light seeping through the blinds.

"Tell me about the margaritas," she said.

"You're probably right about the husband, if that's what he is. What happened with your cake?"

"She's such a phony. They fed each other pieces, and everyone applauded."

"We're going for a hike this afternoon to Jenny Lake."

"You are? Now this is exciting. How'd you manage it?"

"It was her idea. I think he has something wrong with his feet, so he couldn't go. By the way, what's her name?"

"Are you serious?"

"It just never came up."

"Elizabeth Moore. Boring, huh? Hey, I need you to tend bar for a couple of hours tonight. Larry's band has a gig, so I gave him the night off."

He sat up farther in the bed. "Okay. I gotta get going here," he said. "I have a boulder to finish, and then later I get promoted to cattle."

Straight wasn't at the studio, but he'd left scrawled instructions on a couple of Post-it notes. The first read, "Do Cows." On the wall behind the easel there was a rough sketch of what the finished painting was supposed to look like. One cowpoke sat resting against a boulder, holding out a cigarette, while another leaned down toward him, his hands cupping a lighter. A bit to the right was a horse, and in the distance, moving up and toward the vanishing point, were lots of cows, represented at this point by lightly sketched shapes.

Do cows. On the canvas itself, Straight had already penciled in the closer cows, as well as their faces. The ones that receded into the distance were probably what he meant, but Kaufman, who was used to working from photographs, had an idea. He poked through the stacks of art books piled against the wall until he found what he wanted, a fifteenth-century Flemish nativity scene. The Christ child at the center, casting light outward onto the faces of Mary and some admiring angels, and just off center and far less well-lit, a bovine face, almost thoughtful. Kaufman mixed some paint and set to work copying it onto the face of the second cow back.

At one p.m. he was by the front desk, waiting. The air was even smokier today than yesterday. Coverage of the fire was national—*Good Morning America* had reported that over three thousand acres were ablaze, with no rain in the forecast. Elizabeth Moore came in with a small black backpack and Italian leather hiking shoes.

"Sorry I'm late," she said. "You ready?"

"Your car or mine?"

"You honestly don't want to see me drive."

She smelled like vanilla and nervous sweat. He was somewhat embarrassed about the state of his car, which was still full of the detritus from his cross-country journey—empty fast-food bags, mostly—but she made no comment. They drove up past the airport, toward the mountains that jutted into the sky like jagged blue teeth. She chewed Tic Tacs, shaking another one out of a container every few minutes.

"They sang to you, huh?" he said, after a while.

" 'We've Only Just Begun.' It was humiliating."

"I warned you."

"It's harassment. Can't two people just be left alone on their honeymoon?"

"You don't get something for nothing. You wanted a fancy room, you're paying for it. Lots of people would be happy with free cake."

"I bid on this and won. I guess I should have known the place would be on fire."

"Sort of spur of the moment for a honeymoon."

"Hey," she said. "I'm that kind of girl."

They arrived at the parking area and set out on the trail, which went first through forest, paralleled by a gurgling brook, then emerged into an area which was far more open. There were lots of shrubs and short trees, but very few of any size, although quite a number of dead ones poked up like broken phone poles as far as they could see, their silvery trunks the color of polished bone.

"This area burned in the early eighties," Elizabeth said. "I read about it in my book. That's part of what makes it such a beautiful hike. You can see all around you."

It took an hour to hike to the lake, and they made small talk as they went. She was originally from New Jersey. She'd once thought she'd like to be a dancer. She loved dogs. Her favorite movie star was Vincent Price, her favorite movie *Theater of Blood.* They found a spot to sit. "I brought cheese and an apple," she said, poking in her bag. "And these." She held up two brown and beige items about six inches in length. It took Kaufman a moment to recognize them as shoe inserts. "Orthotics," she said. "I snuck them out of his shoes last night. He's out wandering the town right now looking for a present for his kid, and I'll bet his feet are killing him. Funny, huh?" She made a strange sound in the back of her throat, and her eyes filled with tears. "This is what I'm reduced to. Stealing people's orthotics."

"Look," Kaufman said. He arranged her apple and the piece of cheese on top of the rock beside them.

"At work, I'm known as the funny one. I did tell you I cry a lot. What is that, a still life?"

"Ever paint one?"

"I'm not what you'd call artistic. I'm funny." She sniffed.

"Look at the apple." He moved over so that he was right beside her. The light was coming from a slight angle. "What colors do you see?"

"Red," she said.

"Anything else?"

"I don't know. Darker red? Some brown where there's that spot."

"Good. How about underneath, just above the rock?"

She sniffed again. "Purple, maybe."

"Something close to that. It's the reflection of the rock itself. I think it's more a blue gray. But you're right."

"Are you going someplace with this?"

He wasn't sure. He only knew that he needed to keep her attention. "Being able to recognize colors is the key. That shadow, that's going to mostly be cerulean blue. Our red on the apple is going to range quite a bit. I see at least five different shades there, not counting what's reflecting up from the rock. The colors are in the light, you know, not the object. They travel in waves. Opposite colors—yellow and violet, for instance—actually seem to tremble when they're next to each other, because our eyes can't adjust for both at the same time."

She picked up the apple and took a bite, then held it out to him. "They're actually called *orthoses.* That's what he calls them. *Orthoses.* It sounds like calling dibs on birth control pills."

Kaufman took a bite of the apple and chewed.

"See, I told you I was funny." She got up. "You want to head back?"

He didn't move. He shouldn't have started lecturing her about colors. People didn't care about colors. Most people didn't. It occurred to him that he might never have a normal interaction with the world again. All those days he'd come into his class waving *The New York Times,* saying, "Who can tell me one thing about Liberia?" or "West Bank! West Bank of what?" That person seemed someone he'd dreamed.

"Wait," she said, and turned around. "Come stand behind me. Close."

He did this, almost touching her. She reached back and took his hands, bringing them up under her shirt, placing them on her breasts. "Just hold me," she said.

He looked out at the flat lake, its surface reflecting the blue sky, but darker. They stood that way for a minute, and he closed his eyes, and it was Jackie's breasts that he touched, though she had never let him—not again, after her diagnosis. After a few months, she'd moved out to be with her family, down in Virginia, which was where she'd finished up, spending her last days designing gardens in a small sketchbook. He'd gone down, of course, taking sick days, vacation days. But he'd missed the very end—she'd just slipped away one night while he was putting together a lesson plan. Her mother asked for her photograph albums; her brother wanted her books. The house he'd bought the following year had a small garden, but he'd never done anything with it, just let it grow wilder and full of leaves.

They took a different route back to town, one that brought them close to the burning mountainside. Kaufman had almost forgotten the smoke after this afternoon in the relatively clean air at the lake, but now he found it irritating to his eyes. On the news, they heard that the fire was twenty-percent contained, which didn't sound all that promising. From various points on the road, they could see it pluming thickly off the mountainside into the sky. He thought again of those train cars stuck in the tunnel, glowing white with heat.

When they got back to the hotel, her rental car, a green Dodge Neon, had been decorated with shaving cream, "Just Married" spelled out across the back window in thick, white letters.

"You could admit it," said Kaufman. "I'm sure she'd let you keep the room."

"Never," said Elizabeth Moore.

Irving Straight came by a few hours later, while Kaufman was tending bar, wearing a freshly pressed tan shirt and a bolo tie. "I was over to see a guy this afternoon, lives in the Indian Paintbrush subdivision. He has to get out of there by tonight. They're spraying all the houses with slurry in case the fire moves any further down the valley."

"Friend of yours?" asked Kaufman. It was eight p.m. Earlier he'd served two nice-looking older women who stared right through him like he was made of glass, but now it was just Straight at the bar. No sign at all of Elizabeth Moore or her not-husband. He had the TV on, sound off, tuned to a cooking show.

"Customer—owns three paintings. Shouldn't never have built up there in the first place," he said. "None of them. Just a matter of time. These people with money get *arrogant.*"

Kaufman thought of the painting from Pompeii of a woman picking flowers. Of course, it wasn't a resident of the town, just a decoration on someone's wall, but he'd always thought of it that way, as if he were looking at one last pretty moment in a life before the sudden wave of lava swept down and stopped time.

Rhonda came in, wearing a black silk shirt, open at the collar, jeans with high heels, and some dangly Native American–looking earrings. She touched Straight on the shoulder. "Ready?"

"I'll be there in a second."

Noticing the surprise on Kaufman's face, she smiled. "Have fun, Skip."

When she was gone, Straight looked at Kaufman and poked him in the chest with a meaty finger. "Sint Jans," he said. "*Nativity at Night.*"

"I thought a classical reference might be fun," said Kaufman. "Hey, it rhymes with 'Injuns.'"

"It took me over an hour to make that cow back into one of *my* cows."

"Sorry," said Kaufman.

"Any references in my paintings are going to be to *Stagecoach* or *The Searchers,* not the Northern Renaissance." Straight downed the rest of his drink and smoothed his mustache. "Damn nice brushwork, though," he said.

"You think?"

But that was all the man was going to give him. "This isn't a joke," he said. "This is what I *do.*"

Kaufman closed up at eleven, locking the register and hitting the lights. He made a brief, unsuccessful attempt at conversation with Shari, the Navajo girl who was working the front desk, then figured he'd go read in his room for a while before bed. Through the lobby doors, he saw Elizabeth Moore putting luggage into the trunk of her rental car.

"Number 5 check out?" he asked.

Shari flipped the page of the *People* magazine she was reading. "Not to my knowledge."

He pushed his way out into the cool night. “Howdy,” said Elizabeth Moore when she saw him.

“It’s late.”

“Exactly. But not too late.”

The air was full of tiny specks of white ash, suspended, almost weightless, nearly invisible. An owl made a noise like a distant train.

“What about what’s-his-name?”

“I killed him,” she said. “He’s back in the room.”

“Killed him how?”

“Brained him with a mandolin. I’ll need to get going now so I can keep a couple steps ahead of the law.”

“If they catch you, they’ll hang you.”

“I reckon.” She shook his hand. “I want to thank you for the lesson in colors. All that time I thought they were just sitting there, and it turns out they were trembling.”

Words were like bricks in his mouth; he might have been a sixth-grader asking a girl to dance. “If you ever come to Baltimore,” he said.

“Don’t even say it. I’m not coming to Baltimore. I barely know where it is.” She sniffed her shoulder. “All my clothes smell like smoke,” she said. “I bet they will forever.” She looked at him, smiled. “Next honeymoon, I’m going on a cruise.”

After she left, Kaufman walked around the grounds. No lights were on in Number 5. He sat on a carefully placed boulder at the edge of the path and imagined her driving to the airport—where else could she drive to?—perhaps sitting in the parking lot for a while, determined to make her point, whatever it was, staring up through the windshield at the same ashy sky that stretched over him now.

His colleague who died had taught biology. On April Fools’ Day, his heart had simply given out. A faulty valve or whatever—there really wasn’t much to say, no lesson to draw from it. He hadn’t smoked, had drunk only moderately, played basketball once a week with some other faculty members. His wife had thought he was kidding around. Their kids were in college—the whole next part of their lives was coming up. They’d been having a beer and peanuts together at a pub, and he’d suddenly put his head down on the table and started to snore. She thought he was making fun of the story she was telling. By the time she realized, it was already too late.

From within, Kaufman heard the muted, tinny sound of mandolin strings being tuned. One of them kept slipping; there was the gentle climb toward unison, a moment where all was right, then a quick falling away. Probably, something was wrong with the tuning pegs, and yet the guy kept patiently at it. Kaufman could see how that sort of thing could drive you nuts.

KATHERINE BELL

The Casual Car Pool

He had jumped a radio tower and a cliff in Norway, but never a bridge. He chose a Wednesday morning when the fog was expected to burn off early and called in sick to work. At dawn, he climbed the tower. The riskiest part, he thought, would be landing in the water, where his friends would be waiting with a boat.

While he fell he counted to three and pushed it to four though he'd promised he wouldn't, and his canopy opened without any trouble, exactly as it should. But a freak wind came and lofted him—he didn't remember this, but it must have happened—and now his chute was snared in the steel ropes of the bridge, and he was dangling like a hurt insect a hundred feet above the morning traffic. His right arm had snapped inside its Gore-Tex sleeve, and though he wanted to tuck it close to his body, he couldn't. He couldn't reach his radio, either. He looked down at the cars on the top deck. They glittered in the sun as they streamed toward the city, the very edge of the continent. It was stupid to have jumped so close to rush hour.

Now, because of him, more than eighty thousand people would be late to work. Across the city, deadlines would be missed, meetings cancelled, stores understaffed. The host of the nine o'clock show on KQED would not arrive in time; at every major hospital, surgeries would be postponed. The driver of the Nissan Altima stalled near the end of the Yerba Buena tunnel would be late, and so would the woman beside him. The girl in the back seat did not have a job. School had already started, but that was behind her, before the bridge. She had never planned to go.

Ian tapped the steering wheel and stared hopefully at the tunnel's bright mouth. Usually, when you came out from under the manmade island, the traffic sped up until it hit land and clogged again. The pattern was roughly the same every day. If you hit the 880 loop at the right time, you could slip straight into the carpool lane and not stop until the toll plaza. That's why it was worth it to pull off the freeway in Oakland to pick up passengers—you saved the two-dollar toll and at least twenty minutes. It always struck Ian as odd, the idea of ferrying strangers across the bridge. He couldn't help feeling responsible for their safety and comfort. He limited the mess in the car to the floor behind his own seat and drove more cautiously than he did when he was alone. Until Oakland, he listened to the symphonies and concertos that bored his wife, and sometimes the outdated pop music that embarrassed her, but after Oakland he turned the volume down and switched to news, the least political of the stations, with weather and traffic repeated every fifteen minutes.

He stole a look at his front-seat passenger, her dark head bent over a stack of papers. She'd unhitched her seat belt when they reached the bridge, which meant she'd lived in the Bay Area long enough to remember the earthquake in '89, to prefer the risk of a car accident to the risk of being trapped under rubble.

The girl in the back had never put hers on. She couldn't sit still, kept shifting her limbs about, running her nails back and forth along the beige velour edge of her seat, leaning her head against the window and clouding up the glass. She'd rather be on the train, hurtling under the Bay, unstoppable. But the train was expensive, the car pool was free, and though her parents had money, plenty of it, she didn't have any of her own. Their money came weighed down with rules and obligations that Julia, a month and a half before her sixteenth birthday, did not want or need.

The first couple of times she'd ridden the car pool into the city, she'd felt a little thrill of danger as she waited in the parking lot under the overpass for the first car to drive up. Her mother would kill her if she knew. It was like hitchhiking, only more organized. The drivers were usually men in luxury cars, who could afford parking in the city, who draped their suit jackets over one backseat window, obscuring the view, but Julia wasn't naïve—she knew that they could be rapists or murderers, too. Even this guy, who looked so ordinary, so suburban, so *nice,* could stop the car at any minute and put a knife to her throat. The fact that two random passengers rode in each car helped; it meant that there was a chance they could work together to overpower the driver if he turned on them, although the woman in the front could be his accomplice—they could have planned it so that she'd wait in line behind Julia, and maybe she'd be the one to pull the knife. Except they were stuck in traffic inside a tunnel, trapped in the middle of five lanes, where you couldn't pull over to go to the bathroom or change a blown tire, let alone to commit a crime. Julia listened to the weather report for the third time. It hadn't changed—outside the tunnel the sky remained an immaculate blue, and the temperature was still sixty-four degrees. Nothing interesting was going to happen.

"It's bad today," the driver said.

Hannah looked up from the papers in her lap. "What is?" she said.

"The traffic. We've hardly moved in ten minutes."

When she'd moved to Oakland for Kate and started commuting across the Bay, something she'd always said she'd never do, Hannah had been relieved to discover that the casual car pool was not casual at all, but a complex and predictable system which operated under its own code of etiquette. You had to get into the first car that arrived, no picking and choosing, although women could skip pickup trucks and two-seater convertibles in which they'd have to ride alone with a man. The first person in line always took the back seat, unless he was unusually tall. Worse-than-usual traffic and worse-than-usual weather were the only acceptable topics of conversation, after *Good morning* and before *Thank you, have a good day,* and passengers were expected never to speak unless the driver spoke first. No one ever explained the rules, but they were so clear and universally accepted that you figured them out yourself the first day you took the car pool. Hannah had only witnessed someone break the code once, a middle-aged white woman driving a Volvo station wagon with a "Free Tibet" sticker on its rear bumper. There'd been a news item on NPR about a black kid beaten to death by the police, and she'd started apologizing to the suited, briefcased black man in the front seat. In back, Hannah had cringed, but she hadn't said anything. Later, she wished she had.

She looked at the blue-lit clock on the dashboard. Seven thirty-eight. She'd been running late all morning, in a foul mood, snapping at Kate for hitting the snooze button one more time than Hannah could tolerate and for buying the wrong kind of coffee, but on her way out she'd discovered in yesterday's unchecked mail the thick manila envelope that might change everything. She should have taken the envelope back into the apartment as a peace offering, should have wanted to open it with Kate—it was addressed to both of them—but instead, she brought it with her, leaving the rest of the mail for Kate to find when she finally left for work.

Reading in cars made Hannah feel sick to her stomach, especially in traffic. It helped to train her eyes on the horizon or on anything far enough away that it didn't appear to move, but today she couldn't resist the packet in her lap. Luckily the driver shifted gears and changed lanes smoothly and only when necessary. As soon as he'd merged safely onto the freeway Hannah slid her nail under the envelope's seal and drew out a stack of papers, each two sheets, stapled, letterheaded *The Bay Area Cryogenic Center,* containing a brief description—not only physical but biographical, medical, and genealogical—of a man Hannah would never meet, who had agreed, in advance and for reasons of his own, to become the father of her child.

Only it wasn't going to be her child, not only hers, but hers and Kate's. Which meant that this preview, this flipping through profiles in a stranger's car, felt like a small betrayal.

Ian squinted at the headlights reflected in his rearview mirror, trying to determine if the car behind him remained at a reasonable distance, or if it had crept closer, the way he'd eased off his own brake to shorten the gap between his car and the one in front. He knew it was pointless, this edging forward, but he could not help feeling anxious to get out of the tunnel. If he was going to sit in traffic, he wanted a view: the silver lip of the city, the roll of fog cushioning the Golden Gate. He thought about how the prisoners on Alcatraz used to hear the boisterous city at night, the sounds of glass and laughter. Nothing was very far away. He checked his mirror again, and this time saw not the river of lights but the girl, the one in back, with her arm bent at an awkward angle, shoulders bare, T-shirt noosed around her neck. He glanced at the car in front, then at the woman beside him. She was oblivious, still completely absorbed in whatever she was reading.

"Is it warm back there?" Ian asked. "I can turn the air on if you want." Ian never turned the air on. He liked to feel the climate change as he drove to work. Most days, the temperature dropped ten degrees between home and Oakland, and another ten as he crossed the Bay.

"It's fine," Julia said. She was an expert at changing her clothes without revealing anything more than her shoulders and a couple of inches of belly, parts that other girls showed off all the time. She'd spent a long time choosing the T-shirt she changed into: fading black, emblazoned with the name of a band she'd never heard play, slightly ripped along one seam. She envied people who lived casually, who did not need to try as hard as she did to pick out the right T-shirt, or to think of the right things to say. She snapped a studded leather bracelet around a wrist, extracted a hook of silver from a tiny Ziploc bag and threaded it through the nearly imperceptible hole in her nose. Watching in the rearview mirror, Ian thought she looked as though she were dressing for work, or for a performance, and in a sense she was. If she made it off the bridge alive, if she did not die of boredom first, Julia would take the streetcar to the Castro, where she would sit on the gum-splotched sidewalk outside the Ben & Jerry's next to Isaac, a fourteen-year-old runaway Mormon from the shore of the Great Salt Lake. She would put a coffee cup in front of her, a few coins in the bottom for seed, and stare into Sweetie's eyes while she waited for change. Sweetie, Isaac's half-grown pit bull, was good for protection but discouraged donations, while Julia, with her wispy blond hair and new-to-the-streets fragility, elicited sympathy and dollar bills from the older women and straight men who were immune to Isaac's charms. It made no sense that passersby rewarded cleanliness among panhandlers, but they did. Julia bought Diet Cokes with the money she earned, and cookie-dough ice cream cones for both of them, but at the end of the day she turned what was left of her takings over to Isaac before boarding the F Market to the Embarcadero and then the bus back across the bridge.

Later, lying awake in the pink room she'd slept in since she was small, she thought about Isaac. They didn't allow dogs at the shelters, so he either camped in the park with the other street kids, or he let someone buy him a sandwich and take him somewhere where afterwards, if he was lucky, he might be able to sleep for a few hours. Julia wished she could bring him home with her, but she couldn't; her parents, though they donated to several charities and dropped loose coins into Styrofoam cups more often than not, would never open their guest room to a runaway kid and his dog, no matter how sweet and desperate they looked, no matter how much Julia pleaded.

She'd met Isaac in the summer, when she started riding the car pool into the city to escape the boredom that hung over the East Bay like smog. Julia had no friends. She used to have a friend, her best and only friend, Serena. Serena was the kind of girl who liked to keep only one friend at a time, and for almost two years she adored Julia. Her attention was bright and uncomfortable and hard to resist. They spent nearly all their time together. Whenever Julia spoke to anyone else, or mentioned another girl's name, or, worse, a boy's, unless it was in a mean way, Serena acted possessive and jealous, like a boyfriend. Then, in the spring of their freshman year, she replaced Julia. She found a new best friend who'd just moved to Oakland from Florida, who needed her more than Julia did and who would do whatever she asked. Almost overnight, and with no explanation, Serena stopped talking to Julia entirely. It was too late in the school year to make new friends. Everyone was organized already, into twos and threes and bigger groups; it didn't matter. No one, not even the outcasts, would make room for Julia.

She wanted to get a summer job, but her mother wouldn't let her. She said she wanted Julia to enjoy herself, to do whatever she pleased, within reason. In the future there would be jobs and SAT prep classes and trips to Europe. This might be the last summer she could be completely free.

"You used to have such fun at the pool with Serena," her mother said.

"I hate Serena," Julia said.

Her mother threatened to send her away to camp. Julia hated camp. She hated even the idea of camp. She refused to go. She went to the pool once by herself and felt so conspicuous and so alone that she never went back. After her parents left for work, Julia lay on the sofa in her underwear and a tank top, drinking cold milk with Hershey's syrup and watching TV reruns from before she was born. By July she was so lonely she wanted to die. One day she went for a walk and noticed several people standing in a parking lot. A fancy car pulled up, and two people got in.

Julia walked over to a woman in a cranberry suit who reminded her of her father's secretary.

"Where are you going?" Julia had asked.

A space opened up, and they fell out into the light. Ian switched off his headlights. Now he could see that the traffic extended all the way to the city, a two-mile ribbon of wasted time.

Hannah was thinking in control statements: *If (these conditions are true) then this will be the outcome. Else if. Else if. Else.* She'd worked as a programmer for a couple of years before she'd begun to think in code. Now, she found that it calmed her; it helped her to make decisions. *If* (the father is a mechanical engineer, six-foot-one). *Else if* (a Russian lawyer, in perfect health). *Else if* (a musician, with light-brown hair like Kate's and a slight risk of cancer on his mother's side). *Else if. Else.*

There was a reason to reject every profile. A disappointing academic record, an alcoholic grandparent, acne scars left over from adolescence, dishonesty or arrogance discernable in the way he answered the question "Why did you decide to do this?"

Of course, on terms like this she'd reject Kate. She'd reject herself. In their immediate families, she could count three alcoholics, two early heart attacks, three types of cancer, a paranoid schizophrenic, a case of multiple sclerosis, and one probable suicide. Kate sunburned easily (why was that a question on the profile; did anyone reject a donor for that?) and was frequently depressed. Hannah had an unimpressive college GPA and a late-blooming career.

She read the next profile. A twenty-three-year-old computer scientist, five-eleven, a hundred and eighty-two pounds, brown hair and eyes. No health problems, either mental or physical, no evidence of male pattern baldness. He was half Armenian, half Greek. Under cause of death for three of four grandparents he'd written "civil war."

She knew things about these men she'd never bothered to ask Kate—their blood types, the occupations of their aunts and uncles—but she didn't know if they were charming or considerate, if they could be trusted. She knew the particulars of their appearance, their eye color and so on, but she couldn't tell if they were handsome or ugly or strange. Hannah had been a bartender for most of her twenties. She wished she could watch the possible fathers from the other side of a long slick bar. She would listen to their voices and assess their looks. She'd notice their liquors of choice, how much they tipped, whether or not they carried drinks to their companions before they came back for their own.

Hannah looked at the driver. She could decipher almost as much about him as she knew about the possible fathers. He appeared to be in his late thirties, average in height and weight, his dark hair cut short to control the curl. He looked as though he worked out, though not every day. He wore a narrow wedding band (which meant, she thought, that he'd married while still young and relatively poor) and the sort of business casual attire—wide-wale corduroy pants and a carefully ironed, un-tucked white shirt—that suggested a media job of some kind.

"Jesus," he said. "What's that?" Now that she was paying attention, Hannah noticed his voice. Beneath evidence of education and moving about, she could hear the trace of an accent.

She squinted up through the windshield. "A helicopter," she said.

"No, look at the bridge."

Hannah looked. A butterfly: enormous, implausible, trussed in the steel cabling of the bridge.

"I don't know," she said. At such an angle, in the early glare, she could not be sure of the scale of the thing. Perhaps it was only a kite. Except that a helicopter fluttered mechanically near the suspension tower. Up ahead, in the right lane, several police cars, a fire engine with its ladder raised, and two ambulances waited, and in the Bay, beside the bridge, were two Coast Guard boats.

"Maybe it's a suicide." Suicides usually preferred the more romantic and accessible Golden Gate, so many they'd had to install phones with direct lines to counselors, but Ian liked the Bay Bridge better. It looked like a piece of the city, a cord tying it to the rest of the continent, while the Golden Gate was purely decorative.

"It's turquoise," Hannah said. "I think it has wings. It must be a hang glider."

"A hang glider could never make it this far."

"Someone with a parachute?"

"They're probably just filming a movie," the girl in the back seat said. She didn't care what was happening ahead on the bridge. If a person wanted to fly, he should stay away from bridges. If he wanted to kill himself, he should do it privately, not at rush hour.

"I don't think so," Hannah said. She often saw camera crews filming chase scenes or commercials on hilly picturesque streets in the city, but this looked like a real accident, not a made-for-TV disaster.

For his thirty-eighth birthday, Ian's wife had given him a skydiving lesson. A calculated risk in the form of a gift certificate. Miranda had driven him to Napa and sat on a blanket in a yellow field, reading a book, while he climbed into the hold of the little plane and flew up into the cloudless sky. The fall had not been as terrifying as he'd hoped. He just closed his eyes and jumped, that was all. He was tethered to the instructor the whole time. Later, during lunch, as he poured the last of an expensive bottle of chardonnay, he asked Miranda if she'd been watching as he plunged toward her, and she said yes, of course she'd watched. He knew she wasn't telling the truth.

He fiddled with the radio dial, against car-pool etiquette, to see whether he could find out anything about the person (he was sure, now, it was a person) caught above the bridge. But there was nothing; not even the traffic reports included the backup on the Bay Bridge. Ian wondered if he'd imagined the traffic, his two passengers, the parachutist. The morning had begun ordinarily enough. He'd eaten his usual breakfast: two slices of rye toast and a glass of grapefruit juice. He'd had a pleasant conversation with Miranda before leaving the house. He'd backed the car out of the driveway and into the street, without hitting the awkwardly placed mailbox or scraping the paint on the untrimmed hedge. As he veered onto the freeway, he thought: *If I wanted to, I could leave today and never go back.* This was a shock. It wasn't the first time he'd had such a thought—everyone entertained such ideas, no matter how content, how responsible, how in love they might be. But it was the first time Ian had thought this in quite this way, purposefully, as if it were possible. As if it were true.

He forced himself to look out, rather than down. White sails flecked the water. The city shone. He was used to seeing the Bay from above; he'd been skydiving for years. But stilled, the view was smaller, painful in detail. The tiny whitecaps looked like accents:

grave, acute. He was in pain, slipping in and out of consciousness. His right arm was useless; with his left he clung to a steel rope as thick as his waist, although if he let go he would not fall. His rig was caught in the suspension wires like a bird in netting. In his most alert moments he felt more embarrassed than scared.

Julia leaned her head against the cool window and stared at the sliver of visible city. She wished Isaac would send up a balloon or raise a flag to signal her. In the closet in the front hallway of her house, behind the coats, there was a white cloth safety-pinned to a wire hanger. Julia, at nine or ten, had insisted on it. Across the fabric, a square ripped from a linen tablecloth, she had colored in the letters O and K in dark blue magic marker. If there were another fire, she would hang the sign from a window, so the firemen would know she and her family had survived.

She'd been only six the last time, but she remembered everything: the too-bright sky, her mother's panicked, resolute voice. Before the fire came close, they packed a bag, just one for the two of them, and went to stay with one of her mother's friends in a small mint-colored bungalow far down on the flats. Julia's father was in Europe, on a business trip. Julia called for her cat, but Samson was off hunting or curled somewhere napping, and he didn't come. She sobbed for three days, inconsolable, until her father, who'd flown back from Europe as soon as he could, took her as close as possible to the ruined house. They stood among charred eucalyptus, calling and whistling for Samson. Of course he never came.

Her parents built a new house with the insurance money. A bigger, better house made of wide redwood planks, with walls of windows facing the Bay. Julia was allowed to help design her new bedroom. She wanted a window seat with a secret compartment. She wanted everything painted pink. Their neighbors on one side built a monstrous Tudor mansion, while the family on the other side chose an Italian villa with trellises and a red tile roof. All of the new houses, too big for their lots, looked as if they might fall off the scorched hill at any moment. For years, there were hardly any trees.

She did not know exactly what happened to Isaac at night—he'd never tell her, no matter how many times she asked—but she knew it was bad. She came to believe that he needed her, that her attention kept him safe. Whenever she climbed onto the F, he said he'd see her soon, and because he'd promised, he would. It was as though she'd imagined him, and she had to see him to make him real. It was harder now that school had started. In the first week and a half she'd skipped two days, and she hadn't been caught yet.

"What are you reading?" Ian asked his front-seat passenger.

Hannah resisted the urge to turn the papers upside down. She didn't want to get into a complicated discussion. "Applications," she said. It was true, in a way.

"What do you do?"

"Tech stuff, nothing very interesting." *If,* she thought, *we sit here forever on this bridge. Else if. Else.*

The girl in the back seat put headphones on. Hannah could hear the hiss and static of her music. She pulled down the sun visor and looked in the little mirror. The girl nodded in time with the rhythm. She looked even younger, Hannah thought, in black.

The possible fathers made her anxious. She tried to imagine the twin-helixed thread of a stranger's DNA wrapped two-ply with her own.

"Do you have children?" she asked, surprising herself.

Ian shifted and closed the gap between his car and the one in front. "A daughter," he said. "Natalie. She just turned six."

They'd flown to Beijing to get her when she was eleven months old. For weeks before he saw her, Ian had carried her picture everywhere with him, a tiny, wisp-haired girl, unsmiling in a red smocked dress and white shoes. Those weeks before they finalized the paperwork, when she was still an ocean away, had been torture. And then the plane ride, the longest he'd ever endured, longer even than the journey home, Natalie on Miranda's lap with the stiff posture and stern mouth of a judge. In the hotel room in Beijing those first numb, amazed nights, Natalie had whimpered and refused to eat, and they'd had no idea how to calm her. Ian held the baby so awkwardly his shoulders had ached for days.

"You're lucky," Hannah said.

Ian nodded. "You don't have kids?"

"Not yet."

He had no idea how difficult it could be. She could not believe she'd ever thought it was easy herself, that she had worried about getting pregnant by accident. When she was younger and slept with boys, it seemed as though all it took was a single mistake, but now that she wanted it to happen, the process was fraught with complications. She and Kate had made a list of possible fathers, men whose appearance and intelligence they approved of, whom they could trust not to panic or steal the baby away. They asked Kate's cousin, their gay friends Salvatore, Danny, and Tim, and Hannah's college roommate, the one she'd dated for a short time in her final effort at straightness. All of them said they'd think about it, then all of them said no.

An unknown donor was simpler logistically and safer legally, but still, Hannah worried. Several of their friends used the sperm bank in Berkeley. What if one chose the same donor as Hannah and Kate? In California, only twelve children could have the same unknown father, but the number of babies wasn't restricted in the rest of the country, and she'd read that England had started importing American sperm. She couldn't stop thinking about all those half-brothers and half-sisters, possibly hundreds of them, meeting accidentally as adults. What if two of them fell in love?

If only they could make a test-tube baby from two eggs, fusing one of her X chromosomes with one of Kate's. It had to be possible scientifically, although she'd never heard of a successful case. There were social and ethical implications, of course, but Hannah would gladly settle for girls.

He couldn't help it: he looked down. A river, glistering. He was confused, until the river broke into rectangles. Cars and SUVs and buses. He counted three white tops of buses, and counting roused him. Who was down there? People he knew, certainly. Coworkers, maybe an ex-girlfriend, people he knew but didn't know: security guards and bank tellers. Somehow, by jumping, he had stopped the morning. He thought: *I could shake this tower and break this bridge.* His shoulder hurt. He would not fall. He thought: *All of us are going to die.*

"That poor man, I can't imagine what he's going through. If it is a man." Hannah had always been afraid of heights. "It might be a woman," she said.

"Less likely," Ian said.

He watched a firefighter rappel up the nearest tower. He hoped the rescue effort wouldn't take much longer. He was almost out of gas. His habit of letting the needle drop into the red zone drove Miranda crazy. She worried about exactly this type of situation: Ian stranded on the bridge. Irresponsibly, he'd let his cellphone run out of batteries. He considered turning the ignition off, risking a rear-end collision if the traffic behind him started suddenly, but decided against it. He could hear someone singing, far away, behind him, a sweet faint voice, but he couldn't make out the song.

Julia tried to distract herself with music, but it didn't work. Two leather-clad men zoomed past on Harleys, in between lanes of stopped cars. She wished for a motorcycle, or even an ordinary bicycle. Once, not very long ago, a man had ridden his bicycle across the bridge, eastbound. Julia had seen it on the news. When the police tried to stop him, he pulled a gun, and they shot him. Julia wanted to get out of the car. She was thirsty, and she had to pee, a combination of sensations so irritatingly contradictory they must have been used for torture in China, or somewhere. She had to get out of the car. She could hitch a ride with the next motorcyclist to pass, or she could walk. She'd be perfectly safe. The traffic was hardly moving. The cops were busy with whatever was stuck up on the bridge like a kitten in a tree, and anyway, they'd be unlikely to shoot at a girl.

"Did you know," Ian said, "this bridge is actually three bridges?"

No one said anything.

"In the middle of the western span," he continued, "just up ahead, there's a block of concrete thrust into the floor of the Bay. More concrete than the Empire State Building."

"How do you know?" Julia asked.

Ian shrugged at his rearview mirror. "I read it somewhere. I don't remember where."

Over the guardrail Hannah could see Treasure Island: a hopeful name for a gray plate of landfill striped with military housing.

She pointed. "Imagine living there," she said. "Marooned in the middle of the Bay. You couldn't go *anywhere* without crossing the bridge."

Julia wrapped the cord around her headphones and zipped them into the front pocket of her backpack. The coating on the door handle had begun to peel. She worried it with her nails, etching flakes of rubber away like sunburned skin and flicking them onto the floor. She kicked a child's toy she hadn't noticed before and leaned to pick it up. An action figure, a lithe plastic girl wearing a silver costume, her ponytail frozen in mid-swing, arms upheld in a karate pose. Julia's door was locked; all four of the Altima's doors locked automatically when the car reached five miles per hour. She pressed the button to unlock it, but nothing happened. The child lock must have been turned on. What if the driver *were* a kidnapper or a rapist? She'd be trapped. Julia did not panic. Instead she tried to pry open the lock using the karate girl's slender hand. The driver looked back over his shoulder at her, but he didn't say anything. He looked like the kind of man who never said anything until it was too late. She tried again, but she couldn't lift the lock.

"Excuse me." Julia leaned forward. "Could you unlock the doors, please?"

"I don't think that's a good idea," Ian said.

"I'd just feel safer, that's all," the girl said.

"Safer?" Ian said.

"Yeah, I mean, I'm in a stranger's car. Anything could happen."

"Very little could happen." Ian gestured vaguely at the surrounding traffic, the water only slightly touched by wind. "We're stuck."

Julia sighed loudly and switched tactics. "Please?" she said. "It's not like there's anywhere I could go."

Ian didn't feel like arguing. He looked at the woman in the front seat. She was doing her best to ignore the conversation. He clicked the locks.

"Thanks," Julia said. She opened the door and stepped out onto the bridge, calmly, as if onto a curb.

The girl slammed the door harder than necessary. Ian's first reaction was irritation. Why did she have to slam the door every time? But this was the first time, the only time, and she wasn't his daughter grown tall and sullen. She was someone else's kid. What was she doing in the car pool, anyway? He'd never let Natalie ride with strangers, not at sixteen, not at twenty-two. This girl was lucky she'd ended up riding with him. Not that he'd kept her safe—he hadn't even managed to keep her in the car.

"Damn it," he said. "What does she think she's doing?" He'd been responsible for her, and he'd failed.

"You can't just let her go," Hannah said.

"What else am I supposed to do?" Ian glared at her. "You could have said something before."

Hannah looked up at the man on the bridge. At any moment he might fall. She pictured him plummeting to earth, breaking every bone in his body when he hit the surface of the Bay. The girl was already several car lengths away, darting between cars and SUVs and minivans, her red backpack bobbing. Hannah was quick in a crisis. She opened her door and half-fell onto the tarmac. She hadn't expected the wind on the bridge.

For a second she forgot why she was there. The whole bridge vibrated, tens of thousands of engines idling at once. She looked up, felt dizzy, looked back down. People shouted at her through car windows, but she couldn't understand them. The girl up ahead, running. Hannah chased her between the stalled cars. It felt like she was running on a conveyor belt; she was sure the bridge beneath her moved. The air fumed with exhaust. She was out of shape, and her chest began to hurt almost immediately. She didn't know the girl's name.

"Hey," Hannah yelled. "Slow down."

Julia didn't hear and neither slowed nor turned. Nobody paid attention to her. No one ever noticed Julia when she didn't want to be noticed.

A News 24 helicopter had joined the police helicopter near the tower. They floated, noisy as bees, the beginning of a swarm. Alone again, Ian waited for the woman to catch the girl. His phone was dead; he couldn't call 911. Should he abandon his car and follow them? He was tempted to lock the doors and put on some Bach, the partitas or a cello concerto, something soothing. Let them chase each other to the city. He didn't mind waiting for the man on the bridge to be rescued. He reached over and picked up one of the résumés the woman had left on the passenger seat. It looked more like a police report than a CV, the word RESTRICTED stamped in red across the top. The first page listed the applicant's vital statistics: height, weight, age, et cetera. There was a full medical history. He turned to the last page and read: "My children are the most important thing in my life, I want to give someone else the chance to start a family. Also, I think my genes are worth passing on."

It wasn't a résumé.

Ian gave up before Miranda did, even though she was the one who endured the painful tests and treatments, the weeks confined to their bed. She refused to believe that her body had failed her this first, important time, but after three years of worry and disappointments, he'd had enough. He wanted a child, but he was willing to live without the thrill of combining his genetic code with hers.

Hannah couldn't keep up with the girl. She slowed her pace enough to look up at the man still clinging to the steel ropes that held them all up. For the first time she wondered if he was already dead, if the helicopters, the emergency crews, the traffic jam, if all of it were a wasted effort. Why should the girl wait on the bridge with everybody else? Why shouldn't she walk across the Bay if that's what she wanted to do? She'd be safe enough, as long as she kept to the white line between lanes, as long as she watched out for motorcycles. She would reach the Embarcadero in fifteen or twenty minutes. Hannah let her go.

Julia stopped when she reached the flashing lights. She couldn't help it. She stopped and looked up at the glittering bridge. There was a person up there. For a moment she forgot about Isaac. She forgot about Serena, about school and her parents and the coins she'd have earned if she hadn't been stuck on the bridge. All she could see was a slip of turquoise, like a tatter of fabric caught in barbed wire, but she knew there was a person up there.

Hannah made her way back to the car, peering through windshields. Everyone looked sad and separate. How would she recognize the car? She could not remember what make it was, or what color. She did not notice that she'd passed it until she'd nearly reached the tunnel's opening. She considered climbing up onto the island; she had no idea what she'd find there—an enclave of houses, more military buildings, a bird sanctuary? But then she heard her name behind her, at least she thought she heard it over the din of cars and radios and helicopters.

The woman stopped, and he called again: "Hannah, Kate." He didn't know which of the two names on the envelope was hers. She didn't look like a Hannah—too small and dark—but he wasn't convinced she was a Kate, either. She must have been one or the other, though, because she turned and started toward him. As she moved closer, away from the tunnel's grip, she appeared to float above the tarmac. He wasn't sure what caused the effect; perhaps simply the strangeness of watching someone walk where he'd never seen anybody walk before.

"What happened?" he asked.

"I couldn't catch up with her."

Ian went to the passenger side of the car first and held the door open for her. He wasn't sure what brought on the gallant gesture—once he'd prided himself on opening the passenger door before his own not just on dates but all the time, no matter what his intentions towards his passenger were (he even did it for men, and for Miranda after he married her), but when he bought the Altima, with its electronic key that locked and unlocked all four doors remotely, such courtesy began to seem excessive.

He turned the key in the ignition. "So are you Hannah or Kate?"

"Hannah," she said. "How did you—?"

He nodded at the manila envelope. He'd put it on the dashboard; its reflection glowed faintly in the windshield. "After a while I wasn't sure you were coming back. I checked for an address in case you didn't."

He wanted to ask about the contents of the envelope, but she seemed so enclosed, staring through her side window at Angel Island to the north.

"I wonder what was so urgent," she said. She missed the girl in the back seat. With only two passengers, the car no longer qualified as a high occupancy vehicle. Officially, it didn't matter, because the car pool lane ended at the toll plaza. But inside the car, the rules disappeared.

"Everything's urgent when you're a kid." Except for his daughter, who was more patient and reasonable than most adults he knew. It unnerved him. He looked sideways at Hannah. "See what you have to look forward to?"

Hannah picked up the envelope. "Did you open this?" she asked.

"I shouldn't have. My curiosity got the better of me." Ian watched her face change. "I'm sorry," he said.

"It's private," Hannah said, although it wasn't. She'd already dealt with the unnaturally buoyant staff of the cryogenic center, already endured a lesson on optimal sperm insertion from a midwife who'd once been on a blind date with Kate. And then there were the possible fathers themselves.

"I really am sorry," Ian said. Hannah ignored him, but he was nervous now, and when he was nervous he could never stop talking. "It's quite a process, isn't it? My wife and I tried everything: bed rest, hormone shots, in vitro, acupuncture, awful smelling herbs. Nothing worked."

"Really?" Hannah couldn't keep the surprise out of her voice.

"We ended up adopting."

"That's great," Hannah said. "I mean, it's great that it worked out. Your daughter's very lucky."

"We're all lucky. Natalie's a great kid."

Hannah shook out the profiles. "So did you see anyone you liked?" she asked.

Ian's smile flickered. "I liked the Armenian."

"I was curious about him, too."

"Couldn't you just ask someone you know?"

"We tried that. Everyone said no." Hannah looked over at the driver as she said this. Sitting there beside her, tapping one hand on his corduroy thigh, he seemed as plausible as any of the possible fathers. In programming, you had to take into account every parameter, every circumstance, every possible factor. Hannah thought she'd done that, but she hadn't. Here was proof of her mistake: another option. If she wanted it to, it could happen. She felt absolutely certain of that. She'd never have to see him again. But there was Kate, who by now would be at work in downtown Oakland, beside the garlanded lake. Kate, who would not yet have heard about the man with the parachute.

Someone knocked on Ian's window. A cop. He put his gloved hand on the rim of the door, leaned, and peered in, then motioned to Ian to open the window.

The girl from the back seat was standing next to him, her cheeks flushed from running, her small chin pointed and defiant. She was still holding the silver-clad karate girl.

"This your daughter?" the cop asked.

"No," Ian said.

"Yes," Hannah said at exactly the same time. She did not know why she felt such a compulsion to lie for the girl.

"Which is it?"

"He's my stepfather," the girl explained. "We don't get along."

Inexplicably, Ian felt hurt and tempted to defend himself.

"I caught her wandering on the bridge," the cop said.

"Thank you, officer," Hannah said. "We were worried."

Ian gave the girl the most punishing look he could muster. "Get in the car."

The cop opened the back door like a valet. "Please watch your daughter more carefully in the future. We have enough to deal with as it is."

"Oh, we will," Ian said.

Julia slipped in behind him and slouched in her seat.

"You're lucky we covered for you," Ian said. "You could have been in serious trouble."

"Thanks," Julia said.

"What happened?" Hannah asked.

"I stopped to look, and that guy saw me," Julia said. "I didn't want him to call my parents."

"So you lied," Ian said.

"I guess."

"Could you see any more from up there?" Hannah asked.

"Not really," Julia said.

The jumper watched his rescuer draw closer, sidestepping along the suspension cable, a high wire acrobat above an audience of thousands. The man appeared to shout, but the jumper couldn't hear him above the din of the helicopter treading air above him. For the first time since smashing into the bridge, he blistered with panic. He watched as the man lowered himself onto the spun-steel cable and cut the lines to his canopy.

He did not fall. He did not plunge three hundred rushing feet and hit the water, and he did not arch into the cool sea-level air. His rescuers (suddenly there were two; he did not know where the second had come from) tended to the wound on his neck, splinted his arm, and wrapped him in a silver blanket. A basket fastened to a cord appeared, and they lifted him into it. He shut his eyes and let them haul him up to safety.

JON BILLMAN

Inkneck

The crusade had been brewed up over empty stomachs and ulcer bomb margaritas made from reconstituted lime juice and ice cubes older than the tequila. Bob's tequila-idea plan was simple: He—we—would become minor anecdotes by driving to El Paso, Texas, finding Cormac McCarthy at the pool table, challenging him to a game of eight-ball, beating him, then walking into the neon infamy of morning having whupped what Bob called "the best living writer to ever live."

"This," Bob said, "will ensure us our very own asterisk in the annals of American letters." He studied my face for a moment. "How hard can it be?"

"Damn hard," I said.

"He's a shark, for sure—I'm not gonna try to pull any wool about that." Bob was talking as if he knew this guy, had scouted him out. "He's beatable."

"I just don't know," I said. "El Paso, that's like, like Detroit with better Mexican food. We'll find nothing but trouble there. You've heard the song."

"You been there?" Bob said. An El Paso notch in my pistol grip would have impressed him.

"No," I said. "I've read about it."

"Yeah, me, too." His eyes wide green shooter marbles of possibility. "But that's why Cormac's the real deal. He could afford to live anywhere. The Big Apple. Key West. Palm Springs. A three-story cabin in the middle of the town square in Jackson Hole, for chrissakes. But he's too leathery and steely for those velvet-codpiece puff towns."

"Velvet codpiece? You gotta quit reading for a while."

"That's what I'm getting at. Cormac walks the streets of El Paso, baby!"

The man with the little hammer had paid us both a visit. Midmorning, and I was entirely removed from my good sense—this with nothing but what I think may have been a housecoat to cover up with—on the shag carpet on the living room floor. Bob had sprung with new life from his own couch to make pancakes since Allison was still at the hospital, working, but would have made them for us had she been home. Not only did Bob remember the idea best left in the tequila tank, but he started making on-the-ground plans right along with the just-add-water pancake batter as if I remembered all of this cockamamie plan, too, and no further discussion would be necessary. Oh, how simple it would be: We'd drive his 1972 Volvo from Laramie to El Paso, find the wordsmith at the tables, and take his lunch money and with it a story that would last us the rest of our lives. "He's good," Bob said. "Semi-pro quality, I hear."

"Where do you hear this stuff?"

"You know, Cormac chatrooms."

"They have those?"

"Blogs and chatrooms, sure. Then there's the Cormac McCarthy Society, but that's kind of officious, and they don't talk much about pool."

"How do you blog about a writer?" Bob looked at me like I was a blank sheet of typing paper. "How would us beating him even be in the cards?"

"We practice."

"Hold on," I said. "Running a 'semi-pro pool hustler' from El Paso, Texas, is way different than beating peewee league–play eight-ballers from Wheatland."

"Why," Bob said.

"Just a feeling I get."

"Maybe we're on our game and Cormac's off his."

"Or vice versa."

"Naw, we'll have the momentum of travel on our side. Wyoming road men coming to your town, unannounced."

"Never mind his home-table advantage, huh." We followed through, anyway. Even after Bob bailed on us taking his Volvo and insisted it would turn out just fine if we took the Flower Ranger van instead. The van was my work vehicle, before we took it to Texas. A 1990-something Dodge minivan, new-banana green with the red Flower Ranger bucking bronco bouquet airbrushed on both sides.

"What we really need is a hearse," Bob said. "You know, for intimidation. Wouldn't even have to break down our cues. But this'll do. It's like something Harrogate would drive." Harrogate being Bob's favorite character of literature, the off-his-nut Tennesseean who goes to jail for violating muskmelons in Cormac's novel *Suttree.* Huck Finn on a hearty diet of lead paint.

Bob is one of those guys who are led around by their obsessions as if obsession were a weather balloon and Bob was tethered to it at the navel with parachute chord. Some days the wind is up. Some days it's howling. The term "fanatic" is a bit mild when talking about Bob's affliction for Cormac McCarthy. It's like a budding guitarist's might be for, say, Eric Clapton. No, it's worse than that. Bob has read Cormac's *Suttree* twenty-two times and plans to read it again. "I figure I've got sixty more years in me before I'm quit of this world," Bob says. "Conservatively figuring if I read it twice a year, that's one hundred twenty more times. One hundred forty-two total."

I read *Suttree* once. Most of it. I guess I liked it fine, especially the carp-fishing scenes. It seems to me that you leave a book with the immediacy of life, and it lasts for about an hour or so. But then after three or four days turn into weeks and months, you look back on the book when you see it there under coffee cups and beer bottles or leveling up a card table or even tucked back on the shelf next to cookbooks and telephone directories and self-help manuals on how to improve your marriage, and there's only one image—Ishmael clinging to the floating coffin—that you associate with that respective work. The *Suttree* image I hold is of Harrogate, overalls down around his ankles, moonlight reflecting off his hairy peach ass, violating those muskmelons.

"It's a Southern thing," Bob says, as if that should explain it, no need to keep beating that dead horse.

To tell you the truth, I never even finished *All the Pretty Horses,* even though Bob gave it to me on six cassette tapes that read "Books on Tape for the Visually Impaired. Property of Albany County Library." I played it in the van for a while, but kept ejecting due to that feeling that news was fomenting out there in the world and I might be missing something on the AM.

"He must be an athlete with a pool cue, an extension of his

genius pen," Bob said. "A dancer with a fencing foil. Anyone who writes like that. He's insane. Mad. Captain Ahab of the Chihuahuan Desert." Bob has to take a break to swallow the spittle that isn't hitting me when he talks about this guy we're driving seven hundred miles one-way to shoot against—that is, if we can find him. "It's not like he's out on a book tour somewhere," Bob said. "Hey, you know what's so brilliant about Cormac?"

"No."

"It's that inside that whack world of crazy nouns and adjectives and explosions of verbs, there are definite rules. No one knows what the rules are, of course, except Cormac, which is why he's The Man with a typewriter. Herman Melville of the border landlocked."

"Herman Melville we can beat at pool," I said.

"I saw Herman Melville's grave once, years ago," Bob said. "In the Bronx, New York, not far from Yankee Stadium. I expected a shrine to rival Jim Morrison's or Mark Twain's. But it was a smallish leaning limestone marker, not extraordinary at all. I don't remember the epitaph, but I remember how the words were weathered down so that the gravestone was nearly flat and coarse. And there were no flowers, no sir. No bottles of sherry, no anything left near it—it was like no one had visited him in months. Hey, you know who else was in that cemetery?"

"Who?"

"Bat Masterson."

"*The* Bat Masterson?"

"Yup, that one and only. Know who else?"

"No."

"Miles Davis."

"I thought he died in a gunfight out West somewhere. Arizona or someplace."

"Miles Davis?"

"No, Bat Masterson."

"Naw. He went back to New York and became a sportswriter."

Where are the Bobs of the world, making pilgrimages to pay respect to the father of Moby-Dick? So maybe this pilgrimage to beat a still-living genius wasn't that bad an idea—maybe it was a procession of respect for the man while he's still alive.

"Battalions of English professors are working 'round the clock on cracking Cormac right now," Bob says. "Think of the resources employed in the cause. Harness that energy, and you could light all the neon in every bar in Laramie."

This trip would be good for me, I figured. Maybe I'd find my head and bearings in El Paso. Maybe I'd be motivated to finish commercial driving school or commercial carpentry school and make a better situation for Jeannie, my wife, and Hogue, my three-year-old son. Maybe they'd take me back. But the licking of a novelist at billiards wasn't something I needed—who but Bob and his blogger pals would it impress? The act seemed akin to saying you beat Mark Arn, the local weatherman on Channel 5 out of Cheyenne, or even the Governor of Wyoming, what's-his-name?— who would care? But then, because it's in the darkest pockets of our already-black souls, what we did not want to do was to *get beat* by a novelist, not even a ham-fisted one like Cormac McCarthy.

So we practiced. Upstairs at the Buckhorn Bar down by the Union Pacific switchyard in old Laramie. The Buckhorn is the closest you can get in Wyoming to the image in our minds of El Paso, Texas; the rest of Laramie, Wyoming, in general, are the Horse Latitudes of Culture. But in the Buck there are bullet dents in the pay phone—not holes, but dents, where a .38 Special's slugs tried and failed to pierce the old and reliable communication device. No one still here knows the story of whether or not someone was on the phone and between lead and miracle material at the time of the denting. "Why don't they just build cars and airplanes out of that stuff they make those pay phones out of?" Bob says.

"Bob, man," I said while working on a kick shot. Bob caught the balls so they wouldn't drop and cost us another fifty cents just to practice. "I just hope your expectations aren't too high."

"Whatdoyamean?"

"I mean, this guy Cormac doesn't sound like he's trying to outreach to readers, exactly. He doesn't read down at the local coffeehouse. He doesn't do *The Today Show.* He doesn't even tour after he writes a new book. No interviews. No lectures. He's like the Dick Cheney of novelists. Maybe we can work up a game of eight-ball, but I just don't want you to be surprised if we don't leave El Paso F-O-C."

"What the hell is F-O-C?"

"Friends of Cormac."

"No, no, hell no. What did you think? We're like gunslingers in the Old West. Those cats didn't have friends. Didn't need 'em. What's a gunslinger with a friend? A corpse, that's what. They just wanted to rule a territory. And the baddest, the baddest of the bad would at times ride into some other gunslinger's territory just to kick lead in the other gunslinger's face. Then they'd go back home. That's what we're gonna do."

You might want to know this about Bob. I first met him at the bowling alley one morning after I'd let the Bluebird-load of middle school kids off, before I had any scheduled deliveries for Flower Rangers. He had been an attorney in Michigan, had had drive, ambition once, but said he found himself standing in front of Lane 4 one afternoon and thinking, What am I doing? I don't just not enjoy going to work—I outright hate it. Being a lawyer is unlike any lawyer's life I'd ever read about—Atticus Finch, my ass. I can't leave it, I bring the ambulance home with me evenings, and can't sleep because I'm thinking about plaintiffs in neck braces and jowly paid expert witnesses. I'd like to just bowl.

"The last straw," he says, "was when I came home from the office one afternoon, and on my driveway was a copy of the new phone book, white and yellow pages. And there I was on a peel-and-keep baseball card begging anyone with a phone and a finger to call toll-free for a free accident consultation." Bob blows a crown of Kool smoke and watches it drift over his monologue. "When I first moved to Laramie, I was looking for a place to hang out mornings. I wandered into the Buckhorn, and bowling turned into billiards. You know, bowling balls are so heavy in those early hours. Anyway, Cormac doesn't bowl. I don't know any novelists who bowl. Good novelists, anyway."

After a couple of beers that morning, that first time we ever hung out and over together, he told me this: "I want to be a reader. Know what I mean?"

"You mean a writer?" I said.

"No, I want to be a reader. Go full-time with it. I'm better at it. You know, than writing. And I like it more. The world doesn't need another grocery list from me."

"Is there a future in that?"

Bob just shrugged his shoulders, like that question had never really occurred to him.

Bob is married to an incredible woman named Allison. Allison is a nurse. She works Intensive Care, and they live in West Laramie, the not-so-quaint part of town. It's on the windward side of the city and takes the brunt of the Wyoming Wind Corridor, which is essentially the jet stream touching dirt, so that by the time the wind hits East Laramie, it's worn out, tired, needs a break, needs to catch its breath before revving up over the mountain and down again onto Cheyenne. His trailer-park neighbor to the north is a methamphetamine chemist. His neighbor to the south is a hard-drinking mechanic named Chester who works nights out at the Petro truck stop. Allison is a certified nurse and punches graveyards at the hospital. I've seen her there when I've been running late and just getting to fill the refrigerator with the twelve-dollar arrangements when she's going on shift, and her aura is that of an optimist, a smiler in scrubs the color of wine who believes even though in her heart she knows her husband has been bitten—by an affliction worse than alcohol or meth or golf—and she's the one wearing the scrubs in the family for the foreseeable future that could so easily stretch into forever and death did we part.

She gets Bob free antibiotics with which he kills a sinus infection about twice a year. "That's all the sick I ever get. Zythromax is the bomb," he says. "But you gotta make sure you eat yogurt with it because it'll kill even the good bugs in your gut." Allison works so hard. Bob is still asleep when she gets home after the sun has only been up a few hours. And she showers the hospital off and crawls into bed next to him. Then he gets up and eats cereal while she sleeps. By the time she goes back off to work, Bob is at the library or Second Story Books or practicing at the Buck with me. She's incredible, and I love to watch her working so hard for people who need her, her black hair tied up and her skin sweating in those scrubs, making calculations about IVs and injections, and I think she is beautiful. So improbably beautiful when you consider Bob's latest prospects. I'm not sure what she sees in him anymore except that Bob used to be an attorney, still is, I guess, technically, if he's kept his card up. And he can play "Old Plank Road" on the banjo. "What did the banjo picker say to the dentist?" Bob says.

"I don't know. What?"

"This might hurt a little."

I gave Bob a little piece of Spanish news. I'm not sure what that means, but it sounds good in Tennessee Williams. "I know what you are," I told him. "You're a redneck who likes books." Swallow. "You're an. An. An... *inkneck.*"

Bob regarded me for a moment. He made wax lips with his. His marbles conflated and brightened. He seemed proud of that, that moniker: Inkneck. "Yeah. Right on, then. I'm down with that. Makes me sound like a modern-day Queequeg—the tattooed harpooner of bookmobiles." He sipped more beer. "So if I'm an inkneck, what're you—a redneck who delivers children and flowers? The dandelion cowboy?"

"Just that, I guess." I hadn't really thought of a definition of the picture of myself in a long time—I'd been putting it off. There I am, interfacing with all those people taking blood pressures, setting bones, saving lives. Here I am, a taxi driver for small plants. Travis Bickel with baby's breath.

There's still so much stuff out there Bob hasn't read; entire librariesful—he needs to stay with it. Ask him sometime to show you the tattoo on his deltoid of the knife stuck into the book and the book is bleeding and the blood has pooled so that you cannot read the title. "I was going to have the title on the book read *Allison,*" he'll tell you. "But when I got it done down at Tiny's Tattoo Rodeo, you know, the place at Ivinson and Owen Wister, Tiny asked me how do I spell her name, and I was so messy that I couldn't remember if my Allison was spelled with one *l* or two. Then Tiny says, Is it with an *i* or a *y*? Tiny didn't know either, so all I can do is sit there in the barber chair and stare at Tiny like he's a man on Mars trying to remember one *l* or two and do I gamble on it until Tiny looks at me like I'm so lost he doesn't even feel right about inking me at all anymore, like I don't deserve it. It's not like we could have called her and asked her at that ungodly hour—she was working."

It's dark in the back room of the Buck, like a casino, and you lose the sensation of time—a guy could spend a lifetime in there, and it would only feel like a stage he was going through. The Buck smells of a combination of cigarette smoke, old books, and cat urine. Bob has this habit of powdering his hands with talc about every third shot, caressing the phallic cone like it's a work of art and he the master potter. Talc fills the air when he claps ritualistically. I'd watched Bob slipping since he'd dreamt this Cormac plan, and now he saw the entire world through bad-metaphor-tinted glasses. "It's like being in an asbestos mine," he said. "We're like bats in here, bats playing pool and drinking bat beer in an asbestos mine."

"Bob," I said over the pool table, under the Falstaff naked lady light, one afternoon. "You think it's possible to read a life away?"

Whatdoyamean?

"To never live, just exist vicariously through characters from someone else's imagination. Someone else's heart. And all the while your body is dying, atrophying, sagging and burping and decaying and gassing and cells are shitting the bed and begging for a few antioxidants in order to go buck the molecular inevitable one last futile time?"

Bob took a long pull of beer. "Yes I do," he said while banking the nine-ball into the northeast corner pocket, a nice pinch of backspin on the whitey.

"Nice shot," I said. Bob speaks in semicolons, so I just waited for him to reply to my question. The question scared me, made me think of my own life, and how working driving a bus for the school district and delivering flowers are great jobs with flexibility if you like to drive around town and listen to kids screaming and the world revolving on the AM radio, and I just call in sick whenever I feel like it, but maybe there's no future in that, either, when the bottom line is both jobs put together with overtime don't pay fertilized squat. Bob dropped another one, and he was after the black eight. He stroked it a little too hard, and it jawed between the corner tits and hung in the pocket for me to take on home.

"You on the lemonade?" I said. "It's not like you to miss that one."

"The sun was in my eyes."

"Care to expound?"

"On what?"

"On the point that you agree that it's possible to read a life away in some sort of bibliophilic Margaritaville."

"Well," he said, stealing a tall quaff from the shell glass that paints the mustache of his goatee white with foam. "That could happen to a cat like me. So that's why we're shooting now, practicing, working out. Training; so we can go down to El Paso and box Cormac's ears."

Chester looked Bob's old 1972 Volvo bucket over and said it probably wouldn't make it to Tie Siding, let alone El Paso, but that we could always pull the license plates and thumb it or catch the Greyhound back to East Laramie if the car goes south. "It's those damn Swedes," Chester said. "They rolled out that insane Bosch fuel injection years before it was ready, thinking they were getting the jump on the carbureted world. It was like taking a box of empty guns to a knife fight."

"Thanks, Chester," Bob said. "For ten bucks will you tell us what we want to hear?"

"Hell, I'll tell you what you want to hear for five. But if I were you I'd take your sister's flower van there. Just top off the tank when you get back, and no one will notice."

"No way in hell," I told Bob.

He smiled his big goateed Mephistophelean beat smile. "But there's a way in Hell-Paso!"

And that's really the beginning of—if you were drawing this out on a napkin—the parabolic arc leading from the bad idea, over the hump of consequences, and down into damn dubious resolution.

We hit the tripmeter on the van at the cement plant at the south edge of Laramie. Leaving Laramie is a little anxiety-inducing—to go off the standards of semesters and happy hours and hunting holiday and buy-nine-lattes-your-tenth-one's-free down at the Pony Expresso. From this windy Lotusland we are sucked through the sewer pipe that is I-25, down the diabolic vortex of the Front Range. Traffic in Denver is—no surprise—phantasmagorical. No one in Denver is happy. In fact they're pissed off most all of the time. Round the clock, like it's their job and they work hard at it. That's because no one there is from Denver, they all bought into the John Denver Theory of the Universe and, mistakenly thinking they were moving to Colorado, up and U-Hauled away from all their family and points of reference to the Mile High City instead. When they got there so much of their stuff was broken, and they quickly learned the city is polluted as any on whichever dream coast they'd come from, skiing was still two hours away on a good day, and the one thing they brought with them that they should have left back where they'd come from was themselves. Besides, their baseball team, the Rockies, is a perennial turd. That, Bob and I say, is why they drive this way.

I'd never used the air conditioning in the van before—never needed it in Laramie. Also I knew it didn't work. Down about Fort Collins Bob turned it on, and it kicked out a bug-gun plunge of dust, then some hot air, then less-hot air, then air just as hot as the air outside. "Ha," Bob said. "This is travelin' ice wagon style. I'll bet, though, we can get some Freon at the border, from some Freon smugglers." He liked the word, Freon—it sounded dangerous and illegal. "We oughta stock up on Freon for this baby." He was sipping on another beer from the block-ice flower cooler in the back. "This reminds me of my friend Puker's hearse he drove in high school. Had a ski rack on the top and a pressurized keg system in the back. We took it skiing."

"I didn't know you skied."

"I just went the once with Puker. I don't like being outside in the cold all day. I guess it wasn't all day, just an hour or most of it. It was really icy so I kicked it by the fireplace in the lodge with a book."

"You remember what book?"

"Yeah, it was *The Red Badge of Courage*. I love that one. I sat there and read it twice, I think. It's pretty short."

Before they flew flowers into Cheyenne and rushed them over the pass to Laramie, Wyoming got the dead and dying flowers they swapped out of hospital coolers all over the country—that's where they all went, along with watery avocados and black apples and chocolate-colored bananas: Wyoming.

This isn't true, of course, except for the fruit, but it makes for an anecdote to tell patients and orderlies and nurses and custodians as I'm swapping out the cooler. Now sometimes there are flowers left over—an order is mixed up or messed up or I'm refreshing the hospital cooler with tulips and roses just off the airplane, so I get to keep the old stock—when you're already there there's no Wyoming for us to send them to. That's my favorite part of the job—I'm the Shepard of Sunshine then. Jesus of the Geraniums. I'm free to dispense the irregulars! I often take a bunch to Jeannie, though she knows I get them free when the flowers are tired and their end is near, and I suspect she's weary of just-this-side-of-wilting-so-soon-to-be-compost chrysanthemums. But I have time to kill, and I take them by, anyway, our place—her place now—on Custer Street. I'll try to be clumsy and leave the window down with the AM blaring Gordon Lightfoot or Jim Croce or someone, and maybe Jeannie will come out and catch me leaving flowers on the doorstep, and maybe Hogue will be on her leg, wondering who it is and are they brandishing possibilities.

Sometimes I'll give those flowers to someone in a wheelchair and a smock who could use a boost. And if I still have a vase or two left, I take one into Rosie, the afternoon barmaid at the Buck. Rosie has been the afternoon barmaid since before they built the railroad. I have a pop—just one—before I have to get bus number six and deliver kids. When I get back to the Buck in two or three hours, those roses are on the bar, standing up to all that smoke, doing their best for as long as they can. "Don't forget to put a pack of sugar in the vase water," I tell Rosie. "None of that damn Sweet'N Low."

And once I left some roses in baby's breath at the Intensive Care desk with a note: "For Allison, from someone who cares and appreciates all that you do." I hope she thought they were from Bob; I hope he didn't screw it up when she got home.

At Raton Pass the sign says all commercial vehicles must stop at the inspection station. I pull in and shut down on the scale in front of the flat-roofed inspection building. The Inspection agents inside don't even get out of their chairs—they wave me off, and they're laughing, very animated through the glass, maybe at a joke one of them told.

Wyoming is not a food state. South of Raton, New Mexico, we stop to eat at Heck's Hungry Traveler in the middle of a tumbleweed field. Heck's Hungry Traveler is nothing to read at home about, and you have to be famished just to finish the chicken sandwich and soggy fries. I am sad to report that in Wyoming, Heck's would be tops. Then Las Vegas and Elephant Butte. "It really does look like an elephant," Bob says.

"All ridgelines look like elephants if you stare at them long enough," I say. "Elephants and Sleeping Indians." Truth or Consequences.

"I think that's a portent," Bob said. "A sign. You know, we're seeking the truth about Cormac. The consequences of not seeking the truth would have been that you'd have to hear me speculate about the Cormac truth, the shattering of the myths, until hell freezes over."

I wanted to throw a switch on the metaphilosophy. "Man, think of the badass hanging judge this place was named after back in the day. Gavel-pound-wham—give me truth or be damned to the consequences!"

"Actually," Bob said with his especially informative tone. "The place is named for the game show. From back in the day. *Truth or Consequences.* Sad but nonfiction—I read about it."

"Anyway," I said, "the place looks just like West Laramie."

"You think?" said Bob.

The strip buffets and furniture marts and pancake houses are stacked like teeth along I-25 through Las Cruces, where the crusty ass-end of the Rocky Mountains is pounded flat before ramping up again in Mexico's Sierra Madres. South of Las Cruces, pecan orchards turn into dairy farms that turn into creosote fields. At the border we pass a horseracing track, then Exit 0, and Bob takes it as a sign. "Exit 0! There can't be an Exit 0—we've entered a new dimension." There is a line in the road, and the pavement goes from New Mexico decent to Texas sketchy. "We've reached Cormac's Van Diemen's land," Bob said. Past a glowing steel mill. "There's the blacksmith in the village of the damned." I think Bob expected witches in sombreros and bald giants with croker sacks full of bats and children—croker sack being one of those Cormac words Bob especially enjoys.

The sky over El Paso was capped with a pollution cloud the color of the plastic-jug tequila that goes by the name of Potter's. Bob had read on several of those Cormac-worshipping websites that caution you not to ring the writer's doorbell that Cormac really does not live underneath an oil derrick, not in a rough stone hovel without running water, but rather he lives in engineered seclusion in a regular neighborhood in El Paso, and in the afternoons he grabs his stick and runs the tables on the locals. "Coffin Avenue," Bob said. "I have it on good authority that Cormac lives on Coffin Avenue. I want to respect the man's privacy and just beat him at pool, not interrupt his next divine epistle." We'd start at one pool hall, talk to the lokes, get a lead, and go from there. Bob seemed to think, once we were on the ground and shooting pool, that Cormac would come to us, the cosmic practicality of it synchronizing smooth as a new transmission.

Unless we won some money right away, enough to afford a motel room for a night or two, we planned to sleep in the flower van and use it as our war room. We donned cowboy shirts that we'd bought at Corral West Ranchwear, the discount chain store, on the way out of Laramie. Mine was a simple-yoked job in a modest cinnamon-toast plaid and round faux-pearl snap buttons. Bob's a solid burnt coffee with double-diamond onyx snaps and pollen-yellow arrow slit pockets. "This is a shirt Suttree would wear," Bob said. It did go nicely with his sneakers, vintage black canvas basketball models. "Harrogate maybe," I offered, trying to keep the pre-game light.

"Naw, definitely Suttree." I'd learned this on the nature programs on the Nature Channel: there's a certain moth in Mexico or someplace that, in times of danger, stands up on its toes and opens its mothy wings and makes itself appear to be two, three times larger than it really is. We wore our shirts untucked to give us some casual authenticity while at the same time making us look bigger and forces not to tangle with.

"We'll need our strength," Bob said. "Come on, let's fortify ourselves with tacos."

One thing I noticed right off was that there are more houseflies in El Paso than in Laramie. But they're slower, probably from the heat. It takes a lot more energy for an airplane to take off in the thin, hot air, so these jumbo-jet houseflies have to work hyperdrive just to make it to the *menudo* drippings on the counter, let alone get out of the path of the whiffled head of a fly swatter traveling one hundred twenty miles an hour. But since no one else in the place seemed to notice them, those fly swatter swings were nonexistent at best.

The salsa. Ha, I've had salsa. And this was pink—"*picante effeminente,*" I said to Bob. Kinda the color of Pepto-Bismol. The salsa came in a Negra Modelo beer bottle—probably because they're dark glass, and they don't have to wash them very often—and you had to pour it onto a chip yourself: I drowned a greasy, stale chip with this stuff the viscosity of vomit, popped it in my mouth. My face began to melt off like red paint stripped from an antique rocking chair.

I had to stand up. The little room spun and bucked. I had to step outside. I couldn't feel my scalp and my ears rang and El Paso spun like a nightmare carnival ride. Booths and the countertops and the lights over Mexico went Salvador Dali, and I strode Hell's midway, and barkers and midgets and savages and little girls and patchy dancing bears were laughing at me and the atomic puss that was pouring from my orifices. I thought I was gonna pass out, and I think I sat down on a curb, but I don't remember the actual motion and repose of it. I do remember thinking that if I did pass out, the world would be quiet and I could be at peace. For sure a taxi running over me couldn't have hurt any worse. This is the chemical they make bear spray out of, I remembered. And I ingested it. On purpose.

I felt my face with my hands, then hunted just south of my eyes for my nose. My ears were still ringing, and I couldn't taste the inside of my mouth. Bob was there poking a glass of manila-colored milk in my face and saying at first he thought it was funny, but not if he had to drive the Flower Ranger van all the way back to Laramie with me on ice and tell people I'd been picanted to death in Old El Paso.

Bob checked the Yellow Pages, and we found a pool hall called Click's in the sprawl not far from the university. There were college students and a platoon of Army boys from Fort Bliss there, shooting mostly doubles on a couple dozen tables. We played well, got loosened up, enjoyed the camaraderie, but how good can college students and soldiers be when they've got to go to school or work or both part of a day, so all we did was go around the world a couple of times and made beer money and enough change for the jukebox so that I could play "Pinball Wizard" and

"Folsom Prison Blues" and that trucking song about Tucumcari and weed, whites and wine, but not much else. Then the soldiers we'd been shooting with went back to the base, and Bob and I drove downtown looking for Cormac like he was the Wizard of Fucking Oz. Which he sorta is.

We'd asked around about him at Click's, no one had heard of him. Or they were protecting him from groupies and the literary paparazzi. Perhaps he wore a funny hat and shot under an alias? That's okay, Bob said, he'd recognize him. "He won't be wearing desert three-color camo fatigues and a crew cut."

"Maybe that's just it," I said. "Maybe he does wear camo, to blend in with all this camouflage. Sergeant McCarthy."

"I doubt it," Bob said.

We parked off of San Antonio and walked, our cue cases like violin cases from *The Godfather,* to a little row of shotgun bars just off of a street called Stanton. From here you can see the border to Mexico, all lit up with security lights, like a prison or a baseball field during a night game.

The windows of the bars were either plywooded over or smoked opaque from the inside, where it was dark and smoldering and part of you was afraid, but they had tequila and beer and a jukebox with Johnny Cash to buck you up and help you remember that The Man in Black had been there, survived, come out the other side, and so you could, too. Unless of course those songs were all just fiction, he hadn't lived any semblance of that life at all. Which, I suppose, was possible, and all those formative years I'd just taken the word in his songs for gospel.

We stepped into the Bar with No Name. I could feel the pressure equalize in my chest as the door swung closed behind me. "This place is the cat's ass," Bob said. "I told ya it would be, didn't I." The warm green felt of the pool table drew at us like a lodestone.

There were drains in the floor under the row of barstools. The bartender was dozy drunk. Sometimes this works, like with Rosie, so that she overfills your drink and maybe doesn't bother to charge you, but sometimes—like this cat—you pay, he underfills your drink, then demands for you to pay again.

"That's just wrong," Bob said, stepping away and sipping a sad little drip of tequila. "I didn't even get a lime."

"Yeah. You go take care of that," I said. I knew he wouldn't go to loggerheads over our cocktails, but I enjoyed the image in my mind of this guy using Bob to wipe down the bar.

"Let's finish our half doubles and chill," Bob said. "Need to stay sharp, anyway. We're here to shoot pool. Think about the game."

A thick guy in a black leather vest and no shirt underneath broke a loose rack, not scattering the table very wide. We casual-ly-as-we-could opened our cases and slowly assembled our sticks. When the guy shot, a necklace with what looked like a semicolon but was probably a claw or a fang dangled nearly to the baize. Silver studs on the back of his vest spelled H-E-C-T-O-R.

"So, when does Cormac like to shoot?" Bob asked the man in the vest.

"Who?" The guy had a tattoo of a green clown on the fat part of his arm. The clown had sharp fingernails and appeared to be ripping the man's skin from the inside, birthing out from liquid testosterone inside of the man and into the earthly hot and arid consciousness of El Paso.

"You know. Cormac. Cormac McCarthy. *All the Pretty Horses.* He shoots some eight-ball most evenings when he gets done with writing and his nap and whatnot."

Nap? Where the hell did nap come from?

Hector signaled to a couple of buddies that they'd better get over here. "All the Pretty Horses?"

"Yeah, *that* Cormac. The man."

"The man, huh. Where you from, Pretty Horses?"

"Wyoming."

"We got sports all the way from Wyoming. Chalk your cues, boys. Cormac'll probably be here in a little while."

"Good deal," Bob said. But this wasn't like shooting pool in the Buckhorn. The tables were tilted or the baize was nappy or the balls were more dense or the lack of altitude or humidity or barometric pressure was affecting the roll. For whatever reason, these cats took a good chunk of what dollars we had to get to Cormac with. "All part of my plan," Bob said. "It takes money to make money. A date with Cormac ain't gonna be cheap."

Bob was on a roll with the clichés when a shadow walked in the front door.

"What would those chances be?"

"Well, we've narrowed our scope down to pool tables in El Paso. So maybe it is him."

My heart tried to climb out of my chest, just like it had when I'd eaten that salsa.

"Nope, false alarm. That ain't him."

"How would you know? You got a poster of him like Steve McQueen in your bedroom?

"No, just his author photo. The newest one—the one where he's a hawkish, wise, weathered plug of brilliance. That guy looks like he's had a tough week at the dog track."

In my stomach fomented the edges of the sickening feeling of having actualized this ridiculous sortie. *This really isn't happening to me. I'm smarter than this.* The feeling in my stomach was like the time I ate leftover sushi in Casper.

"Cormac looks," Bob said, "like a guy who's been carrying a typewriter around on his shoulders all day. A huge smoking, ringing, coal-fired, trip-hammer, stamp-mill typewriter, forged from the same stuff they make pay phones out of." Bob was getting even more abstract and postmodern as we kept racking and playing Hector and his buddies for beer money and mostly losing it. Neither of us was on our game. At least not yet. "Maybe, just to say no hard feelings for us taking his lunch money at the tables, he'll invite us to sleep over in his guest room. And a beautiful girl, a señorita, will bring us breakfast on a tray."

I'd known guys addicted to fantasy fiction—you know them, the Dungeons and Dragons types. Sci-fi Trekkies. Neo-noir crime freaks. But with only a couple unfortunate exceptions I knew they could always function in the world and not hurt themselves. But not literature. Literary fiction was supposed to be good for you, vitamins for your mind—no more harmful than an accidental overdose of Flintstones chewables.

This writer was still dangerous, still alive, and not all bloated and worn out like Norman Mailer or some other lesser Manhattan fictionist—Cormac was still living on Coffin Avenue in El Paso and shooting pool at gunslinger level. It had become clear as the Lone Star sign that Bob was more than a fanatic, a lunatic aficionado: Bob had been set afoot in Cormac's world, protected by the white space in the margins of a book as if they were velvet bumpers. Bullets now for Bob were no more lethal than periods.

Switchblades no more deadly than exclamation points. Bob had become so necessary to the plot of this story that the writer could not afford to kill him off, at least this soon. In the time it took me to go to the pisser, Bob had become vital. It was now clear to me that Cormac—the myth of Cormac—controlled our reality—our present and our immediate future. And Bob's fantasies and delusions could get us both killed.

I knew I'd left my reality and entered the Cormac Meridian for certain when in walk these two girls, women maybe, with a dwarf. Midget? I guess "little person" would be the PC term. The little guy was wearing a bull rider's hat, a big black Resistol with an ostrich feather in the band. His face only a dark shadow, and he wore a leather vest less like Hector's and more like one you might see on a child. The women were intimidatingly beautiful, athletic in their carriage, with cheekbones and skin the hue of a new latte after it jounces around and the espresso shots mate with the skim milk. Straight black hair like a horse's, hair so shiny you could see your future in it. The little bull rider stood on tiptoes to chalk his cue, then kicked a thick gray book to where he wanted to shoot. He stood on the book and sighted the cue between his thick little thumb and pointy finger. And he used a man's cue, just like he wore a man's hat because his head was still regular—not a youth stick like you might expect him to.

"This is Jarvis," one of the women said. She wore a choker of bone around her neck and black motorcycle chaps that framed her butt in a perfect apple. Tattooed razor wire the color of copper oxidation on the Statue of Liberty banded the muscle part of her arm. The green baize of the pool table was an oasis, a golf course in the desert. The light hung myopically low, the fret diamonds on the wood gunwales. They may have been sisters, but who can tell in the lucubrating glow of a smoking pool table light. "Jarvis is the star bull rider in the dwarf rodeo over to Juarez."

"That so," Bob said casual as if they were talking about high school basketball scores. "Didn't know there was such an event. I see that book you stand on is a reissue of *Middlemarch*." Then, while the dwarf looked down, "You like to wager a little added money, Jarvis?"

The little cliché nodded, hopped up on his book, then dropped two on the break, a big one and a little one. He read the break, set up for solids, and sunk three in a row, click-thunk, click-thunk, click-thunk, kicking *Middlemarch* around the gritty floor with the heel of his little boot.

"That must make you run in large circles in the greater Juarez/El Paso metropolitan area, riding bulls in the rodeo and all." Bob shot and missed. "You know a friend of mine in El Paso, by chance, guy named Cormac?"

"Cormac." Jarvis' voice was a little tinnier than Bob's. "Dark-haired fella. Kinda intense. He shoots in here now and then. Haven't seen him in a few days, but then I've been working on the dark side."

The other sister wore an amulet with something—something liquid—the color of blood through antique medicine glass. She'd disappeared and came back with a pitcher of drinks the color of green Kool-Aid. It tasted strongly alcoholic and medicinal, like nighttime cold medicine.

We beat Jarvis, then the girls, one-on-one and in teams. They won one, then we beat them again. We kept drinking the green liquor, and they apparently had lime Gatorade on the rocks like real athletes because the table for me got fuzzy, but they seemed to laugh and chalk and shoot sharp as new Bic shavers. It wasn't long before we were poisoned as mescal worms, and they beat us without interruption.

While they were beating us, instead of thinking about the game, this is what I'm watching instead: These women play with the grace of a cat in the crown of yonder tall cottonwood tree. Witches. Who are we to judge the world by Laramie standards? Dancers' finesse and librarians' flexibility. And Jarvis, remember him, the little sable bull rider and that damn thick British novel of his—together, novel under dwarf, they are better than the best pool player in all of Wheatland. The atmosphere filled with the precise percussion of Belgian balls ticking together like an antique clock as if this were a measurable thing, a sport of time.

Another thing about billiards. It's not like cards—pool is nearly impossible to cheat at; it's put up or shut up. Bob and I couldn't touch them with a bridge, couldn't run three balls together, and they were flashing lipstick rodeo teeth and laughing in Spanish, table-dancing apparition-like on the rails when Bob asked when Cormac usually shows up on a Saturday night, and the next thing that happens is that Hector—whom I'd forgotten all about—steps from the binding shadow and starts talking to Jarvis. Hector said something about how Bob and I are two dimes down, and it's a good time to even up so Jarvis and the sisters can get some beauty rest before the sun comes up.

It wasn't the money. Well, of course it was the money, but they'd not only beaten us thoroughly, they'd made us *like* it—we owed them two grand, not counting drinks. But more than losing this kind of cash, it's what would happen when they saw we didn't have anything but more air-barrels in our pockets.

I needed to get Bob out of here; I needed to get *me* out of here. He needed to get back to Allison and maybe into some sort of program for fiction addiction. But first we had to get away from this table and Jarvis and the pretty girls and Hector and all of Hector's crows sitting, pacing in the shadows like auxiliary characters trying out for a manuscript.

Hector spoke: "Friends, I've got a solution to our situation." I didn't trust his gray smile. "I know where there's an ATM. Let's just stroll around the corner, and I'll bet—even down here in the Third World—our ATM will read your Wyoming ATM card. As if it were magic."

"Okay. Sure," Bob said.

"Wouldn't hurt to have a little cash for later, too," I said. "Buy some more of this tasty green stuff."

"Good thinking," Bob said. "For when Cormac shows up."

"Ha!" It was Jarvis. He pointed his little buffalo fart finger at Bob and barked at him: "Cormac moved to Santa Fe, New Mex-i-co, a month ago!"

The handle of a pool cue swinging through the air has the same physics, just a little less mass, as a baseball bat. I needed to hit Hector square and not foul off his head or he'd turn around and crush me and again. I rose above myself like cigarette smoke, looked down, and could see myself swinging the cue in Kyros time. So strange, this violence from me—it was as if I'd been reading about the act, and it wasn't me but a paper protagonist committing this manic swinging of dangerous sporting goods in order to save something for a scripted dénouement. Up there, from where I watched myself do this visceral thing, I could see Bob and Jarvis and the horse-angel sisters. In the bruise of shadows are all the black crows, sound of nervous feathers when they hear the cue handle hit square. Hector's head did not explode like a melon. I watched Hector fall in slow motion, like the statue of Saddam Hussein, falling headlong, then crashing against the table, then the tile floor. I could see me yell something incomprehensible, drop the cue like a baseball bat after a single, then follow Bob to the exit.

We stepped through the atomic cheese-wedge of neon and floodlight that cursors the door. The two of us made it past the crows, who must have been stunned that someone would do this to their Hector. Outside it was still Baghdad-hot, and my running shoes made a sucking sound on the greasy tarmac.

We ran. "Not the van," I yelled. "They'll be waiting for us at the van."

"Right." Bob sounded like he was hyperventilating. We kept running on heavy legs, past the square gray correctional facility, past Amigo's Bail Bonds, we ran on adrenaline and lost time because, as you'll read in Einstein, time is relative to what it is you are doing. We ran some more. Asphalt turned to soft earth as we pulled up in the middle of a dark lot, a place to build, a hospital perhaps, a library. It felt safe there, in a relative sense. We stopped to blow, hands on our knees, trying to heave as quietly as possible. "I need to sit down for a minute," Bob said. I did, too. We were tired in that way that if you knew you'd never wake up it wouldn't matter—all that matters in the world is going to that quiet; Heaven is a nap, but the sheets are clean.

I awoke to the sticky tickle of flies big as black olives walking around the snoring rimrock my lips made. I could hear the Sturm und Drang of diesel machines. Something the size and shape of a silver dollar had stuck then dried to my cheek. I turned my head and saw magnanimous brown, antennaed roaches fighting over a splintered bone with scabs of meat still hanging on it at a knuckled joint. There were more pieces of bone, and I'd fallen asleep on some of them. My cowboy shirt was torn and stained in an inedible color I didn't recognize. My wrists and forearms were tacky with dried blood. The morning became literal. "My God, I've been savaged!" I yelled.

Bob had propped himself up by the elbow in order to survey his morning glorious because it was not in an office, not on a street, not part of the mainframe of progress. If he'd had a stem of wheatgrass he'd have chewed it like a minor character out of *On the Road*. Bob relished this bookish lifestyle. "Take it easy," he said. "I think it's chili sauce. Too dark for ketchup. And you've got a pickle stuck on your cheek."

The bones were chicken bones. "Church's," Bob said confidently. "I can tell by the color of the batter."

"Well, why don't you just have a little for breakfast," I said. "I'm sure we can find a scoop of coleslaw and half a biscuit to go with it."

We must have been in the City of El Paso's landfill. One of them, anyway. How had we managed to find the one-hundred-yard section of cyclone fence that had been torn out, probably for expansion? The rest of the landfill was railed with cyclone fence and concertina wire. I guess they didn't want anyone coming to the Land of Opportunity through the landfill. "Isn't this great!" I'd had just about enough of Bob's intrepid enthusiasm. "Cormac may not still be here, but think of all his leavings. Cormac detritus. Old combs, paper plates, magazines with his address, empty tins of kippered snacks, junk mail with his name on it—an alias maybe—bourbon bottles from his Drinking Period, old notes and manuscripts, an Olivetti typewriter ribbon, grocery lists—the possibilities are bottomless! In a hundred years armies of archaeologists from English departments all over the world will be out here mining this place for POC."

"POC?"

"Proof of Cormac."

I closed my eyes and could see the page-three headline in tomorrow's *El Paso Times* on the backs of my eyelids: "Man Murdered at Landfill." The traction atop the spongy overburden was not excellent, but the chicken bones gave me enough purchase to propel myself just high and far enough—Superman-taking-flight-with-his-fist-style—to hit the little weed sucker right in the Adam's apple.

"Ow!"

"You need to snap out of it," I yelled. "This is a nonfiction situation. I'm without my nonfiction flower van, and I owe nonfiction money to psychokillers and a rodeo dwarf. I may have killed a guy last night, trying to save the paper-thin skin on your ass." Exhausted, I made a slow overfill angel on my back, staring at the sun with my eyes closed because it felt good on my head. I needed water.

"My God, what's gotten into you?" Bob rolled up on his butt and felt his throat. "You never used to be violent. It's this place, isn't it. The borderland. I warned you, and now you've injured my thrapple, for Godsakes."

I rolled my head to look at him. Everything went still and silent. The wind stopped. Flies lit and became frozen. The diabolical diesel Cats shut off their engines, and the sun ducked behind a hot cloud. "What did you just say?"

"I dunno. Something poetic about the borderlands."

"No, you injured something. What was it?"

"My thrapple. You've bruised my damn thrapple."

I sat up. "What the hell's a thrapple? No, wait, before you tell me you'll listen up and now, you little ex-attorney: this thrapple you're talking about better not be what I think it is." I was pointing at him like a middle school principal at the kid who just pulled the fire alarm. Bob *regarded* me, the Cormac term for the thing he was doing.

"All right, then it's not," he said.

"Not what?"

"Not what you think it is."

"What is it, then?"

"Nothing. I feel better, crazy man. Leave me be."

"Wrinkle not thy reptilian brow at me, my friend." I was channeling now. "You're gonna tell me. You're gonna tell me what in split-wide-open hell a goddamned *thrapple* is."

"No I'm not."

"Don't make me do something Holden on you."

"Ha. Just put it on the shelf right next to all the other foolishness we've gotten into in Hell Paso." Bob grinned. "I ain't telling."

"It's a Cormac word, isn't it."

"It's just a word. A word for the thing on my person that hurts right now. Thanks to you."

"Yeah, and it's a Cormac word. From that Godforsaken two-hundred-dollar dictionary he keeps on the six-thousand-dollar pool table in his hundred-thousand-dollar living room. In Santa Fe." I tried to say "Santa Fe" like an invective. "Just admit that it's a Cormac word. I ain't happy about it, but admit it and we'll forget the whole thing."

"No."

"It's gonna mean the difference between epigraph and epitaph for you, Bob."

"Forget I said it."

"I will not."

"You're really starting to scare me."

"You need some fear in your life."

"If I admit it, will you shut up about it and we can go get some breakfast?"

"We'll see about that."

"Pancakes. Eggs. No, I know: *huevos rancheros.* With pancakes. And a tortilla—a flour tortilla the size of a hubcap. Coffee."

"Maybe."

"Orange juice."

"We'll see."

"Okay, it's a Cormac word."

I'd meant to keep my own word about forgetting the whole thing, but I snapped again, my nerves sanded thin as they were. My fight-or-flight mechanism got crosswired and sideways with my benevolent self, and I grabbed a drumstick Henry VIII style and went for him. We ran around Commercial Construction, past Steel Salvage and Biodegradable Organics, but avoiding Domestic Pickup where I think he knew there would be diapers and Kleenex and condoms and other unseemlies. Where did his energy come from in this hellishly hot hungover state?

Bob ducked out of the landfill and was an earth-colored man about streets and statues and sidewalks. He remained one block ahead of me, vectoring around the city, careful to cross with signals. I couldn't be sure, but my hunch was that he had bearings enough to find where the van had been when we last saw it.

The van was there. It appeared untouched except for a parking ticket pinned like a goose feather under the driver's wiper blade. In no way did I anticipate this, such fortune, a happy ending. My anger had been exorcised on the run, and now I just felt volumes of hope because the van seemed real and whole.

"We could disappear in Chihuahua." Bob was catching his breath, sitting on the bumper. "Go to Mexico and never come back. Just like Ambrose Bierce."

I thought about that, and the image was the two of us on mules under sombreros the size of poker tables. There were buzzards and a three-legged dog. "Naw," I told him. "Allison wouldn't like it."

We had to pay for gas with Allison's Texaco card. We bought snacks with it, too, because the clerk never bothered to look at the name on the card. If a clerk had looked and told Bob he didn't look like an Allison and some picture ID would need to be produced, Bob could say that we were on a crusade and had been licked and were heading home. He could say that Allison would approve of these corn chips and bloody Redbulls. That while she humps it at the hospital, helping people not to die, someone needed to be down here representing the readers, making sure writers didn't move to places like Bozeman or Jackson Hole or, most of all, Santa Fe. He did not get to say this to any filling station clerks. If he'd been questioned, what he really would have said was "Allison's my wife. The only one I got. Maybe you could call her?"

On the way home we didn't talk much for a long time. I'd been thinking that when we got back to Laramie I'd cook something, something for three, launder my World's Greatest Dad shirt with the mustard stain Hogue gave me for Father's Day when he was one, and take a picnic over to Jeannie's, a casserole maybe, because Hogue likes tater tots and cream of mushroom soup. With a cold salad. I wouldn't tell her I went to El Paso with Bob in the flower van. What for? She'd ask and then I'd be stuck having to tell her we were trying to hustle a novelist she'd never heard of and never would care to read and then I'd be back in that place in our relationship when kicking me out seemed like the smartest, most immediate thing in the world.

As for this trip, like most of my miscues and dropped pop flies I'd decided I would chalk it up to experience and try to forget it. Near Socorro, where the earth starts to bunch up like a Sunday tablecloth before cresting and falling through so many Hot Sulphur Springs and Sleeping Indians, Bob said something about how down here the sun rises and sets differently than in Wyoming, the way it blots and spreads and fades at the periphery like chili sauce on hot broken eggs.

North of Albuquerque there were billboards for Brooks Brothers and Ann Taylor and then SANTA FE NEXT FOUR EXITS. We passed the first exit. "We could pull in," I said. "Couldn't be all that hard to find Cormac at a table in Santa Fe. Probably air-conditioned."

There was a pause. Then:

"Naw," Bob said. "It's not the same. Santa Fe. A far, far cry from El Paso. Cormac might as well be Tony Hillerman. Anyway, he's probably collecting postage stamps now or something instead of pool."

I'd seldom felt that kind of relief, but I had known something like it before—it was the feeling of getting a busload of middle-school kids back to town on icy roads in visibility-zero.

"A pool shark in Santa Fe is like a—like a pirate on a Carnival Cruise," Bob said. There was a long funereal pause. "He deserves flaccid sales on his next book, just like he got with *Cities on the Plain*. And worse. I liked that scene with the rabbit heads in the radiator grill, but he deserves to be remaindered from hell to breakfast."

Colorado. It had been quiet and peaceful between us, and I was thinking soft thoughts, how we could go back to spending our mornings at the Buck, shooting just for fun and quarters, when—north of Trinidad and not yet to Pueblo—Bob starts in, cooking up this plan to drive to deep-woods Arkansas and see if we can find Charles Portis, the mastermind behind *True Grit, Dog of the South, Gringos,* and challenge him to a bird-hunting contest with dogs and birds and shotguns and whistles and bourbon. I told Bob to shut the hole under his nose and that's the last I wanted to hear of it.

FREDERICK BUSCH

The Bottom of the Glass

The cousins made a rough crossing, they'd have said, if they had thought to complain. They mentioned but didn't lament the time in the air, the late arrival at De Gaulle, the bus ride to catch the train at the Gare Montparnasse, or the long wait for the Très Grand Vitesse to Bordeaux. They did joke about the man in the car rental agency at the Bordeaux terminal who spoke no English and who resented that they spoke some French. He cost them a half an hour of futile searching for the car he pretended to direct them toward, nearly shouting his exasperation: "*Les voitures, ils restent là, à droit—là, monsieur! Là!*"

Eleanor could imagine them, with their several heavy bags, their sacks from the duty-free, their great, damp slabs and mounds of muscle and fat shifting and trembling as they panted in and about the station and, finally, through the darkness of the garage beneath it where the rentals, *les voitures,* were parked. She imagined Eugene's French, with its awful accent and its wonderful vocabulary, as he breathlessly sought to entertain the traveling salesman who, speaking French with native fluency and English with a transatlantic businessman's ease, had offered to lead them to their car.

Now Eugene sat at the table in the kitchen of the rental house, which he called, quite properly, a *gîte.* They had never met, and her husband had never spoken of these enormous creatures who, it seemed, were kin. Eugene had embraced her on arriving in their sporty convertible, climbing out from behind the wheel with slow, laborious motions to hold her neck in a yoke of moist, thick fingers, kissing her head with the greatest delicacy until Bertha had pulled her away to smother Eleanor's bowed face in those enormous breasts that shifted as if they were independent creatures trapped beneath the baggy tan traveling dress she matched with tan strap pumps and a tan leather handbag that looked as though it were weighted with stones.

"No la, no la-di-da, and surely no parked vultures, dear girl," the cousin of Eleanor's dead husband chanted. "The fellow knew we'd never find them. The Sino-French gentleman, a manufacturer's agent for *plastics*, if you can believe it, unless he meant explosive *plastique*, now that you mention it, finally showed us where to go. He'd been there before, of course, and he was waiting in the corner of the rental office with that polite tranquility of theirs—"

"Not that my dear husband wishes to be mistaken for a racialist," Bertha warned.

Eugene smiled damply at the table in the kitchen they had planned, she and Sid, to use during the rest of June and all of July. While Madame Panifiette, their landlady, took the advice of her husband and several friends in the area to consider whether—here she had made a number of faces involving downturned lips, raised brows, and a half a shake of the head—given the legalities involved, she could release Eleanor from the remainder, as she said it, of "your obligation to me."

Eleanor had said to the tiny Madame Panifiette, with her alabaster complexion, in front of Eugene and Bertha, "You never liked me, did you?"

"Well, now," Bertha had said, in sweet, slippery syllables, "we don't want to necessarily accuse anyone of anything, do we?"

Between them, Bertha and Eugene weighed seven hundred and fifty pounds, Eleanor would have bet. On a better day, she'd have guessed it at six-fifty. But this was only a few days after Sid had looked up from the little corner table on which he leaned toward his white, lined pad with his fine-point fountain pen. She had been sitting at the pine dining table in the tile-paneled kitchen, writing postcards home at maybe eight in the morning. She looked up as Sid did. They caught each other's eyes. She thought he was going to say something rueful about his work. She was ready to smile and cluck and go back to the cards that told what a fine time they were enjoying. But it stopped, inside his eyes, and they went out. He fell sideways from his chair. She went to him, she called to him, she blew her breath past his teeth and felt it going nowhere except back up at her mouth. That night, after following the ambulance to the regional hospital and after talking to a man from the gendarmerie who seemed too young to drive, much less take charge of her husband's death, she used Sid's address book and her own to call home and speak to eight or nine people. She did not call her daughter, Margo, and every day that she failed to, it seemed like a more impossible task. It was an overdue account, accruing a terrible interest. Of the people she did call, Sid's cousins, whom she'd never met, insisted that they come to her. They flew from Baltimore to Roissy–Charles de Gaulle, they took the train to Bordeaux, and they navigated their rental car over the small roads of the wine country of southwestern France, and here they were, managing, among other elements, her grief. Over some days, the details of their journey emerged, and she came to think of them as her big, fat heroes.

They were probably sixty, she thought. Bertha was as tall as Eugene, with beefy shoulders and thick, rounded arms. She dyed her hair black as if to match it to the hair of her shaved mustache. She wore either dresses or skirts with matching tops, nothing tucked in, which was a vanity that Eleanor found moving. She could see the breadth of Bertha's vast thighs as she walked briskly, in dressy high heels, through the echoing, cool, white or white-and-rose tiles of the floors and walls of the *gîte.* She "straightened things up," she said. "Not that it isn't as neat as a pin. But one tries," she said, "to help. The best, the most useful help, they say, is order. So one picks up."

Eugene, who ran a rare-books business in Baltimore, on one of the streets near the revived waterfront area, looked every day at the few French books Madame Panifiette had supplied, as well as the couple of stacks that had taken up too much of the space in Sid and Eleanor's rolling duffel cases. When he wasn't reading in books he clearly didn't like, or looking at titles he didn't want to open, Eugene spoke on the telephone, using his credit card, to arrange in his blatting but quite correct French for the passage home of three vertical Americans and one who would, as soon as his body was released by the authorities, travel prone.

"Assuming," Eleanor told him as he hung up and sighed, "that Fifi LaPue over there lets me out of the lease. She had a little hankering for Sid, by the way, would have been my bet. What the drug people call a jones? Though I don't know her position vis-à-vis the African American dead."

"Perhaps, then, she'll be glad to see you go, now that you're on your own. I *am* so sorry," he said. "Forgive me. Sidney—"

Eleanor nodded. She didn't know what else to do with her face, so she put her hands over it. Sidney and I, she nearly said to his cousin, would not have made it from the June we are in to the start of autumn. They'd been a middle-aged couple in a second marriage for each that was going as sour as the wine their landlady's husband produced in what was little more than a very large, old stone garage. Now Eleanor was a middle-aged widow whose husband had died of what the very sweet young doctor, who smelled of a citrus soap Eleanor had thought clean and sexy at once, called *une attaque*—a stroke.

Then the doctor had added, not hesitantly at all, for she was a sophisticated woman of France, after all, "*Les nègres*—" She did pause on Eleanor's behalf to say, "Do you know this word of ours for, er, the Negroes, madame?"

Eleanor took a deep breath in order to shout at her, to screech, she realized, about her experience as a teacher of French at the sixth snootiest prep school for girls in the City of New York. She was going to scream in impeccable French. But the woman's kind, tired light green eyes, her obvious concern for the dead man's wife, silenced her. She touched the doctor's forearm with the fingers of her right hand, and she nodded.

She let her breath out, and she said, "*D'accord.*"

"*Eh, bien,*" the doctor said. "*Donc. Les nègres, ils sont très vulnérables des attaques. Je regrette, madame.*"

It had seemed to her before he died, and it seemed to her afterward, that they had remained in love. The sorriest part, she was beginning to believe, was that love did not necessarily make it possible to live, together or alone. And a desire to live, something beyond the animal drive to not be killed off, she had reluctantly come to think, was the most necessary and most elusive of feelings. Thinking of the size of Sid's mistake and hers in marrying, she wondered if Eugene suspected something of the great error in which Sidney and she had courted and married and traveled abroad. Here he was, because he thought it right to come to the aid of his nephew's white wife, this gentle, vast, and elegant pear-shaped cousin from Baltimore, sweating through his white duck trousers and his dark blue long-sleeved shirt, waving his white, broad-brimmed straw hat as a fan between them while they sat at the kitchen table and checked their little list of what to do after a husband's death in a rural rental house among the rows of the Panifiettes' sauvignon blanc vines at the end of a very warm June.

She knew that Bertha's whiteness could be all or some of an explanation, but she doubted it. His hairless café-au-lait head shone from the heat, and she thought she could feel it, like his decency, radiate from him across the yard or so of polished pine.

"I'm sorry the weather's so uncomfortable," Eleanor said. "And I'm so glad you're here, you and Bertha, that I feel *treacherous* about my relief—on account of your discomfort. But thank goodness."

"You're a cousin. A cousin-in-law. I do not know *what* you are, in legal definitions, Eleanor. You are our family. If you want to be. If you do, then you are. If you don't, consider us a very, very large pain in the ass until we see you safely home."

She took his beefy, moist hand, the one that rested on the table near his coffee cup, and she set it against the side of her head.

"Dear girl," he said.

Bertha walked in, moving as gracefully in spite of her size as Eugene did, whether it was to lift a cup of coffee or cross a room. Eleanor could imagine them as they somehow, helping each other quite cordially, made their slow, breathless way up the stairs of the Très Grand Vitesse and stowed the bags at the end of the first-class carriage. She could imagine them murmuring to one another—"Are you all right, dear? If you'd give me your hand..."—and could envision them as they faced each other across the little table of their compartment, stomachs folded doughily over the table's edge, great arms flattening on its top, arranging bottles of Evian and sandwiches, wedges of cheese, perhaps, and chunks of fruit that Eugene cut for them with a folding wooden-handled picnic knife while the train gathered speed. She saw his vast hands manage with delicacy the division of a Cavaillon melon or a crescent of brie, saw hers distribute napkins and plastic cups.

"I have just been having another word with Madame Panifiette," Bertha said. "She was most accommodating of my accent." Her smile might have excused Madame or indicted her own French, but it was kind, somehow. "She expects to 'achieve a resolution' quite rapidly."

"I'll bet you money," Eleanor said, "that it costs us extra money."

"I will expect her to do better on our behalf," Eugene said, with a little steel in his voice. "But some money might pleasantly change the equation. I *could* see that."

Bertha asked, "Did Eugene tell you that we were cooking tonight?"

Eleanor shook her head.

"Well, we're cooking," Bertha said, "so you might prepare yourself."

"Is that a stressful situation?"

"No, dear," Eugene said. "It's noisy, a little, and sometimes quite messy, but I wouldn't call it stressful. You are in one of the superb culinary districts of the world, and not at all far from St. Emilion, such a great wine center, as I'm sure you know. We're off to shop, and then, when we return with food and drink, you are invited to a meal prepared by relatives. Are we your in-laws?"

Eleanor shrugged. She tried to smile brightly.

"Outlaws, then," Bertha said, and she laughed like a girl, though her eyes seemed sad as they slid toward Eleanor and then away.

"Outlaws it will be," Eugene said.

Begging her pardon for seeming intrusive, they moved about the room, opening cupboards and inspecting the refrigerator, each naming items for a list while Eugene wrote down, on one of Sid's green-lined white legal pads, what they would need to buy at the open-air stalls in the square of St. Macaire and at the supermarket in Langon.

Eleanor, who was tall and broad-shouldered and, according to Sid, "the slightly repressed all-American lifeguard at the country club pool," was thinking of Margo, also tall, slender, and broad-shouldered, who suddenly, it seemed, was in graduate school for the study of some kind of cell physiology that her father, a medical doctor, seemed to understand, while Eleanor could only decipher the meaning of "cell" and "physiology" without formulating an intelligent sentence that used both words. She was remembering how, early that winter, Margo had come home from Madison, Wisconsin, to Eleanor's place on West 9th Street to stay the night and register her opinion about Sid and her mother before spending the weekend at their old apartment, now her father's, uptown.

She said, "Mother, for Christ's sake. Have an *affair.* It's an itch, so scratch it. Get over the thrill of it. Then learn how to live alone like the rest of us, for Christ's sake."

"And have you considered that it could possibly be more than sex?"

"When a forty-five-year-old divorced white woman gets a jones for a slightly younger, fairly hot black man who writes books, one of which she happened to read *before* he picked her up at the Metropolitan Museum show of those Vienna Whoevers who did the highly sexualized paintings? Ma: *duh-uh.*"

"I don't know where to begin," Eleanor had said. She remembered stumping back and forth on the broad, painted planks of her little Village living room. "I don't know whether to shout terrible things about your not knowing the Vienna Secession, or calling their paintings 'sexualized,' like you're the Dean of Correctness at a second-rate college, or portraying me as this overstimulated matron who just wants to get *laid* by the nearest black man, who, like all the rest of them, you know, *you know,* is a phallic engine who cannot stay away from dumb and oversexed white women. Margo: *duh-uh.* How could you? And why are *you* so lonely, handing out that living-alone stuff? And since whenever do you say I have a *jones*? I don't know where to begin."

"Don't say anything I can't forgive, Mother."

Margo had called her Mother since the divorce, which they had conducted like a small war while their civilian casualty was in the eleventh grade. Eleanor said, "Margo? Are you really that alone? Are you saying that *I* am? Are you accusing me of being in despair? How desperate do you think I *am*?"

"How much do you weigh, Mother?"

"How much—"

"How much do you weigh?"

"One thirty-three."

"I thought it was, like, a hundred and forty-five?"

"No comment."

"Right. So I'd call you roughly a hundred and forty-five pounds of desperate. That's how desperate I think you are."

Margo sat in silence then and watched her wander in the living room, from the wall of bookshelves to the long sofa to one of the windows onto 9th Street. Finally, Eleanor let a long sigh slide between her lips and said, "I've been holding my breath. I've gotten so strung out by you, I forgot to breathe."

"Then you know the principle of blowing dope. Hold it and hold it and then let it go. I could roll us a joint."

"Of marijuana?"

"What did you think it involved, Mother?"

"I don't want to know."

"All right."

"Do you smoke it a lot?"

Margo looked at her with the pity of the young. Eleanor had seen it on her students' faces. That it was undisguised made it cruel, as if they had never considered the possibility of an elder understanding the gulf between them. You decayed before their eyes, it said, and you didn't know how close to dead you were.

"I think you're learning to value yourself is all," Eleanor had said when they told each other good night. "It's not easy. I know."

"And do you?"

"Do I what?"

"Mother, do *you* value yourself?"

"Of course. And I know that Sid values me. Oh," Eleanor had said, "not a great answer, is it?"

"You're still learning, too."

"Life is long," Eleanor remembered telling her.

"It better be," Margo had said, about to go inside the guest room, "because you are one slow learner."

Which apparently was true, Eleanor thought as, in the French rental, Sid's great cousins prepared to drive into St. Macaire to purchase butter and cream and duck breasts and two kinds of mushrooms. "We can bake in those little ramekins instead of metal molds," he said. "Absolutely no harm done. And that's a reminder," he instructed Bertha, "about milk for the timbales. We cannot forget the milk."

"You're making the list, dear."

"Yes, I am," he said. He told Eleanor, "The preparation of food, you will not be surprised to learn, excites me. I get forgetful."

"He can also be dictatorial and quite like a master chef—decidedly cruel," Bertha said, smiling. "It gets quite dangerous when we cook."

"The danger," Eugene chanted, as if from memory, "lies in running short of reliable duck confit, not in any slightly bruised feelings among the sous-chefs."

"Who said that?" Bertha asked.

"I did, of course."

"You can see," she told Eleanor, "he grows brutal."

There was a rustling of linen clothing, a seizing of lists, and a counting of currency, and then they were off in their black convertible, down the stony drive to turn left onto the little connector road, then right onto the paved secondary, and then to wander the turns past vineyards and the sheds that sheltered stainless-steel storage tanks and the descent into St. Macaire with its ramparts and its small, plain cathedral, and its narrow streets. She thought for a moment of the cousins as they loomed over the small, taut French while they inspected the wares of the seller of Basque sausages and cheeses, or the local man so proud of his harsh Armagnac, and the butcher who always seemed to sneer over his duck legs, his unplucked chickens, his thick loins of pork. She could hear their murmurs to each other and their charmed, polite replies.

In the master bedroom, which like the dining area opened into the vineyard, she moved folded clothing about and tried to pack. There were two large bags and two small ones for carrying books and bottles of water onto the plane; they hadn't brought more than thin summer clothing and a cotton sweater apiece for a cool night, but there seemed to her to be too little room in their luggage. It felt important that she leave nothing of his behind, although she suspected that, eventually, she would give it all away in New York. For now, though, she wanted to bring him home with everything he'd carried abroad.

Did that include her? She wondered if they would have returned together, assuming the small matter of his not having died of an explosion of blood in the brain.

"Probably," she said to the chugging of insects outside, the slow droning of fat bees in the waist-high pots of rosemary next to the house.

"Of course," she said.

Looking at the herbs and thinking of the cousins at their list-making, she thought of the preparation of food. She remembered the first formal date with Sid, who had taken her for dinner to Jarnac, the restaurant in the West Village. He had insisted that they order the cassoulet, which was better, he said, than the cassoulet with white beans and duck and pork sausage that he had eaten in the Fifth Arrondissement of Paris the previous year. A stocky, jolly, but tough-looking woman came out of the kitchen while they ate, and she circulated through the small room. She and Sid embraced, she patted Eleanor on the shoulder, and she moved on.

"The chef," Sid said.

"I can't help it," she told him. "I'm impressed."

"That was the idea."

"It was?"

"Oh, yes. You're who I'm determined to impress."

His thin face, which she thought had as many muscles in it as an athlete's arm, was a little darker, with a little more putty color, she thought now, than Eugene's. Sid kept his coarse hair short, and she had enjoyed inspecting the beautiful shape of his head. She could imagine a mother holding her hand around the back of that head. She could imagine her own hand there. He saw her speculating, and he suddenly grinned, a big and boyish happy smile.

"What?" he said.

"Never mind. Although I suspect you can figure it out."

"I hope so," he said.

"I'm considering matters," she said. "So tell me something."

"About what?"

"About anything besides me. Tell me something about your work."

"You said you know my work. Now I'm disappointed."

"What you are is like a boy about it."

"I'm like a boy about everything else, too," he said.

"Never mind. Tell me about what you do. I read the one about the women who robbed banks. Very cool, as my daughter might say. A bunch of right-on women, she'd say, except for the part about shooting people. Your detective cries. People seem to like that."

"Margo. Your daughter."

"Yes, Margo. So what are you working on now?"

"Why, you."

He had never mentioned any relative except his mother. He had certainly never referred to his cousins, the vast Caucasian Bertha, and Eugene, the giant brown purveyor of rare books who would return chirping to the house to prepare something involving magret de canard in order to nourish the widow. And here was the widow, trying to fit too many clothes into too few cubic inches of luggage that, a couple of weeks ago, had accommodated everything.

Eleanor slept among the stacks of neatly folded undershorts and T-shirts and olive-green cargo pants and the socks she had bought him at Brooks Brothers. She had been frightened while she slept. She had awakened herself by calling out, had looked about the room and closed her eyes and gone to sleep again. Now her mouth was gummy and foul, her face felt greasy, her left hand hurt from clenching it. She showered but put on the same clothing she'd worn—khaki shorts, a wrinkled white camp shirt. She brushed her teeth and worked her hair into a ragged bun. She went barefoot into the kitchen, where she drank iced spring water while watching the sun hang huge and orange over the hills at the far edge of the grape vines cultivated by Monsieur and Madame Panifiette. The sun appeared not to move, though the insects chirred louder, she thought, and the bees worked harder now, and the hills began to go dark, almost as if they were a silhouette, even though the brilliant orange sun appeared to be directly over them. You would think it would light them up, she thought.

"Stand by, Eleanor," Eugene called. She heard the throbbing of the engine of their Saab, and then she heard the slamming of doors, the rustling of plastic sacks, and the panting of very fat people moving across the hot slate walk at the back of the house.

She and Sid had not slept together during the week before he died. They had agreed, though they'd said nothing aloud, to continue to sleep in the same bed, to kiss each other good morning and good night, to walk naked from the shower to their bedroom, to use the toilet without hesitation or shame, and to in every other way manifest their intimacy. The making love had stopped as though a mechanism had broken without any other symptoms. They had malfunctioned without a fight, only slightly acknowledging the increment of tension between them. Sid was making some progress with the book, his fourth, about a black detective of the upper middle class who solved crimes out of his affection for the victims, but never quite learned how to love the woman who, by the end of each book, loved him.

On the night of her learning about the breaking down, they lay in the dark in bed, he in pajama bottoms and she in sleeping shorts and a sleeveless, scoop-necked top, not touching, at the start of their sleeping this way every night.

"I keep wondering," she said. "I mean, about how, where you are—at the start of it—you could go off to France for a couple of months and work on a book that depends on being in New York, where your people are—"

"My *people*?"

"Now, you know what I mean. Your *characters*. You couldn't have meant—you didn't think that *I* meant anything about race."

"No, El, of course not."

"It doesn't sound like us," she said, "talking that way. I mean, making that kind of mistake about each other."

"No."

"We don't do that."

He shifted. He sighed. "We surely didn't used to," he said. He teetered on his side, and then rolled onto his back again. "We didn't. We mustn't." He turned toward her and kissed her upper arm, letting his teeth gently close on her flesh.

"You're trying to turn me on," she said.

"I am."

"So that—so that what, Sid?"

"So that you know."

"It's a part of the argument, then?"

"We aren't having one."

"What are we having?"

"I don't know."

"A power struggle," she said.

"El, come on."

"Well, I'm not hard to get," she said.

"That's not what I meant."

"I don't know quite what you meant," she said. "But I do think we're a little old to be wasting our time on so much talk about what we aren't doing when what we *could* be doing is making each other happy."

He lay beside her, he didn't move, and the orange sun hung in the early nighttime sky.

"Except we aren't," she said. "Am I guessing it right? Happy, I mean. I mean, we're *not* happy." Here they were, she thought, two adults who functioned in terms of language carefully chosen, and it was as if neither spoke the other's native tongue. But the attitude of his body, his distance though he lay so close, his silence, now cut through the words they didn't or couldn't select. It's as simple as that, she thought. We are not. "What we've been doing, maybe," she said, "has been hoping. Maybe what we did was mostly hope."

"Mostly hope," he said. "Nothing ignoble in that."

"We tried."

He said, "We did our best."

"Oh, Sid," she said.

After a while, he said, "That's right. Oh."

And finally, she had returned his kiss, on the hard curve of the top of his shoulder, letting her lips come away slowly from his bronze-tan skin that always smelled to her like spices—and she thought of their names, although she never cooked with them and really didn't know one from the other: mace and cloves and nutmeg—because it seemed likely, she thought, before she turned over to face away from Sid and from the enormous, ragged sun, that they had just kissed goodbye.

Bertha and Eugene cooked, and they did their best to entertain her. They made drinks of Campari and soda over ice, and Eugene warbled bad renditions of tragic French arias while Bertha complained about the mysteries of the stove mechanisms.

"I am using dried crêpes," she told Eleanor, "along with chopped shallots and milk and no more than one half a cup of heavy cream to make a kind of gâteau of mushrooms. They're really called timbales. You know the term? After we combine over heat, we'll bake. You'll find it echoed in the heavy cream, the port, and the shallots of the woodland sauce that my brother, the fascist chef, is coercing together for what will, after all, be simply sautéed duck breasts. Are you hungry, dear?"

Eugene was gliding from the sink to the table to the stove, wiping at his sweaty forehead with a dishtowel hung about his neck. The evening breezes came in over the grapes while the air of the kitchen took on the aroma of the reducing canned chicken stock he apologized for using. "We bought it at the hypermarché outside Langon," he said. "It's a travesty, of course, but there hasn't been time to make real stock. And we had better hope, by the way, that the co-fascist to my left"—and here Bertha actually performed a half a bow, her huge breasts falling against her dress—"knows that I require some of those crêpes for my sauce. And, darling," he said to her, "can you scoop me five tablespoons of butter?"

She said, "Eleanor, would you mind awfully grating some nutmeg?"

Eleanor said, "Why?"

Eugene stopped washing parsley at the sink. Bertha, panting as she sautéed mushroom strips and chopped crêpes with a knife in one hand and a tub of butter in the other, paused, then turned to Eleanor, looked at her face, and said, "An unpleasant association?"

She almost spoke, but only shook her head.

"It's hardly necessary, dear," Bertha said.

Eugene danced, immense over his relatively narrow, small feet, toward the table where she sat. "I must make you another Campari-soda," he said.

"No," she said. "No, thank you."

"Some of the dinner wine? If you know me, then you know I brought enough. I have Chateau St.-Georges-Côte-Pavie, which is a St. Emilion from nearly up the road. It's supposed to be very fleshy and full of blackberries. It's breathing on the counter, let me pour you a glass."

"I can grate the nutmeg," she told him. "That's all right."

"And I can pour you a glass of wine," he said. "And *that's* all right."

She held her palm out, and Bertha deposited the little tin grater with its small compartment that held the nuts. Eleanor leaned to sniff at the compartment. That was the smell of nutmeg. She said, "I wonder if you could excuse me?"

"Dear girl," Eugene said, "it's all too, somehow, celebratory, isn't it? We were afraid it might feel that way. Although one *could* celebrate Sidney. Perhaps one ought to, even. My brother's boy. And aren't genes *so* treacherous? Arthur, my brother, also died too young. And he was healthy. Anyway, he was slim. Broad at the chest, but slender all the same. He was a dancer for a couple of years, a professional chorus-boy hoofer in Philadelphia and New York. You'd have thought that one of us was adopted, my mother used to say, because we were made so differently. Of course, I happened to them twelve, nearly thirteen years after my poor mother thought she was done with bearing babies. Arthur believed I was this pick-me-up-off-the-street creature, but I wasn't. I was born to them, and we were brothers, the poor soul. We both of us adored Sidney. He was more like a brother to me than Arthur, now that you mention it, who was, if you'll forgive the psychology, a little bit more of a *father,* if you can believe it, as we got older. So maybe the meal's for him. But it's also for you, Eleanor, because Sidney loved you and you loved him. God bless you both."

Bertha said, "She's all done in, Eugene. She's exhausted. She should sleep. Eleanor," she said, "you must have a nap. At once. We can worry later about food. Do you hear?"

Bertha insisted on shepherding her from the kitchen table and past Eugene, who leaned to kiss the air beside her face, around the corner, and down the short corridor that separated her bedroom and Sid's from the room in which the cousins slept. She smelled the nutmeg, she believed. And she smelled Bertha's heated skin, and a floral talc, and the astringency of a deodorant. Bertha held a vast, round, heavy arm about Eleanor's shoulder, and she murmured to her, making noises but not whole words, little cooing sounds of encouragement, as she saw her through the bedroom door. Inside the bedroom, as she lay on the bed beside the open French doors, Eleanor heard them moving across the tiled floor of the kitchen, heard the sputtering of sautéed food, the clatter of implements against crockery and pots, the thump of the oven door, the gurgle of liquids measured out. It all calmed her, and she let herself listen to the sounds of their cooking as, when she was a child, she heard, from her room, the noises made by her parents as they cleaned up in the kitchen at the end of a dinner party, her father's voice tired and grainy and deep, her mother's voice rich with satisfaction as she gossiped about her guests.

Eleanor woke to the sweet smell of grapes outside the bedroom, and the creamy, thick odor of the chalky soil in which they grew. Over those smells lay the dark richness of roasted vegetables and seared, sauced duck. She was lying on Sid's side of the bed, among his scattered clothes, closer to the open doors onto the fields, in the darkness of a cloudy sky lit coldly now by the pale, small moon. It would rain in the morning, she thought, and the day would be humid. Eugene and Bertha would be uncomfortable in high humidity, and they would soak through their traveling clothes. They would suffer, and so might she, she thought, but none of them would look up, like Sid, and then, like a lamp extinguished, go out.

She put on clogs and went into the kitchen, passing the closed door to the silent extra bedroom. A bottle half filled with the St.-Georges-Côtes-Pavie glowed in the low light the cousins had left on. She tugged at the cork and poured some into a kitchen tumbler. In the refrigerator she found sliced duck wrapped in plastic, and she sat at the table and ate. The wine was fruity and rich, and the taste of the duck made her hungry for more. But when she thought of the smell of nutmeg, although she couldn't make out its taste in the duck, she removed the partly chewed meat from her mouth and threw it into the garbage pail under the sink. She took a swig of St. Emilion and spat it down into the drain.

Walking past the great pot of rosemary, and among lavender bushes, she slowly carried her wine down a row of grapevines. Something flew close to her head, but when she looked up she saw only the rows of cloud, like the serried layers of flesh on a fish, lit from above by the dim moon. She squatted, suddenly, and coughed, waiting to be sick. Nothing happened, though. It was as if they had eaten the corpse, she told herself, and she gagged again. But nothing more happened except a strangled cough, and she turned from what she thought of as her theatrics, sipped at the tumbler, and then walked the short distance back to the French doors of the bedroom, where she sat cross-legged on their bed and emptied her glass and thought of the sorry sweetness of their confession to each other that, at barely their beginning, they were failed.

A night bird at the far edge of the grape vines called, another answered, and then she heard Bertha's rich voice. It had made a kind of whinny in the bedroom across the corridor. She moved from the bed without thinking, and she crouched at her closed door. Breathing raggedly, shallowly, she pressed the empty glass to the door and her ear to the bottom of the glass. She heard the whining of what she knew were bedsprings in the extra room. She heard the shuffle and brush of bedclothes, and she heard their skin. They were probably running with sweat, she thought. They were naked and their bodies were wet and they were making love. She had never thought of them this way. She had considered them delicate of feeling, gentle of motive, bound inside themselves by their fat and the difficulty with which such large creatures moved, no matter how graceful they might appear. But now she heard them whisper with pleasure, she heard the smack of lolloping, floppy skin, the suction of their flesh as they moved together and apart and then together again.

Eugene said, low, "Oh, for God's sake, my *dear*est girl."

Bertha made a sound of pleasure at her wickedness.

"God," he said.

She thought of the hundreds of pounds of flesh that shifted and slid, of the way a mounded stomach was stuck by fluid and friction to the loose, damp canyon of a crotch. She was excited by what she heard, but she was also suddenly aware that what she ached with now was not the grief of this morning or of the days and nights before. It was envy, she thought. She didn't breathe out, and didn't breathe out. She kneeled at her door, one hand closed on the knob and the other holding her eavesdropper's glass as she listened to the long silence in the room across the hall. Then one of the sweat-slicked, gargantuan lovers held by death at bay whispered words she couldn't distinguish. Then one of them shifted great weight, the guest bed groaned, and Eleanor began to breathe.

LESLEY DORMEN

Curvy

One day I get tired of crying and feeling sorry for myself—I'm not starving, I'm not in a war, I'm not crippled—and decide to track down my real father's phone number. Isn't it about time? I'm practically thirty years old. *This* is my life, right now.

I call Cleveland information. I don't know why I'm surprised when they give me the number. Irving Brandwein, as present and accountable as Macy's. I write it down on the corner of a takeout menu from Hunan Royal.

It's the Fourth of July weekend, a few weeks before Prince Charles is supposed to marry the shy kindergarten teacher. Everyone—meaning my ex-boyfriend and some crazy girl he broke my heart for—has left the city two by two. When all that's left is me and my carefully chosen pile of new books (*The Complete Novels of Jane Austen Volume 1, The Interpretation of Dreams, Strangers on a Train*), armature against the heavy air, the Sunday stillness every day, the whoosh of the occasional taxi, the Doobie Brothers coming from someone's open window. The soundtrack to the end of the world.

I don't know my father, not really. My mother divorced him when I was six, replaced him with a new father right away, then another one when that one turned out to be defective. The last time I saw him I was—what? Twenty. He called to say that he was passing through New York for a sporting goods convention—that's his business, sporting goods or sports clothes or maybe sports trophies, something like that—and could he take me to dinner. Very polite. The time before that I was ten, when he took me to lunch and asked me why I wanted to change my name. This was in Cleveland, where we lived. My mother took the same care dressing me as I took dressing my dolls. For lunch with my father: patent leather Mary Janes and my brown tweed Chesterfield coat with the velvet collar. (The bowler hat with streamers felt babyish. I left it in the car.) I didn't have the heart to tell this almost stranger that Mother had changed our names, unofficially at least, the moment she remarried. "I just want my last name to be the same as my mother's last name," I said primly over chicken in a basket. My initial sense of importance—my younger brother, Alex, wasn't included—had been worn down by my father's soft, persistent questions with their alarming implications. I wanted to go home, to my biography of Abigail Adams and the new puppy our second father got us.

The last time my real father called, I asked if I could bring my best friend, Phoebe, along to dinner. As I said, I was twenty. Nothing that happened to me was real unless it happened to Phoebe, too. My father was shorter than I remembered. Phoebe and I sat beside each other on the banquette, smoking and drinking gin and tonics, telling what we had studied at college and how we liked our first jobs, the two of us scrupulously avoiding each other's eyes for fear of collapsing into awful helpless laughter. The memory makes me cringe. "I'll wait for *you* to call the next time," my father told me kindly at the end of that evening. I guess it wasn't a great strategy on his part.

A few days later, I get up the nerve to dial the Cleveland number. She answers the phone. His wife. I ask for him, for Irv. That's how we refer to him, Alex and I. He's the original one-name celebrity. "It's Grace," I say. "His daughter." I feel like I'm calling the President.

"It's nice to hear your voice," my real father says when he gets on. His voice has the gentleness I remember, a little bit shy. He definitely sounds surprised. We say a few formal things back and forth, but it doesn't matter what they are. It's like he's been waiting for the phone to ring. I know the feeling.

The next thing you know, Irv and his wife are going to stop in New York for a day just to see us—me and my brother—on their way to a wedding in Florida. The first Saturday in August. They'll arrive in the afternoon and spend the night. So there's going to be a reunion: Me, Alex, Irv, and his wife. Not Mother.

"Have you told her yet?" my brother says. He has zero memories of Irv—he was only three when they divorced—but he's onboard with the reunion. "Because you know she'll want to be in on it." Nope, I haven't. I've been relishing the secret. It's like walking around town with a concealed weapon.

"This has to be about *us,* not her," I say with big sisterly authority. It occurs to me, though. Telling would be like actually using the weapon.

I say I'll explain it.

"Good luck," he says.

I take the subway to my mother's apartment on a Friday afternoon. We only have to stick around the office until noon in the summer. I work for a consulting firm that tracks novelty item and condiment trends. I write up reports for Howard and Josie, the two partners, put together focus groups, attend luncheons sponsored by Pez and the Pimento Council. Look, it's not the job I'm supposed to have. I can't even go into all the reasons I have it.

My mother and I sit on the terrace. She lives in an apartment house that takes up the whole block, but her apartment is on a low floor, and you can see directly across the street into a firehouse that's been remade as a sculptor's studio. What an excellent New York view. I feel sorry for the sculptor, though. All he gets to look at is my mother's mammoth white brick building.

My mother has made iced tea for us to drink with the biscotti I picked up on the way. She's perfectly dressed, in pale linen afternoon clothes. She looks like she's just come from or is going somewhere. Where? She doesn't have a job, she doesn't see a therapist, she doesn't volunteer, and she has no hobbies. A mystery as usual.

"Grace, you know me. I only want this to be a good experience for you and your brother," my mother says after I've made my speech about who can participate in the reunion and who can't.

"Okay, well, good." I sit up a little straighter. I like this feeling—gently but firmly forbidding my mother to suck up all the available attention.

We each sip our tea.

"Although I'd be curious to see Irv after all these years," she says. "That's natural, isn't it?"

Who knows what's natural? I ask people to share their feelings about tiny pickles. Is that natural?

"Have you discussed it with Dr. Gold?" my mother says.

"What do you mean?" She means, Did you tell her before you told me.

"Does she think this is a good idea for you right now?"

"Why wouldn't it be a good idea?"

Recently my mother called Dr. Gold and asked her what she should be doing to help me. She and Alex hover impatiently around my prickly unease like diners waiting for their table. "Be her mother," Dr. Gold says she told her. I wish I had thought of that.

Instead of going downtown to my empty apartment, I let my mother persuade me to walk around the corner to a neighborhood boutique she likes. My mother chats it up with the saleswoman while I peel off my T-shirt and jeans and try on a bunch of stuff in the dressing room. I come out in a strapless cotton dress with a matching jacket and consider myself in the mirror. I don't feel like me exactly, but do I feel like someone I might like to be? I try to picture my father seeing me for the first time in ten years. A sophisticated young woman. Nice shoulders, curly hair. Sexy. My mother runs her hand thoughtfully across the back of the dress with a small frown. I know that touch. It's code for stand up straight. I see what she sees: I'm crooked. One shoulder is higher than the other. I have no idea what happened to make my spine curve that much and no more. I don't even think about it. I'm tilted in a certain direction, and that's that. I adjust my shoulder.

"I love that on you!" my mother says with a great big smile.

"And it's transitional," the saleswoman tells my mother.

I get the dress and some other stuff. My mother pays for everything while I pretend to be mesmerized by a scarf and jewelry display at the front of the store.

The next day I go to Bergdorf's for shoes. I tell them to put it on my mother's charge. I sign her name on the slip and write "Daughter" in parentheses.

The following week, Dr. Gold and I start out with the upcoming reunion and how I feel about it and what my fantasies are of what might happen. I feel good, kind of excited, I have no particular fantasies. "I just want him to know what kind of person I've turned into," I say. But what kind of person is that?

I tell her about the shopping trip. Last winter Dr. Gold and I spent three sessions on whether or not I would accept a raccoon coat my mother no longer wore. Telling her about the new clothes is like confessing to some kind of junkie relapse. Just when I think I'm about to finally understand the nature of my bargain with my mother, a fog fills my skull and settles around my brain like a fairy-tale spell.

"That dress I got—it's not even my style," I tell Dr. Gold. I sound combative. Is the spell her fault?

"Well, how would you describe your style?" she says.

"Less, I don't know, *structured.* Looser. More flowy." I get a picture in my mind of Joni Mitchell, then Virginia Woolf, then Julie Christie in *Darling.* Folkloric hippie? Droopy thirties tea dresses? Mod London? A furious ball of misery and complaint has lodged itself in my throat. My eyes fill up. Why don't I have a style? Dr. Gold uncrosses and recrosses her legs. Now I worry that I've inadvertently insulted *her* style. Not that she has a style. When I started seeing her at the clinic two years ago, she wore jean skirts and sandals. "I'd prefer to see a man," I told the director of the clinic when he asked if I had a preference. "No particular reason." They gave me Dr. Gold. She was so new then she didn't get to go away in August. Now she wears silk blouses and tailored skirts and spends the entire month in Greece or Sardinia or Wellfleet. One of those places. It's almost a relief when people go away.

I find a room for Irv and his wife in a hotel on Park Avenue South. A good weekend rate and equidistant from my brother's apartment and from mine.

I call up my brother to tell him.

"I know that hotel. They shot a scene from *The Verdict* in the bar. Paul Newman slaps Charlotte Rampling across the face."

"So do you think I should take it?" I picture us all meeting in the dark woody bar after they've had a chance to unpack and get settled. I hear myself telling Irv and his wife that a Paul Newman movie was filmed here.

"Do whatever you want," my brother says. "This is all your idea."

I have a few memories of Irv as my father, that's all. I've combed through them with Dr. Gold: Irv giving me a stuffed monkey named Zippy, Irv hiding colored Easter eggs under the sofa cushions, Irv's pale calves sticking out of a bathrobe. Mother was the one who'd asked for the divorce. Why? Unclear. She's remarked that Irv could be "sarcastic," that he wasn't "ambitious," that he was "a little too short on the dance floor." She's said that it was a long time ago. Don't even try making someone remember something. It's like telling someone who to love. Irv remarried right away, too. My brother and I used to make fun of his new wife's name—Bettina. Wheatina, we called her. Peals of laughter. My mother laughed, too. We were big laughers.

"Who made that joke?" I ask my brother during one of our planning conversations.

"Probably I did," he says. "Why? What are you saying?"

"I'm just asking." Everyone is so touchy all of a sudden. Is there a law that says I have to find the same old jokes hilarious? This one happens to strike me as mean. And why does my brother still have all the basic facts wrong? He thinks Irv is from England.

"He's not?"

"He was *there,* during the war. But he's not *from* there. They were Polish Jews."

"Didn't he fly in that battle over Holland? The *A Bridge Too Far* battle?" We have a few photographs of Irv from World War II. There's one of him in his lieutenant's uniform. A bomber jacket and a cap. His face—his kind eyes, the shape of his mouth—is deeply familiar to me. "I thought Irv's mother was English or something," Alex says. He says it like he doesn't care one way or the other.

"I think she *lived* in England for a while. As a young woman." Actually, I'm hazy on the details myself. "Irv's parents—our grandparents—were socialists," I say. I feel proud of this.

"I wish I had that leather jacket," my brother says.

I imagine we'll eat at a nice bistro in the West Village on Saturday night. Should I get theater tickets? No, it won't be that kind of visit. We're probably going to want to spend most of our time talking.

"If this is just going to be some superficial thing, if we're not going to talk about why he left, then I don't want to be part of it," my brother says on the phone one evening. I'm surprised by his sudden burst of feeling.

"What's he so angry about?" I ask Dr. Gold at our last session before her August break. "He thinks Irv *wanted* to leave. Where did he even get that idea?" I don't know why I feel so indignant. These are mostly rhetorical questions, and Dr. Gold doesn't answer them. I talk some about work, about how the business is shaky and if it fails I'll probably have to go on unemployment and if that happens how will I even be able to see her because if I don't have a job where would I get the money? After that there's not that much to say. In the silence I can hear the clock ticking. The session is almost over. I wonder if we'll hug. When Dr. Gold asks me how I feel about her going away, I say, "You, you, you. It's all about you." It's not like I expect her to laugh. As far as I'm concerned she's already gone.

I met my ex-boyfriend—he's a writer who does freelance stuff for us—through James. James is our office manager.

"So what's his story?" I asked James after spotting this cute guy in the office one afternoon.

James is ten years older than I am, ugly and kind, with a large, pale head, doleful blue eyes, and thin hair the color of sand. The week I was hired, two years ago, a pipe burst in my office—we're on the third floor of an East Thirties brownstone—and I had to share with James for a month. We got to know each other. I learned that his marriage, to an attorney for the health and hospitals union, was faltering but that he didn't know whether he wanted to save it or leave it. Like me, he loved Fred and Ginger movies and old popular songs. He collected vintage postcards and tropical fish and rolled his eyes at the temperamental business practices of our bosses.

The game wasn't something James and I decided, exactly, just something we slipped into. We pretended that we worked for a company that made some nameless widgety product. James was Mr. Appleton, and I was Miss Hanford, the sexless boss and the spinster secretary. We were formal and repressed with each other, as if it were the fifties. When I moved back to my own office, Appleton Products stayed in business.

They're like small vacations for me, the game days. I forget to be afraid.

Other days, James wanders into my office mid-afternoon, deposits himself in the chair opposite my desk, and tells me stories—about his mother who bakes pies and his father, a state trooper in Oregon. Or I tell him about my life, such as it is, and he tips back in his chair, hands resting on his belly, listening like there's nowhere else he'd rather be. I feel happy when I can make

James smile his whale smile or shake silently with laughter. For minutes at a time I feel good.

"I don't know. Good writer. Kind of an asshole," James said.

He *was* good. I'd read some of his real writing, in one of the men's magazines. Sexy, too. Muscular and compact in tight black jeans, the sleeves on his denim work shirt turned back so you could see the dark hair above his wrist bones. Took me to a steak house on our first date. "You eat like a man," he said approvingly.

I sensed another woman in the background from the get-go. Well, in the foreground, too. An almondy shampoo still owned air rights under his showerhead. A few items of clothing (cute, my size) were shoved to the back of his closet. His former wife. She worked for a United Nations agency whose name I couldn't keep straight in my mind. He said she'd left him for the Palestinian representative to Mozambique.

"Now what?" I asked Phoebe. We were watching television together over the phone.

"*Jeopardy.*"

"No. I mean, *now* what?"

"He's going to dump you five seconds after he recovers from his divorce," Phoebe said. "But wait—*is* he divorced?"

"Well, yes and no—I'm not exactly sure."

"Live dangerously. Ask."

Turned out he was, but only in the letter-of-the-law sense. He confessed that crazy girls held a fatal charm for him. The girlfriend between the ex-wife and me had been a shoplifter. "And how will you describe me?" I asked him once, pretending flirtation. "You?" He pulled me close, and his hands wandered, sweetly tracing the shape of me. "You're not crazy," he whispered. "You're curvy." Curvy! Curvy has its charms, but crazy is love's Super Glue, the mousetrap that never lets go.

I'm the type who gets unhinged *after* love ends. What's saner than that? One night I rang his bell after midnight just to demand a more thorough explanation. "This isn't a police state, Grace!" he admonished. "It's just dating. Dating ends." It *felt* like a police state. "Don't you even have false pride?" he said, helping me off with my clothes. I said I didn't. Maybe I *was* crazy. "That's good," he said. "You only have real pride."

"Well, Miss Hanford, I'm glad to see you back at your desk,"

James said when I returned to work three days later, all cried out. "You're looking well. Your vacation must have agreed with you."

"Thank you, Mr. Appleton. Mother and I always enjoy our yearly week together," I said in my prim pretend voice. That's another thing about crazy girls. They don't have mothers. They create themselves.

The day of the reunion I wake up with butterflies in my stomach. Their plane is supposed to get in at noon. My brother and I do the LaGuardia to Manhattan arrival math a hundred times.

"He'll call me when they get into the room," I tell him again. "Then I'll call you. Then we'll meet them at the hotel. In the bar. Or you and I can meet outside, and we can go in together."

I change clothes a bunch of times. In the end, I'm wearing the new suit.

When the phone rings I think I might be sick.

Alex is pacing back and forth on the sidewalk in front of the hotel, smoking a cigarette, when my taxi pulls up. His face wears a pained, distracted look that gathers itself, briefly, into acknowledgment of my costume. "Different look for you, no?"

I feign disinterest. "Father clothes," I say.

"Well, you look nice." He flicks the cigarette into the street. "Are you ready for this?" My stomach flips.

The bar is pitch-dark after the glare of the afternoon, but I see them right away, at a table in the back. They're on their feet the second they spot us. They look like tourists. Irv. Not too tall. Balding on top and puffy around the eyes. Kind of fit and muscular, though, in a polo shirt. Is that a cigar in his hand? I think I like it. Suddenly I'm remembering a bowling alley—pins crashing and the smell of beer.

Okay, here we go. Lots of hellos and handshakes and awkward embraces. I'm shocked by how *related* I feel to this man. The words form silently on my tongue: My father. Nice hug, and he's just my size, with a pleasing dryness to his voice and again, that familiarity. Plus he's regarding me and Alex with so much, I don't know, pleasure, it seems he feels related to us, too. I feel proud of myself, like I've just given birth. Bettina is beaming.

"What would you like?" Irv says once we've arranged ourselves at the table, me and Alex on one side, Irv and Bettina on the other. No false heartiness in Irv's voice, thank God. A waiter approaches. Apparently, we all drink bloody marys.

But if not false heartiness—what?

Bettina fills in with, "You kids look exactly the same." I smile and nod, still speechless as a fool.

"It's wonderful, really wonderful, to see you both," Irv says then, like a meeting finally called to order.

"Awfully long overdue," I murmur. Am I at tea in an English novel?

Alex says, "Now I know who to thank for my receding hairline," and Irv smiles.

"Doesn't that come from the mother's side?" I say, but luckily no one pays attention.

There's a microsecond when the earth threatens to open and swallow us all (only Bettina survives), but in the nick of time I remember to tell the Paul Newman story—he's even from our hometown—and Irv looks around the bar again, impressed, retrieving from memory the exact scene in the movie which, we all agree, was excellent. From there we slip easily into matters of historical review and record-keeping: Alex accounts for college in Boston, then the two years he spent in South America, running a small leather company. That's the official story, at least. I offer a funny anecdote about my job. I can do that.

"Did you know that your grandfather was an editor?" Irv asks me. No, I did not. "He edited the Yiddish newspaper in Cleveland." Hey. How about that.

Irv and Alex discuss the Red Sox and Indians' pennant chances as if they're picking up an old conversation. Bettina turns to me. "Is there someone special in your life, honey?"

"No, not really, not right now," I say. I'm not interested in doing girl talk with Bettina. I'm listening to Irv and Alex, remembering how our second father took us to behind-the-fence dinners at the stadium. I'm reciting the names of the old players to myself—Minnie Minoso, Rocky Colavito, Jimmy Piersall—like it's some kind of poem. I'm studying the shape of Irv's eyes, hearing the music behind his words and his habit of punctuating his stories with fond, teasing banter directed toward his wife. I'm betting he tells war stories, the same ones again and again, and that everyone listens with real affection even though they've heard them all before. I'm thinking, He reminds me of someone, and then I'm realizing that it's me.

"His all-time favorite book is *Fear Strikes Out,*" I say, indicating my brother.

After that everything quiets down. We all let it.

"You know, I wasn't completely sure I wanted to come here," Irv says. His hands levitate a few inches above the table, hover, then lower again.

My face wears an expression that says, Go on with that.

"I didn't know if I wanted to risk it. If it's not going to lead to anything more than this."

I nod. But I'm thinking: Lead? Lead to what? "I guess we have to start somewhere," I say. "Like, just to get some leverage." Whatever that means. The problem with spending most of your time inside books is you can produce words for any occasion. You just don't necessarily know what you're talking about.

"I have no real memories of you," Alex says abruptly. "I just know that you left. I didn't know why then, and I don't really know why now."

It occurs to me that our second father might have upended the table in response to my brother's challenging tone of voice. That father had a temper. We neighborhood kids used to put on plays in the backyard every summer. I was always the lead and the second lead—princess, queen, fairy godmother. I'd deign to give my brother a minor role—dwarf, palace guard, woodsman. The summer we did *Sleeping Beauty* (I played the Queen and Sleeping Beauty) I happened to be kissing Kenny Baum, the King, behind our garage when Alex walked to the center of the lawn and delivered his one line: "There must be a path somewhere through this forest." Our next-door neighbor, Tommy Lantano, whose job was opening and closing the curtain, a blanket draped over the clothesline strung between our two garages, said, "Shut up, Alex," and I burst out laughing. Next thing you know Daddy has me by the arm and is hauling me into the house—for laughing or kissing, I'm still not sure.

"Well, the short answer is, that's the way your mother wanted it," Irv says. He says it in a resigned way, without a trace of anger.

"Are you sure you kids don't want something to eat?" Bettina says. Bettina isn't resigned.

My brother doesn't remember the day we were adopted by our second father, but I do. We're sitting on a hard wooden bench in the big empty hallway outside a judge's office. This would have been sometime after the day Irv took me to lunch. We're quiet, my brother and me, not even joking. I can feel my scratchy slip under my dress. Someone shows us into the judge's office. He's sitting behind a desk deep as a football field and piled with papers. (Was he wearing a black robe or have I added that?) We already know he's going to ask us which father we want. Even at ten, I know that this is only the pretend question. It's our mother we're being asked to choose.

The judge asks me first: Do I want our stepfather to be our real father from now on?

My mother isn't in that room with us, but my mother can see me no matter where I am. She can see all the way through me, everything good and everything bad. I've hidden my questions in a place so remote even I don't know how to find them.

Yes, I say.

Then it's my brother's turn. When the judge asks him, he says grumpily, "*Why* do we have to choose?"

"But you could have fought harder to be in our lives," Alex says now. "You never did."

"Well, your mother made it pretty difficult," Irv says slowly as if it pains him to say it. "I'd take you out to dinner, and your mother would turn up in the same restaurant. Or I'd come to the house to pick you up for the weekend, and she'd say that Alex couldn't come—he was being punished." I try to picture this: My mother and our second father lurking sitcom style in plain sight. I can even see the challenging hat my mother is wearing. I glance at Alex, who looks frankly skeptical. "But I suppose the real reason is that I didn't think you two wanted me in your lives." Irv pauses. "I suppose I felt rejected."

I'm stirring the swizzle stick around in my bloody mary, poking at the piece of lime. He felt—what? Rejected? *He* felt that. By us?

"Well, we were just children," I hear myself say in my most queenly voice. "I mean, that's what we were." My head is pounding with the wrongness of it. There's a whole new slant being introduced here. *We* rejected *him*. I'm not sure there's room in this reunion for that particular slant.

"It was a very big loss for your father," Bettina says. "It was a tragedy. He loved you kids very much." I understand something about Bettina suddenly: She hates my mother. The knowledge sends a thrill through me. I've never heard of anyone hating my mother. How *dare* she.

By the time the waiter comes around again we've agreed that the meet and greet part of the reunion is over.

My brother and I say goodbye to Irv and Bettina in the lobby, repeating the instructions about the dinner reservation and getting to the restaurant, then Alex and I make our way out to the street, tightlipped, as if we're in danger of being overheard. It's overcast now, and humid, but the two of us stand at the curb, dazzled by the light, murmuring sounds at each other, the gist of which is, Do you believe this? Isn't it unbelievable? A taxi pulls up, we hug quickly goodbye, and Alex opens the cab door. I get in, and he leans in toward me. "I wonder what he thinks of my hands and my elbows," he says. "I wonder what he thinks of the scar above my eye."

It had been a few days before the Fourth of July, when my buzzer rang, startlingly, sometime after ten p.m.—a terrible sound. What had I done? James's voice came crackling over the intercom. Could he come up?

It was the first time James had set foot in my apartment—we didn't socialize outside of work—and the fact of him standing there, his blurred, impassive face and mournful politeness among my things, my furniture and books and bed, made me shy and worried and, as a result, excessively flirtatious.

"It's you! I'm so happy it's you!" I said. He was looking around dismally now, uncertain what he was doing there. "Should I get you a beer?"

He sighed, a complicated soliloquy, and ventured farther in, and for a terrible moment I thought it was Mr. Appleton standing there in my apartment, and for a more terrible moment I thought it wasn't.

"A beer would be welcome," he said. "I just thought I needed some, uh, exercise." With that he sank unhappily into the one easy chair.

"Ah." I nodded and hurried to the refrigerator.

We drank those, and then two more, me curled up in a corner of the sofa, James planted in the chair. As my air conditioner rattled and heaved, we talked about the usual things. He didn't mention what had propelled him out of his own home, and I thought it intrusive to ask. Finally, when he appeared ready to leave—he was standing, not steadily, and I was making thanks-for-coming noises—we wrapped our arms around each other and stood for a moment that way, my head against his chest, breathing together, swaying slightly. He smelled altogether alien through his damp T-shirt. Kissing him was frightening and necessary. The kissing carried us to bed, and once there our heads cleared. Too late, or possibly too soon. Either way, our sympathy for each other was unable to transform itself into anything we could get lost in. He left long before morning, pulling his clothes on like a hurried apology. This I sensed rather than saw. I was afraid to open my eyes.

"Take care, Grace," he said softly.

"*You* take care," I whispered.

My phone is ringing as I unlock the door to my apartment. It's Mother calling, wanting to know how it's going. "It's going good," I say.

"Honey, I'm so glad. I wanted this for the two of you."

Whatever it is she means, I feel a rush of guilt.

"Mom, I'm sorry about excluding you, but you understand, right?"

"Of course I do. In fact, I spoke to Irv just a little while ago. He invited me to join you for dinner, but I think not. Although he suggested brunch tomorrow."

"You called the hotel?"

"Just to say hello. Grace, I hope you're not angry. I couldn't help myself. I had to know what he thought about the two of you." I know that this is at least partly true. "I think he was happy to hear from me."

I picture Irv in the hotel room, sitting on the edge of the bed, talking to my mother. I see the half smile on his face as he lets my mother's warm voice wash over him. I see Bettina, stretched out next to him on top of the bedspread, her shoes kicked off, fuming. I know just how she feels. Still, my mother is the one I'm rooting for. That's just the way it is.

He's a nice man, my father. He's the nicest man my mother ever married. I know how the rest of the visit is going to play out. He'll talk about the past. He'll tell me things about my mother, things he doesn't mean to tell and that I don't really want to know, although somehow I already do. He'll confide in me, wanting to know what he can do to disarm my brother's anger and whether I think it can be disarmed. He'll want to know why I'm not married, and he'll inquire, delicately, if I think the divorce might have had anything to do with it. He'll want me to know that he's there for me, and he'll ask me to promise to stay in touch and let him know, really let him know, if I ever need anything. We *will* keep in touch. We'll exchange dutiful Sunday afternoon telephone calls and say "I love you" before we hang up. It's too late to have a real father, but maybe it's not too late to know I used to have one, once.

After the night with James, I had spent several mopey days believing myself to be in love with him, several more certain I wasn't and was instead responsible for causing some serious harm. In the office, James appeared ambiguously jaunty, then stricken, treating me with an awful counterfeit casualness. Finally, I invited him out for a drink. "Why did you come over?" I asked him. It about killed me to do it.

He shook his head. "I like you so much, Grace."

"And now?"

"I'm married, and you don't need that. God, it's the *last* thing you need."

I let his words, and then the kindness inside the words, seep into my blood and my bones. I said: "I hope I haven't behaved inappropriately with you, James, because I wouldn't want to do that, not with you—you, of all people..." I trailed off. That rickety little speech was the best I could do.

On Friday morning, the start of the Labor Day weekend, Howard and Josie summon James and me into the conference room and tell us that business is bad right now, and the firm can't support a staff. They have to let us go. I knew it was coming; I've known it for months. But now that it's happened I feel devastated. I start to cry. I cry and cry. I'm startled and embarrassed, but I can't stop. How will I survive not being tucked into this little house with my family of coworkers? What will become of me?

James and I each have a cardboard box to pack up the stuff in our offices. Mine holds a few jars of cornichons and fancy mustards, some dumb novelty pens and retro Pez dispensers, but mostly coffee mugs and office supplies. When I look up, James is standing in my doorway. He's holding a white plastic crash helmet with the words "I Saw Haley's Comet Coming" printed on it. It's his favorite novelty crash helmet. He clears his throat ostentatiously.

"Miss Hanford, on behalf of Appleton Products I'd like to take this opportunity to thank you for all your hard work and dedication," he says. He uses the bottom of his T-shirt to wipe off a thin layer of dust, then offers the helmet to me. "I hope you'll accept this small gift as a token of our appreciation."

It's the best gift anyone ever gave me—well, the most heartfelt. When I put it on my head I almost expect to hear the ocean. "Thank you, Mr. Appleton," I say. "No matter where I go in life, I will always remember my time here at Appleton Products." My words feel echoey as they bounce weirdly off the plastic, but I can tell that I'm saying what I mean.

While I finish packing up, I remember James telling me something his father told him, about searching for people who are lost in the woods. The first thing the troopers want to know is whether the missing person is right- or left-handed. Apparently, people tend to get lost in the direction of their handedness. Everyone leans one way or the other. Someone who knows which way will always know how to find you.

PETER GORDON

Celia

In what turned out to be the last year of his life, my father slowly lost touch with the real world. There were persistent but not unpleasant hallucinations, such as seeing red birds in an empty sky, or hearing a nonexistent ringing telephone, so that in the middle of a silent stretch he'd suddenly look up and say, "Isn't someone going to get that?" He invented a dog that lay at the end of his bed but didn't like to be touched by anyone but him. There was also some mildly delusional thinking. He thought he was allergic to certain words, and if you said them in his presence, he'd think he was breaking out in a rash. The words all had to do with medical terminology—nurse, doctor, blood, needle. Also certain colors: you couldn't wear red or orange because he said they shouted at him and gave him headaches. He also came to believe, honestly and truly believe, that I was dead.

In my father's mind I had died twenty-five years before in a tragic childhood accident. He was actually confusing it with a real event, the death of his brother Stephen who had drowned at the age of eight in 1936, in a little river that flowed behind the house where he grew up in Medway, Massachusetts. He was convinced that I was the one lost in the river, that I had been the one whose body was carried nearly two miles downstream and not retrieved until the next morning. He'd begin a sentence, "That awful summer we lost Peter . . . ," or "When Peter was alive . . . ," and I'd be sitting right there in his tropically painted room at the adult care facility, holding his hand, adjusting his lap blanket, maybe spoon-feeding him chicken noodle soup or the plain yogurt he liked to swish around in his mouth until some oozed between his lips like sea foam. Even in abject dependence, my father's face had this regal cast to it, dominated by eyes that were so black and fierce they seemed fake. His mouth was not a crumpled line but still taut, still elastic. His nose had only the faintest streaks of red vein fireworks. Even his deep wrinkles had some aesthetic and satisfying striation to them, as though he lay them out in precise order every morning. His mind had crumbled, and cancer was starting to eat away his colon, but his exterior looked nearly untouched. He almost looked like the handsome dentist he once was.

My visits usually lasted between half an hour and forty-five minutes; I looked at my watch shamelessly. I couldn't wait for my time with him to end, and to that extent the mentally shattered are not unlike the blind—they don't notice your impatience with them, your outright rudeness. Truthfully, I had nothing else to do, nowhere else to go, but I acted as though I did. We'd sit by the window that overlooked a slice of the parking lot, sometimes buffeted by a small breeze that came through the partly opened window, mostly just vegetating there in silence. It was sort of like meditation, minus the inner calm or spiritual destination. I knew he was aware of my presence, that he was cognizant of being with *someone,* and felt the muscle-memory obligation to hold up the social contract of keeping company with another human being. Sometimes to break the monotony I'd get out the family photo album I'd painstakingly assembled and given to him when he first arrived there, comprised of photos I'd accumulated and held on to for most of my life. We'd turn the pages that contained photos of me as a child, and he'd thumb through them with no comment or reaction whatsoever. Just a reverent silence, an unspoken but palpable sadness.

"Do you miss your son Peter?" I might say, to get a rise out of him.

"Yes, I miss him very much very very much." He might steal a glance at the photo of me that was framed and sat on his bureau. I had put it there myself. It was me at age five or so, my cherubic face caught in profile in the artificial amber light of a photographer's studio, the whole effect too beatific to believe.

"What was Peter like?" I asked that question fairly regularly, just to see what he'd come up with.

This was a typical answer. "Very smart. He knew the alphabet when he was a baby." Or this: "He climbed on things. He was a great climber. He could climb to the top of a tree and you couldn't find him and he wouldn't come down, not for anything." He might look at me directly for an instant. "Where are your children?"

"I don't have any children."

"What happened to them?"

"I'm not married."

"You should get married. Have a family. Have children. Have boys." Long pause. A couple of swallows. "Children are a blessing."

"Yes."

Then more silence. Then abruptly, "You have to go now. I need to walk the dog. He hasn't been out all day."

Right around this time I met a girl. I was at a club in the city, one of those subterranean rooms where the light is dirty and dim and you can never be sure that what you're seeing will look the same the next day. She leaned against a wall near the kitchen, and every time the double doors swung open a brief fluorescent wave swept across her. I asked her to dance, and as I was walking away from her soft refusal, she called out: Okay, let's dance. I immediately discovered three things about her: her name was Celia, she was born in California and moved to Boston when she was four, and she was thin enough that I could feel the long angular bones of her shoulder blades protruding like wings when we danced. I suspected she was beautiful, and sure enough, when we met for coffee a few days later, she was. When she got a good look at my face, she told me that I looked totally different than she'd imagined in the dark; not better or worse, just different. She thought I looked older than thirty-three. And that I didn't look like an architect at all, more like a lawyer or an accountant.

I called her every day for a month. I fell in love with her voice over the telephone and with her habit of ending conversations abruptly, with no long prelude or series of false closes. Just click, and she was gone.

I started bringing Celia with me when I went to see my father. She asked me if this was my idea of showing a girl a good time—starting every date at a rest home in the middle of nowhere. At first, she hated to come in the facility and would just sit in the car while I was inside, but gradually the boredom and the sameness of the songs on the radio got to her. She finally moved from the car to the lobby, where she sat stiffly in one of the overstuffed floral-pattered chairs, ignoring the fanned-out magazines, usually staring straight ahead as though she'd been assigned to some sort of waiting room purgatory. If one of the front desk people tried to engage her in conversation, she'd act almost catatonic in her responses. Once, she got up and made it to the women's room, where she nearly fainted; the receptionist found her on her hands and knees in one of the stalls, trembling and hyperventilating. It got to the point where one of the doctors asked me if my friend was suffering from gerontophobia.

"What's that?"

"Fear of old people. Fear of people who are about to die."

"I never heard of it."

"We see it a lot in young women," he said. "It's nothing to be ashamed of. It doesn't denote a lack of humanity or absence of empathy or anything like that. Quite the opposite, in fact. In most cases, it's a case of seeing themselves as old. It's a projection thing. They think, That could be me someday. That *will* be me."

When I told Celia about it, she got really upset. "I'm not afraid of old people. Why would I be? You make me sound like some kind of freak. I just don't like those places. They make me sad."

I tried to convince her to make the walk from the lobby to my father's room. It's only about a fifty-foot walk, I said. You can keep your head down so you don't have to look into any of the other rooms, or see other patients in the hallway, and if the smells bother you, just hold your breath. She got to the point where she made it most of the way to his room before turning back, followed by further advances where she hovered in the doorway, getting glimpses of him. One day I suggested that she have a drink to work up her courage, so she downed one of those pre-made screwdrivers in a bottle in the parking lot and walked right in with me. My father was in his pajamas, bent over in front of the window, talking to his own reflection. "Now that's what I mean, that's what I'm talking about," he said, wagging his finger for emphasis.

"This is Celia," I said in a voice that was firm but not frightening.

He straightened up and walked over to her, trying to be as erect and square-shouldered as possible. She held out her hand (I told her he liked shaking people's hands), and he took it and right away started examining it, turning it over, twisting it slowly as though he were comparing the two sides. He stared at her face, at the freckles on her forehead, the short blond hair that wasn't her natural color but you had to look harder than normal to see that. He traced his finger on the six earrings in her left lobe, the single hoop in her right one, and rubbed the silver chain of her necklace between his thumb and forefinger as though he were trying to grind it into dust. He inspected her neck, smooth and white, offset by two beauty marks set close together like an extra pair of eyes. His face was inches from hers; their noses practically touched. His palm fell below her neckline and landed, momentarily, on her left breast. She flinched but made no motion to stop him. Eventually he pressed his ear to her chest, and closed his eyes. They stood like that, stiff, motionless, fused together.

"Celia," he said. "I used to know a Celia."

She closed her eyes and brushed her lips on the top of his pink, nearly hairless head.

My father had not only forgotten who I was, but never gave a real indication (and I never asked or probed) about who he thought I was now. Nothing about my face, my voice, my mannerisms, triggered any kind of memory, however dim. Probably he accepted me as a benign stranger, a man visiting him by mistake who was too kindly and courtly to get up and leave once he wandered into the wrong room. I must have seemed, I suppose, like a nice enough young man. He never asked what my name was, and he never called me anything. Sometimes he'd recognize me as the person who had visited him the day before, and sometimes he'd say, "That young man who came here yesterday, he smelled bad. You smell nice." I told the nurses I was his nephew, and after a time, I almost started believing it myself. I didn't want to tell them that I was the dead son because that would just cause undue confusion in a place that already had enough confusion.

He dropped stories about his son, Peter, to anyone who would listen—nurses, other residents, the night cleaning crew, guests going by—and it was never the same story twice, even if it started out as one he'd told before. "Once, when he was four, Peter wandered all the way down the avenue, and it turned out he was following a black woman because he had never seen a black woman before." In the next version, I followed a dog that was chasing a bird. The time after that, I chased a bright red candy wrapper propelled by the wind for two miles until I finally caught up with it only to collapse in tears because the candy was gone. Those stories had happy endings; I was found at the end. Sometimes I realized that he was taking and transmuting a piece of something that actually happened to me—like the time I stepped on a beehive at my cousin's birthday party and had to be rushed to the hospital, one of my earliest memories—and other times his plots were lifted straight from the movies or television news, like the time I supposedly saved the family from a raging house fire by going from room to room waking everyone up. (That actually happened in Boston about a year earlier when he was still paying sidelong attention to the world at large.)

Most patients had a running theme, and he had his, tragic but not unique, and wholly believable. He had suffered the most severe amputation a parent can suffer. He'd lost a child. At least he thought he had. Of course, so had Mr. Myers in B-11, and Mr. Mericoulas in B-25, and just about half the women in the C wing. But my father talked about it almost nonstop; he couldn't let it go. It was his aria. I heard him tell the story of how his son, Peter, died so often that I knew every word choice, every transition, every pause where he pulled on the end of his nose to gather himself. That was the strange thing—it was always told the same way, with the same exact details. An act of pure imagination, it seemed to be the one thing that remained clear and constant to him, and he told it slowly, not because he was unsure of where his mind was going to go with it, as was so often the case, but because he knew what lay ahead and he didn't want to get there sooner than he had to.

It was late afternoon. Peter, eight years old, looking forward to a birthday that was less than two months away, was playing by himself near the river near our house. The river was maybe five meters across and two meters deep at the point where the boy (dressed every time in a clean white T-shirt and brown shorts, and always described as being skinny as a stick) stood on the steep, stony riverbank, with water that was a rushing streak of dark dirty brown. It was hot; it was a supernaturally hot day, the worst of the summer. It was one of those days where the heat breaks you down, makes you do things you wouldn't ordinarily do. Peter took off his shirt and hung it over the branch of a tree that stood about ten meters off the bank, near the road. He stepped out of his brand-new sneakers and left them under the same tree. (My father claimed he kept these items, that the police gave them to him once the case was officially ruled an accident. Where he had them was another story, of course, since everything he owned was in the room at the care facility, whether in the drawers of his chest, in the cramped closet, or under his bed, and one day when I was alone in his room, in a pique of boredom, and what you'd have to call an act of madness, I actually looked for the stuff.)

The heat must have driven Peter to the river. Some footprints, very faint, tracked down to the water's edge. You could see right where he waded in. Maybe the boy decided to try to swim, or turned over onto his back to see how far he could float. Or perhaps he was trying to jump over the river; my father's description made it sound narrow enough to give off the illusion that was possible. Once he got in the river the current probably knocked him off of his feet, or maybe he decided to submerge for an instant and got twisted up in the vortex. He was so thin and fragile—you should have seen his arms, the bones were practically sticking through!—he didn't have the strength to fight a whole river. At some point he was overcome and surrendered. The body traveled downstream, and night came on, and very early the next morning some policemen discovered it floating face-up, snagged by standing weeds.

At the end, when he was done with the story, no one would know what to do. You'd look at your hands. You'd nod your head sadly. My father would always lean forward and say the same thing: He was only a boy. He had his whole life in front of him. I wish it had been me.

The convalescent home, Renaissance Village, was at the end of a long road lined with oddly leaning and skin-mottled birch trees, like old men asleep on their feet. It was reclaimed swampland, and retained the musky smell and dampness of cold, wet earth even in summer. The building itself had Doric columns and balustrades fronting an L-shaped porch and other nice flourishes to make the families of the residents think they were getting their money's worth. It was beautiful to behold as you came up the twisting road and caught glimpses of it through the woods, and it was only when you stepped inside that the fantasy gave way to the drizzle of disinfectants and bad bluish light.

The first time Celia heard the story was the second time she went into his room. She had brought him a batch of raisin cookies and a loaf of wheat bread from the bakery where she worked as a cashier and, part-time, sometime baker's apprentice. She put the cookies in a glittering silver tin and put a crinkly green bow on top. But my father was more taken with the bread in its plain white paper bag and immediately hid it under his pillow. Bread was always a good thing to have in case of an emergency.

When he started describing the day when his son, Peter, was playing by himself near the river, Celia looked at him with increasing perplexity and amazement, her eyes opened extra wide, and her mouth hung partly open. She was sitting on one side of my father's bed, I was on the other. He released the story in one breath; it seemed to sap the last molecules of energy he had left; the half-eaten cookie he was holding fell to the floor when he passed out.

She pulled me out into the hallway. "What's he talking about? Does he mean you? Are you the Peter he's talking about? Do you have a brother who's also named Peter, like you're Peter Mark and he's Peter Paul, or something like that?"

"I'm an only child."

"So he thinks you drowned? When you were a kid? His only son? That's so completely horrible. Did you know this?"

"I've heard the story a few times."

"And like, what? That's it? You just listen passively like he's telling you about what he had for breakfast?"

"He doesn't remember what he had for breakfast."

"Don't be an asshole, Peter." I loved how she said my name, landing extra hard on the *r*. She looked up and down the hall and back at me. "It must mean something. It's got to be symbolic of something. Why would he dream something like that up? On some level deep inside there must be a reason why he thinks you're dead." She was pulling on her fingers, her first nervous tic choice. The mouth scrunching would start soon. "Why don't you just go in there and tell him that you're you?"

"You're talking like he's rational, like I could just say, Hey, Dad, look, it's me, and he'd put on his glasses and go, Holy shit, it *is* you, and we'd have a good laugh about it." I was talking too loudly. A woman was scowling at me from her doorway. "His mind is gone. It's like a bridge that got washed away in a storm. Nothing can get from one side to the other. Everything just falls into this big pit. Nothing he says means anything."

"But you have proof you didn't die. You could show him your driver's license. Talk about stuff that only you would know about. It might trigger something with him."

"He's better off not knowing."

"He thinks you drowned. That's terrible for a father to have to live with. You could unburden him."

"He wouldn't want me to. It's his most prized possession."

"I'm glad you're not my son," she said, and walked away.

About three months after we met and three weeks before my father died, Celia said, "I have something to tell you."

"Can it wait?"

"Technically I guess it could wait another couple of months until you figured it out on your own. But I don't think you'd like that."

"What are you talking about?"

"I'm pregnant."

"You're sure?"

"I think I know my own body, Peter."

I didn't say another word. She later told me that my face didn't even register an emotion, which I said was impossible but she said was true. She waited for me to say something, and only a complete idiot wouldn't have seen that she was waiting with the look of someone who expects water to be in the pool they just blindly dove into.

Later, I worked up all this stuff in my mind. I saw the future with the three of us firmly arrived in it, as real as if fully formed figures were standing right in front of me, the baby with the perfect face of one of those toy infants with glass eyes and moveable mouth and workable limbs, its tiny fingers wriggling and reaching out for me, Celia beautiful beyond words, her hair grown longer and her body slightly thicker and more matronly, touches of realism I added intuitively. In the end, she was wrong about knowing her body. Her period came two days later, which I pictured as this dark red wave crashing over a retaining wall and flooding a whole town. I saw myself as part of the scene, washed away with the town's other helpless inhabitants and the livestock and any buildings of historical note. There were no survivors.

We kept up our visits to my father as though nothing happened. Celia brought him loaves of bread that he strategically placed in different places around the room, and that the nurses later removed for fear of attracting mice. I had decided, since the false pregnancy, that I was going to ask her to marry me. I bought a simple diamond ring in a black velvet box and kept it in my pocket at all times, ready to pull it out when the moment was right. I had all the words scripted out on a scrap of paper I put inside my shoe each morning.

The day my father died was all humidity, so thick there was moisture in the folds of the air, but no sun. He had been moved to the regular hospital, on the fifteenth floor, in the cancer ward. It was as though the room was eye-level with the sun, which was trying to push its way through the clouds but the clouds wouldn't budge.

His breathing was forced. He had one hand by his side, the hand that had already given up, and the other one flung through the bed rails, as though he were reaching for something. It was apparent the end was near. The doctor on duty told me to talk to him, hold his hand, bend over and kiss him, that sort of thing. At one point my father opened his eyes and said, "Who are you?" For a moment I thought he was talking to me, but he was only questioning the attendant who had come into the room to check his IV drip and change his bedpan.

I held his hand, but in my agitated state I must have been squeezing it too hard because he grimaced noisily and tried to jerk the hand away. Celia said, "I'll do that. You're too rough."

Hours passed. She started whispering to him nonstop, her mouth perilously close to his ear.

"What are you telling him?"

"Just stupid stuff," she said. "Soothing stuff."

He died during the night. We were out of the room, six floors down getting something to eat out of the vending machines in the cafeteria. We sat opposite each other at a small table, those blue paper coffee cups with the diamond pattern between us. In the fluorescent glow, her eyes appeared to have blackened hoops under them. Her hair had that opposite direction look that comes from holding your face in your hands and then sweeping your fingers up and out.

"Do you think he's scared?" she said.

"I don't think he knows what's happening."

"I think he does. I think he knows."

I bent forward, boring in on her a bit too intensely. "You told him that I'm his son, Peter, didn't you?"

She jiggled the last bit of coffee in her cup and said, "We should go back up."

There was activity in his room, pretty low-key, a few people milling about his bed, and one nurse in a corner of the room folding a blanket with what seemed to me like inordinate care. She's the one who looked up and said, "He's gone."

Celia became hysterical. She flung herself across his body—if he had still been alive, she would have seriously injured him—and sobbed into his static chest. I tried to pull her off, but she screamed at me to get away from them both, to leave them alone.

A month later, we were at a restaurant, and something was wrong. She stared dumbly at her lap the whole meal, not eating, not talking.

"Peter?" The other sounds in the room evaporated. Everything converged upon her mouth. "I can't see you anymore. I just can't."

The waiter was standing in front of us about to tick off the list of desserts, and it only occurred to me later, much later, what a marvelous and intuitive waiter he was, because he backed away slowly and discreetly from our table, sensing, I know now, that the thing about to be served up was the shattering of someone's life.

I said, "Would it be okay if I asked why? Would that be okay? To ask why?"

"We're two different people. We have two different ways of seeing the world."

"Do you love me?"

She bit her lip.

"Is this about my father?"

"No. It's about you. And me."

I tried to call her the next day, but all I got was the answering machine; I deliberately left short controlled messages that wouldn't embarrass her if her roommate heard, but she never reacted to any of them. I e-mailed her at her personal address but got no responses until after about the twentieth one she e-mailed back with just a change in the subject line from my "why won't you answer?" to her "why won't you stop?"

I had to see her. I tried walking by the bakery a few times in the hopes that she might be looking out the big picture window at just that moment and see me, and finally I went in and stepped up to the counter, but she must have seen me coming because there was no one at the counter for about two minutes until an elderly woman in a business suit came out, probably the book-keeper, nervously wiping her hands.

"Is Celia here?"

"I'm sorry, did you want anything from the bakery?"

"Only Celia." I put my hands on the countertop, to show her, I suppose, that they held nothing to be afraid of. "Is she in the back?"

The woman looked up at the large wooden menu sign, as though I'd named an item they no longer carried. "I'm sorry. I wish I could help you."

I took out an ad in the local newspaper. It wasn't a big ad, just a little two column by three column box in the personals. The first one read, "Celia, I'm nothing without you." After a week, I changed it to, "Celia, I'm lost without you," then, finally, shamelessly, to "Celia, I'm drowning without you." It got so that the woman at the newspaper who took the order over the phone felt such sympathy for me that she said that the ad would run for free until I got the desired result, the way you don't have to pay until you sell the car or couch or pair of skis. It wasn't the newspaper's policy to do that with the personals, but she would make it so for me. I told her that wouldn't be necessary, that at some point you just stop trying and I was at that point. "Are you sure we shouldn't run it one more week?" the woman asked.

I thought I saw her, about six months later, in a random encounter in the aisle of a CVS. She pretended not to see me, and buried herself behind a corner shelf of shampoos, conditioners, and hair dyes. It was definitely her hair, big white sweater, scuffed black boots with the side buckle. I still had the ring in my pocket. I went down a parallel aisle and surprised her coming around the corner, where she stood with her head down, examining a bottle of bright green liquid. I took out the ring box, flipped open the lid, and got down on one knee. Celia, will you marry me? There was this short stretch of silence, then another kind of silence that means something else entirely. I looked up. It wasn't her.

Even now, sometimes I wonder. Sometimes I think of this other boy named Peter, completely separate from me, another person entirely. I think, What would he be like now? If I passed him on the street, would I even know it was him? What kind of face would he have, what kind of clothes? Would he be rich? Would he be happy? Would he find someone to love or spend his whole life looking in vain? If he had lived, I mean. If he had made it across that river.

CASEY GRAY

If There's a Hell I Hope You Burn There with the Others

The rain is making this rented tuxedo smell like a wet animal. My sister Rachel and my ex-girlfriend Maggie are standing outside the car while drops fall lightly on their newly done hair and their pink satin bridesmaids dresses. They're looking at me like I should be unlocking the car, not staring at it from a safe distance. But there's a form in the way, a purple-orange spot shaped like an exploding dog. If Rachel and Maggie weren't here, I might call it a ghost. But no. It's only a retinal stain, the kind made by flashbulbs and welding torches and staring at the sun for too long. Still, standing here in the dark liquor-store parking lot holding a brown sack full of booze, I can't bring myself to walk towards it.

Maggie: What are you waiting for, Garvin? Unlock the doors. We're getting soaked.

Rachel: How are we going to sneak this booze into the wedding?

"We're going to drink it before we get inside."

The stain steps through Maggie and disappears by the newspaper stand.

I poke my thumbs into my eyelids while I drive. Thunderclouds are hovering over the wet street. The clouds are purple and orange at the same time, two colors that refuse to mix.

Maggie: What are you doing?

"Press your thumbs into your eyelids."

Rachel: It hurts.

"For God sakes don't press them that hard. Like this."

Maggie: Jesus, Garvin, watch the road!

"Do you see anything?"

Rachel: Yeah, kind of... Maybe. Dark spots.

Rachel is drinking a bottle of Apple Puckers and jamming her thumb and forefinger into her eyes. Maggie is trying to divide a bottle of Dark Eyes vodka into two bottles of Gatorade without spilling any on her dress. The joint pulses red light around the car like an alarm indicator on a dashboard. A fog of sandalwood hair spray comes from Maggie's purse. Soon Rachel and I are asking her to spray our heads so that we smell like anything but vodka and Kentucky ditchweed.

"If I get really drunk tonight you two promise not to get in the car with me." I absolve myself in advance with statements like these.

Maggie: You guys' sister is getting married tonight. There'll be a lot of people happy to drive us home.

"How in the shit are you spilling it? Look how wide the hole is."

Rachel and one of the groomsmen meet in the center of the church. When they reach the third row of pews, Maggie and I walk towards the center. My younger sister, Angie, asked Maggie to be a bridesmaid months ago when we were still dating. It's awkward now, walking down the aisle with my ex-girlfriend. I try not to think about anything except getting our feet to cooperate. *Outside foot—inside foot—don't think about her—consider it a sobriety test—outside foot—all of the guests are cops—inside foot—even the really old ones nodding off and the really young ones that have to be physically restrained from playing in the holy water—outside foot—now part—now stand—now stop swaying like a drunk elephant—stop—be still—still—still. Don't look at Angie walking down the aisle, and don't look at your old man trying not to cry. Don't look at Rachel, and whatever you do, don't look at Maggie. Be still—still—still. Look at the burning candles and the yellow flowers.*

White ribbons are tied to the basketball goals. The lights are low. Apparently, the lady trimming the roast went to high school with my mother.

Mom: Don't be silly, Kelly, there are so many people at this wedding from the class of '77. Let them cut their own roast. How often do we all have a chance to get together?

Kelly: It's my job. You can't trust a buffet line with a sharp knife.

I can tell Mom feels bad about not inviting her, even though they haven't talked in years. She introduces Kelly to the people who are holding up their plates for a helping of roast. When they reach to shake her hand, she holds up rubber gloves covered in bloody juice as if to say "Are you sure?" I take a picture of them at the end of the buffet line with one of the disposable cameras. No photographer was hired, the only pictures will come from the disposable cameras given to the guests as they walked through the door. Angie followed some advice from a popular magazine and asked herself, "Of the three most important aspects of a wedding, dress, flowers, and photography, which is the most important, and where can I find creative money-saving alternatives?" She decided that flowers were the most important, and that photography was the least.

I take a picture of my ten-year-old cousin Curtis, who is dancing very enthusiastically to "Little Red Corvette." Uncle Jay grabs the disposable camera on his table and flashes it a couple of times right in my eyes.

Jay: How do you like it, Garvin?

I flash right back at him.

"Fuck you."

We pop flashes back and forth like dueling cowboys. I see the ghost. *The ghost.* We are laughing now. He takes the flask out of his jacket pocket and adds whiskey to both our soft drinks.

Jay: Jesus drank wine. These Southern Baptists can't dispute that. Can't we just agree on that and have a drink at a wedding without having to sneak it under our coats like teenagers? Get a picture of this.

I snap a photo as Jay opens his coat, holds the silver flask up halfway out of his liner pocket, and looks over his shoulder to see who's within earshot.

Jay: It's prom night, and I'm going to pop my sweetheart's cherry.

Young Curtis has commanded a small space for himself in the middle of the dance floor. The swirling red and blue lights on the DJ booth move in and out of the three-point line and on and off the backboards like opposing teams. Curtis drapes his jacket over one of his shoulders and prances around the court, swinging his hips like a church bell. His stepfather takes a long drink.

Jay: I told that boy it's all right to dance. But a man holds something back, unless you're John Travolta or something. Can you imagine how much wool that guy gets? The rest of us, the teachers and the plumbers and the lawyers, we all gotta hold most of it back. Now look at him, he's miming the goddamn song, driving down the highway in his little red corvette. You've got to believe me, Garvin, I never touched that boy or done anything to make him like this. And I would kill someone dead if I found out they . . . People think that. Especially because I'm his stepfather. They say "Curt didn't start acting 'like he does' until Norma married Jay."

"Nobody thinks that."

Jay: Yeah, well, your aunt Ray and uncle Hugo had the nerve to take him to the Cracker Barrel after mass to ask him if I ever touched him funny.

He burps and puts his fingers to his lips as if he might vomit. Angie's new in-laws whisper and stare at us indiscreetly. Jay slides the flask into my tuxedo jacket pocket.

Jay: I'm not giving you this flask. I'm just letting you borrow it till the whiskey's gone. I'm cutting myself off. Who do people think I am? Am I the only one in this whole darn world that knows I'm a good person? Or am I just the only one who thinks it? Are you the only one? I love that boy, in the natural way that a father loves his son. No matter what. People in this town need a reason for everything, someone or something to point their figurative fingers at. God makes faggots just like he makes horses and all the different kinds of birds.

I don't have the nerve to take a picture of Uncle Jay slouching so that his green tie is pinched in the fatty fold between his gut and his tits. I take a picture of his drink instead. The Easter purple plastic cup is sitting on the table next to one of the centerpieces. A shrub of violet flowers is floating in a clear glass bowl. Clean roots float in the water like a jellyfish. A blue Betta Fish is nibbling on its tentacles. Fins swirl like blue dye that never dissolves.

"If it makes you feel better, Hugo's daughter, Wendy, likes to be suspended by shark hooks they poke through her skin."

Jay: What?

"They poke shark hooks through holes in her skin, holes that have healed over like pierced earlobes. Only the holes aren't in her ears, they're in her back and knees and probably other places. They put these shark hooks through the holes and then hoist her up with an elaborate pulley system some guy built in his backyard. At least that's the way I understand it."

Jay: You're full of it.

"I swore I wouldn't tell."

Jay: Is it a sex thing?

"To hear her tell it, it's a spiritual-vision-quest-enlightenment kind of thing."

Jay: Where can we go from here, Garvin? This goddamn world, it only gets crazier. What's next? You're a young man, tell me what the heck is next. When I was young we would neck for hours and go home fully satisfied.

"Don't cry, Jay. Please. I told you that to make you feel better."

Jay: It does make me feel better in a weird kind of way. Thanks ...What in the hell would make someone want to hoist themselves up by shark hooks?"

"Hell if I know."

Jay: I should take her to the Cracker Barrel and ask her.

I take pictures of the flowers because they'll be dead soon.

I take pictures of the old people after that.

I take pictures of the kids dominating the limbo contest.

I take a picture of Rachel's son, Sam, lapping out of the punch bowl like a golden retriever.

Rachel is sitting in the back corner of the gym. Children gather around her at the aluminum table. They are taking picture after picture of a glass centerpiece with one blue Betta Fish darting around the bowl and one red one, with no eyes and a bite-sized absence of head, swimming aimlessly into the glass.

Rachel: These fish can't stand each other. I don't know how they ever fuck. I named the blue one Shirley. She doesn't take any shit from anyone.

She scoops a red fish into a plastic cup, holds the cup a foot above Shirley's bowl, and dumps it from, what must seem to a fish completely unfamiliar with the concept of free-fall, an unimaginable height. They slash around until Shirley makes her stand in the middle of the bowl. The red fish is named "Jaws" by my cousin Valerie and then "Roosevelt" by Curtis, who deems "Jaws" trite and uninspired. Roosevelt avoids Shirley for a while, keeping tight to the glass. He is trying to adjust and gather strength after being poured from the water that tasted like himself into the water that tastes like his enemy. The red and blue disco lights from the DJ booth pass through the bowl.

DJ: This one is a request. From Rachel to Shirley.

Rachel grabs my cup and takes a long drink. The speakers play: I'm holding out for a hero / I'm holding out for a hero till the end of the night / He's got to be fast / And he's got to be strong / And he's got to be fresh from the fight. Rachel sings along and taps her fingers on the table. Her taste in music is ridiculous for a nineteen-year-old-girl. She only likes the songs that chew their way into her brain like a worm. Mostly pop and commercial jingles. The songs are like screen savers for her mind.

"It must be a disadvantage for Roosevelt, being poured out of his own bowl into a completely new one."

Rachel: But Shirley is getting tired. She has already killed four lesser fish.

I take a picture of the table. There is one bowl in the middle where everyone's attention and disposable camera is fixed. There are six empty bowls scattered at the far end and a pile of dying flowers with roots like Asian noodles. At the near end of the table, five brave Betta Fish have been arranged in an impeccable row.

Curtis: I bet six dollars on Roosevelt.

Rachel: You're on, Twinkle Toes.

Maggie and I slow-dance to an old Gene Autry song that my grandfather requested. The cowboy is lonely, and the woman is beautiful. That's the gist of the song. She might be a whore, but Gene Autry could never come out and say it. I'm too drunk to pay attention to the lyrics. I pay attention to the sliding notes, the high dead voice, the swaying woman and room in front of me. The cowboy is good. He can't go anywhere without an Injun trying to rip his scalp off. He killed a race of people in self-defense. People will believe anything if you tell them enough times.

"I love you, Maggie."

Maggie: I love you, too.

The last picture I take is of Rachel, stumbling through the double doors under the basketball goal, wiping white spit from her mouth. I ask her what's wrong, and she asks me if I have ever seen one of my close friends eaten alive. I tell her that I have not, and I put my camera in the cardboard box with the others. I imagine my father and Angie sitting around the kitchen table organizing the photos. I wonder if Angie will cry when she finds out that seventy percent of her wedding pictures are of bloody fish. I wonder which of my pictures will make it to the album and which ones she will throw away.

"Hurry, before Mom wants to smell my breath." I'm patting myself down like a lunatic. These tuxedos have so many pockets. I find my keys in some strange pocket within a pocket.

Maggie: Can we stop by the Bigfoot so I can get a microwave burrito?

Rachel: I need some gum. I barfed in the graveyard.

Maggie: You barfed in the graveyard?

Rachel: Uh-huh. Can you believe they had their reception in a church gymnasium? Can you believe the DJ, he was awful. He kept talking all the time, congratulating everybody and trying to make people dance. I'm the one with the baby, Garvin. Do you think Angie got married first because she secretly hates me?

"How can you say things like that? Get out of the car while I back out? Make sure I don't run over any kids."

Rachel: It's raining. What about my dress?

"Are you ever going to wear that thing again?"

Rachel: Maybe.

"Fuck it. I just don't want to run over any kids. Say it will be your fault, or go outside and make sure I don't hit one."

Maggie: You guys are being ridiculous.

Rachel: My son left early with his grandparents.

"So you're saying, 'Somebody else's kid getting run over isn't worth ruining my stupid pink dress.'"

Rachel: Don't put words in my mouth.

"Then say it will be your fault if I run a kid over."

Rachel: No.

"I can't look and back up at the same time."

Rachel: Sure you can.

"What I meant was I can't go outside and really—see. It's dark and rainy behind me. Just somebody please go, or a little kid's going to get run over and it won't be my fault."

Maggie: Jesus Christ, I'll go look.

She steps into the light rain and motions me back. I look out over the graveyard as we back up, modest stones on a black hill that rolls easily down to cornfields and subdivisions. It's where I will be buried if I die too soon. Maggie motions me to stop and gets back in the car.

Rachel: Is Angie trying to set a good example or something?

Maggie: Me? I'm damned if I do, et cetera.

Rachel: I'm not talking about you, I said Angie, not Maggie.

"What do you mean by good example?"

Rachel: She's not even twenty, and she's not even pregnant. I don't ever want to get married. I want to live with Mom and Dad and take care of them when they get old.

Maggie: Then who's going to take care of you when you get old?

Rachel: My son . . . or probably a nursing home . . . hopefully better than the one I work at. One that smells like a hotel. If you're able, Garvin, would you kill me if it comes to that bad point and I don't have the physical capabilities to do it myself? I don't want you to do it if you have a family and it could fuck things up. But if you can do it without getting caught, or if you're as miserable as I am, will you promise to do it?

"I'm not promising anything."

Rachel: Every day I go to work I see those old people hooked up to vents and the ones that can only groan with their heads turned towards the wall. I just don't love them enough to kill 'em. But I love you enough.

Garvin: Should I be flattered or terrified?

Rachel: Comforted.

Maggie: I want to be in a death pact. Garvin, do you love me enough to kill me?

"I loved you enough to kill you that first night we slept in your single bed. The air conditioner was broke, and we woke up stuck to each other."

Maggie: Aw. The hot and sticky good old days.

The light is red. I tap my thumbs on the steering wheel. *Life is not like a movie. Nothing we say means anything.* I'm telling myself this more and more lately. I'm like an old Catholic immigrant who looks for signs everywhere. Except I don't believe they're signs from God. I believe that I am watching myself in a movie and that if I pay attention I can guess the outcome. *I am evaluating myself, as well as everyone else in the car. Sometimes I feel like the hero of my own life, and sometimes I feel like the new guy on the Starship Enterprise that doesn't stand a chance. A car full of drunk kids driving down dark country roads on a wet moonless night making death pacts must crash, and if there are three people in the car, one must die. Would it be the one who puked in a grave, the one who saw a ghost, or the one who it walked right through? If I were watching this movie I would predict Rachel to die. Why else would she be here? She inhibits the romantic tension between Maggie and me. Can we find a new way to love each other? That is what this story would be about if my little sister weren't in the car. Then again, why would anybody give a shit about Maggie and me, unless we were played by two über-beautiful movie stars? Maggie is beautiful, but not like a movie star. Her gums are too big, and her teeth are too small. And I've got character actor written all over my face. Rachel is the only one in the car who has suffered enough to make people care about her real self. The scar, spread like putty from the top of her lip to the bottom of her nose, proves it. When people find out how she got that scar, her story becomes a burning sun, and mine becomes just one of the countless shadows it casts. The dominant past is welded to her face. She is the only one that's safe. But I am driving the car. If I die, the audience misses out on all that great, torturous guilt. The real thick drama. The scene where I bring flowers to the grave, throw myself on the mound, and rub the new loose dirt on my only suit. I guess that leaves Maggie. Poor dead Maggie. There are no clues about what's coming next. Sure, we are in a higher-risk category than completely sober people right now. But the deaths in the papers are all crazy drunks going one hundred and six miles an hour. I'm a sad drunk. I am driving five miles an hour under the speed limit because the road is wet and I might have seen a ghost. There is no moral to life. We are certainly not going to die because we want to show people how dangerous it is to drink and drive. That purple-orange spot was not a ghost, or an Angel, or the Virgin Mary, or any kind of warning. It is what happens when brightness burns. I remember staring at the sun when I was twelve. I wanted to burn my eyes out. It was like God himself was daring me to do it. I like the idea that my life is like a movie. I wish I could believe it. But foreshadowing isn't real. The idea that randomness and luck are the only two forces in the universe is the scariest idea I've ever let surface. Or do the words "randomness" and "luck" represent a lack of force? What does that mean?* A foggy ache settles over my brain. The light turns green, and we roll through the intersection.

Maggie: Did you puke on a specific grave?

Rachel: Yep—Ira Head.

"Do you think his soul will haunt you?"

Rachel: No, he's not even dead yet. Just his wife, Noreen. I puked on his future spot.

Maggie: Well, then, that's not so bad.

Life is not like a movie.

Maggie: Pull over, Garvin, I'm going to pee in my pants.

I pull into a cornfield, and Maggie disappears into the stalks holding her dress up around her waist. I roll my window down and let the smell of happy corn with wet roots fill the car. I put my cufflink into my pocket and roll my left sleeve up as far as it will go. I hang my arm out the window and let the drizzle hit my skin.

Rachel: Turn down the radio. Let's see if we can hear her pee.

She rolls her window down and lights a cigarette. All around us there is water, rushing through a ditch and falling from the sky.

Rachel: It sounds like she really had to go.

"I'm almost sure that's the rain."

Rachel: Do you think anyone will want to marry me?

"Sure."

Rachel: Probably not anybody good, though, huh?

"It all depends on what you consider 'good.' It's about where you put your emphasis."

Rachel: What do you mean?

"It's economic. You're worth so much based on your attributes: looks, intelligence, sincerity, money, general coolness—everything. Then you get to choose a person based on your personal worth. It's like buying a car. You have a price range. You choose what kind of car you want within that price range. Do you want comfort or speed? Usually it's someplace between."

Rachel: Do you mean that I could find a really nice guy who treated me good, but he might be boring, or ugly, or stupid, or something? Or I could find a really hot guy who will probably be a shithead because a guy who is hot and nice is out of my price range?

"It's a little more complicated than that. There are millions of features to choose from. You shouldn't sell yourself short. There are a lot of sturdy cars in your price range."

Rachel: What kind of car am I?

"You're my sister. It's hard for me to think of you as a car."

Rachel: Not by blood.

"How many times do you want me to say that doesn't matter? Another hundred million?"

Rachel: Well, if you had to say. Pretend you're someone else so you can say.

"Used, probably."

Rachel: Well, then, you're a chubby car with a big head.

"Most cars are used. All of 'em, maybe."

Rachel: What kind of car is Maggie?"

"She's a three-year-old Maxima with twenty-eight thousand miles on her."

Rachel: What kind of interior does she have?

"Leather. Decent factory sound."

Rachel: Are you two getting back together or what?

"It worries me that I'm thinking about her like she's a car. I was hoping you would tell me that I was wrong. You're supposed to tell me it's more—something else."

Rachel: Do you think big fake tits would help my resale value?

"I really loved her at first, and she really loved me back. It was the first time it happened that way. I was so happy that I don't like to think about it."

Rachel: Like great big custom wheels.

"They're not for everyone, but there's certainly a market for that kind of thing."

Rachel: I hope Sam is waiting up for me.

"It's twelve-thirty at night."

Rachel: I hope that he can't sleep without a kiss from his mother.

Maggie's heels stab into the mud with every step to the car. She offers Rachel the front seat. She declines. I consider it a life-or-death decision. I gently accelerate and then decelerate to a smooth stop before I can get into second gear. A black milk cow with a white exclamation mark on her head is standing in the middle of the road.

"That thing is pitch fucking black." We have been saved by the purple-orange spot burned into the back of my eyes.

Rachel: Is it sleeping?

Maggie: Don't look at me, I'm from Chicago Heights.

I drive around the cow and turn my high beams on. We pass the clicking sprinklers of the golf course and then old farmhouses, with newer ones built in between. Ancient trees line up along Darmstadt Road like soldiers who create a canopy of swords for an officer and his new bride to walk under.

Maggie: We might have hit that cow if I didn't have to stop to pee. It was all black besides that mark on its head.

"It was standing fifty yards in front of us the whole time we were talking, and I never saw it."

Maggie: I don't ever want to hear you complain about me stopping to pee again. I'll say, Honey, remember when stopping to pee saved our lives.

"I saw something strange at the liquor store earlier. It was like a sunspot-ghost."

Maggie: I believe in angels. I've seen one.

"It was a sunspot. Like the spot that's left when a camera flashes and you close your eyes, except bigger and moving.

Rachel: I heard a voice as we were walking to the car.

"What did it say?"

Rachel: Groooowwwwwlllll!

Maggie: It was probably an angel that was sent down to warn us about the cow. I only believe in angels, not ghosts.

Rachel: Baloney shit.

Maggie: I don't care if you believe me. It doesn't make it any less true.

Rachel: How can you believe in angels and not unfriendly ghosts?

Maggie: I don't like the idea of unfriendly ghosts.

Rachel: The good people and the bad people both die in the end. It only makes sense that there are good and bad ghosts, if there are ghosts at all.

Maggie: Only bad people die for real.

Rachel: I wish I could choose what I believe in. I'd believe in a heaven where I go to water slide parks with the cast of *Friends*, and they're all just how they are on the show.

Maggie: Heaven and Hell are tailor-made for each individual person. So, you know, anything is possible. We can't know.

Rachel: What if the cast of *Friends*' idea of heaven isn't going to a water slide park with me? Or being just how they are on the show? Or if they're in Hell? Or if I'm in Hell?

Maggie: God could make a new cast of friends just for you to play with.

Rachel: A fake heaven?

Maggie: Do you know what omnipotent means?

"I wish I would see a ghost. Any ghost. It would take a tremendous weight off of my shoulders."

The Strawberry Hill subdivision is strictly zoned and coded: no unsanctioned structures, such as a club or tree house; no RVs or campers parked outside for what the neighborhood council considers an "extended amount of time"; no pit bulls; no Christmas lights after New Year's. There is a zero-tolerance policy when it comes to divorced mothers who let their lawns go to shit, but nobody is confrontational enough to enforce it. Driving through the subdivision, it's easy to see who they are: Ms. Adams, Ms. Swanson, Ms. Harrington. Their grass is overgrown, and their hedges look like unkempt pubic hair. Except for my friend Max's house. His mother got divorced when he was young. Her "best friend" Tracy moved in shortly after. Tracy mows the lawn in perfect diagonal lines and trims her hedges like a samurai. All the lights in the subdivision are out, except for the red light of the orgy room over the Walkers' garage that is on all night, every night.

Rachel: Lookie, the orgy light is on.

"I wonder what goes on up there."

Rachel: Orgies.

"Yeah, Rachel. I'm sure the Houglands and the Bennets and the Bailys and the Perkins get all hopped up on Bartles and James and Busch Light and say, 'Hey, let's pull off our Dockers and our skorts and have a crazy orgy where we wear leather masks and piss in each other's mouths.' That's just the name the kids in the neighborhood gave it because it's a red light and it's on all night. They're probably developing some pictures, or there's some really boring old people fucking going on up there."

Rachel: You don't know everything.

She gets out of the car and staggers towards my parents' house, right through the neatly trimmed shrubs. She kicks the neighbor kid's soccer ball back at his yard. It hits the sliding glass door with a thud. Nothing breaks. She pushes the button on the garage door remote. Every dog inside of a two-mile radius barks when the door opener starts to pull.

Rachel: It's a good thing everyone in this neighborhood sleeps like a rock!

She lies under the garage door and pushes the button on the remote. The door comes at her neck like a melodramatic guillotine.

Rachel: They say that if you leave your eyes open you can see while your head falls into the basket!

I spin my tires on the wet road when I pull away.

"It's the way you have to handle her, Maggie. Believe me, I know. She stops acting crazy when nobody's watching."

Now it's awkward with just us in the car until Maggie feels my dick through my pants and then I know exactly what to do and I'm so happy that she showed me what to do that it makes me love her again to think about how well she knows me.

Maggie: I want a burrito. That's not a euphemism, either. I want a real bean and cheese burrito from the gas station.

The trees fade away into farmland again. I remember the black cow and slow to a crawl on the stretch of road where we first saw it. The headlights of a Ford truck are shining in odd directions like lazy eyes. I pull to the side of the road. Maggie steps out of the car without looking and slides into a ditch. She takes her shoes off, and I pull her up the bank.

A shirtless teenage boy is standing over a cow lying in the middle of the road. He has the image of Elmer Fudd holding the bloody head of Bugs Bunny tattooed on his shoulder.

Elmer: Ford trucks fuckin' rock! Knocked her twenty-six yards.

Maggie walks to the truck and turns off the ignition. I walk to the boy standing over the cow, and as I walk I wonder if Maggie is smarter than me. The weathered asphalt worked like a cheese grater that left a path of skin and meat between the cow and the truck. Pink puddles of blood and milk form around the cow and then sink into the asphalt. The cow groans. The boy with the Elmer Fudd tattoo walks back towards his truck and makes a call on his cellphone.

Elmer: I got in a wreck . . . I'm fine . . . Your truck is not fine . . . I hit a cow . . . It was black and it is night . . . No . . . No . . . No . . . The cow is still alive, but it's in bad shape... Okay... I was goin' to, but I wasn't sure... I'll call the police before I do... On Kilgore right before St. Johns... Yeah, I'm sure I'm fine.

Maggie walks even paces to the cow, counting to herself. She touches the cow's face.

Maggie: You only knocked her twelve yards.

Elmer: You have to measure from where I hit her. See that pile of intestines? That's where she popped.

Maggie vomits into the bloody milk. Elmer laughs.

Elmer: Ain't you never seen a dead cow before? Ain't you never been to McDonald's.

The cow groans like an accordion.

Elmer: She ain't dead yet. I'm going to shoot her. I just got to call the cops and get a okay. I don't want to get myself in more trouble. Do one of you have a mint or a piece of gum, or a penny—does that work?

Maggie: I have a cigarette.

Elmer: That might help... Hello, nine-one-one, this is no emergency. I just need the number for the police station and I'm on a cellphone in the middle of the country so I got no way to look it up... I guess I could've dialed information... How many emergencies can happen in Evansville, Indiana, one night? Don't act like you're too busy to patch me through... Police? I don't figure this is a emergency. I hit a cow... I'm fine... No, I don't need a ambulance... Yeah, I'm on Kilgore and St. Johns...

There is a red stripe across his chest where the seat belt saved his life. When the police get here and I'm still a little drunk, they will have to let it go because I would have never been caught if I didn't pull over to help somebody out. Will Elmer's father hug him, or punch him, or ignore him completely? I imagine his mother arriving in her nightgown, which is really just a giant T-shirt with an airbrushed Tasmanian devil in his own nightgown, sound asleep. Bugs Bunny is tied up like a turkey in his dream cloud. She smokes Doral Menthols and hugs her son so hard that she jars something loose in her lungs.

Maggie: We can give you a ride to the hospital.

"That's no problem at all. I would be happy to do it."

He waves no with two fingers and talks to his cellphone.

Elmer: I'm fine! I'm walking around. I got a dip and a cigarette in my mouth . . . One more thing is, this cow is pretty bad, I figure I should go ahead and finish her off, but I just wanted to run it by you all . . . I don't know who it belongs to . . . They've got me on hold.

The cow groans, and Maggie groans with sympathy for the cow.

Elmer: I got a gun locked in my toolbox . . . I got my permit . . . It's awful to keep her alive . . . What do you mean you can't authorize it, you're the police, sir, aren't you? . . . I don't know whose cow it is . . . Well, what kind of charges could he decide to press? The brand must have been on the part of her that's smeared on the road . . . How soon? All right."

Maggie: What did they say?

Elmer: They want me to wait for them. They didn't know what the fuck to do. This can't be the first time this has happened.

He lies down in the truck bed. He turns his head and spits on the bed liner. The truck reminds me of a civil war bullet I found on a hike with the Boy Scouts, flat in the front like it hit something hard. I walk to the ditch and take a long beautiful piss into the cattails.

Maggie: Call them back and tell them that all the cow's legs are broken and that his intestines are all over the road.

The cow groans.

Elmer: She's close. Every moment of agony is unnecessary.

Elmer turns his head and spits. Maggie lights a cigarette.

"Why don't you call your folks back and tell them to meet us at the hospital. I'll drive you."

Elmer: You? You're just as drunk as I am and look what happened to me. I'm not drinking and driving no more, and I'm not getting in the car with nobody that's been drinking. I may not drink neither myself, never. My folks are on their way.

"All this has got me pretty well sobered up."

Elmer: Well, you smell like whiskey. I believe you get a warning shot for this kind of thing, and I learned my lesson. No more drinking, period. And I'm not the kind of person that says he's going to do something and doesn't do it.

He folds his hands and looks up at the stars; with just a crack of moon and only road flares lighting the earth, they are bright. The rain is gone; I can't remember when it stopped.

Elmer: I'm givin' my life to you, Jesus. It's belonged to me too long, and I have done nothin' but screw it up.

When the cow groans again Maggie starts to cry.

Elmer: Do you believe in Jesus?

Maggie: Do you mean in a historical sense?

Elmer: "Historical sense." Are you being some kind of smart-ass? Is that some kind of satanic joke?

"Look, we didn't have to stop and help."

Elmer: Help who? You, help me? That's a laugh.

A pair of headlights rolls over the hill. A blue minivan. The driver pulls gently around the flares and rolls down his window. It is too dark inside the car to see his face.

Driver: You kids all right?

Elmer: Yep. My folks and the police are on the way.

Driver: Hit a cow, huh?

Elmer: Yep.

Driver: How far you figure you knocked her?

Elmer: 'Bout twenty-six yards.

Driver: Let's see one of those Princeton, Indiana, Jap trucks do that.

He rolls up his window and drives away. Elmer lies back down in the bed of his truck. It's dark enough to see satellites with the naked eye.

Elmer: Look at the stars. Are you trying to say that there's not something up there shining down on us? The first man on earth looked up there, and he knew it. My dad's going to shit fire 'bout the truck, but he's going to be happy I found the Lord.

The cow groans, and Maggie walks to the car. I follow her.

"Are you okay?"

When we get inside she rolls up all the windows.

Maggie: I can't listen to that fucking cow anymore, and that fucking guy isn't helping.

"I know. It's awful."

Maggie: Let's go, Garvin. He's fine.

"It never crossed my mind that someone else would hit it. I would have tried to move the cow, or I would have called the sheriff, or somebody whose job it is... It's our fault."

Maggie: Listen to me. That kid is drunk. He's been to the same school assemblies as all the rest of us. It's his own fucking fault. I saw it coming. I thought "Somebody could hit that cow" but then I thought "Who the hell would be speedin' down St. Johns at one-thirty at night" and then I thought "Drunk kids, that's who." But I still didn't say anything. I just didn't. If it's anybody's fault it's his fault, and if it's nobody's fault it's my fault. But he's fine so I don't think we should ever think or talk about this again.

"We're here now. We're the only ones here. And we can't leave until we know he's fine. He could have some sort of internal injury."

Maggie: Fine. But I'm staying in the car.

"I should've seen it, too. I'm sorry. It was a logical thought. It was possible."

Maggie: Where the fuck are they?

"Do you have your cellphone? I'm going to call and explain the urgency of the situation."

Maggie: What are you going to tell them?

"I'm going to tell them that he's disoriented and that he doesn't seem as well as he claims to be. And I'm going to call 911. Anything that will get them to hurry."

Maggie: Mine is dead. Borrow his phone. Garvin! Tell him to be careful with his cigarette. There might be gas.

When I open the door Maggie pulls it shut behind me and yells "Hurry!" through the glass. Elmer's feet dangle off of the tailgate. I imagine the truck exploding as I'm walking towards it. A big movie explosion. The thought of flying glass makes me rub my eyes. His cigarette is dead in his fingers. His pudgy belly is moving up and down, a few loose hairs surround his navel. I tap his knee to try and wake him. I take the cellphone out of his pocket and call 911.

Operator: 911 Emergency.

"We need an ambulance. We called the police earlier. What happened was, this teenage boy hit this cow and he seemed fine for a while."

Operator: Is he conscious?

"No."

Operator: Is he breathing?

"Yes."

Operator: Have you tried waking him up?

"Yes."

Operator: What did you do?

"I tapped his knee."

Operator: That's it?

"I didn't know what to do when I called."

Operator: Scream his name.

"I don't know his name."

Operator: Then just scream.

A giant sense of relief and embarrassment fills me. As soon as I yell "Wake up!" He'll be fine. He seems to be grinning now a little, like this is all a joke. Drunk people pass out.

"Wake up! . . . Wake up! . . . Wake up!"

Operator: Where are you located?

"St. Johns, about a half mile before the giant peach."

Operator: An ambulance is on the way.

"They should be on the road. 'Where are you located' should be the first question you ask."

Operator: Was there any response at all?

"Did you not believe me when I said I needed an ambulance? They could be halfway down First Avenue. Tell them to turn the fucking lights on!"

Operator: You should have told me where you were first thing, sir.

"You're the fucking operator guy. Fuck!"

Operator: I know. I know. I'm sorry. I'm new. It's all my fault. Just answer the questions. Is he still breathing?

"Yes. He looks like he's sleeping."

Operator: Very important. Don't touch him.

I see the lights of another car shine over the hill. I leave the chirping operator on his chest, and I run back to the car.

Maggie: What's happening?

I tell her, "We're not supposed to touch him," and we drive away.

ETHAN HAUSER

Nashville

They lived in Tennessee for five months. George had wanted to move there to play guitar, an idea he seized on late one night, in the hopeful, dreamy fog of too much youth and too many beers. When promise is like a drug, the stars are supernatural, water is glass. There, in the bedroom, he took Natalie's wide smile as encouragement, proof that Nashville, with its history and sentiment, was where he should go. Glow-in-the-dark planets, courtesy of a previous tenant, dotted the ceiling. Saturn, a comet with a perfect, cartoonish tail. Sometimes, deep in the evening, a look is all the evidence and spur you need.

They had been together three months, in a relationship born in the manic weeks before college graduation, when everything seemed alternately possible and impossible, serious and trivial. Though they had been in school for the same four years, they barely knew each other—they were friends of friends of friends, that sort of distant, unremarkable connection on a campus of thousands. Early on they figured out they had taken the same introduction to psychology course freshman year, them and two hundred other students stuffed into a lecture hall with tiered rows of seats and a professor overly fond of his laser pointer. One night at a party George had wandered outside and overheard Natalie talking to one of her friends. "I hate my body," she said. "All it does is hurt me." He knew it was far from original for a woman, especially one in college, to hate her body, but he had never heard it so concisely and logically expressed. (Never mind that she had a very beautiful body, one that probably, more likely, only hurt other people, mostly through withholding.)

He told himself that he wouldn't go to sleep until he kissed her. We can end all the hurting from this night on, he thought. *I'll take you away from all that.* They ended up in her off-campus apartment, in her bed kicking the sheets to the floor, surrounded by half-packed boxes and walls scabbed with poster tape and picture hooks. Modern hieroglyphs, people with too much time, too many idols, too much belief in genius. They drank, smoked, laughed. They kissed, turned the stereo up loud, filled the ashtray to overflowing. There was something liberating, something temporary in the room. When you know you are leaving somewhere, you are free; you can atone later, in another city, another time. With a new name, a job and a house and car payments, the furl of responsibilities, the landmarks that begin to sum up your life. A small TV on mute painted the corner of the room different colors. Across the street, yellowed windows of a freshman dorm formed a maddening, unreadable Morse code. There was beauty in the smallest, most unassuming things, and space enough to fuck and fight, be saint or sinner.

Before either of them realized, they were in a relationship. Natalie had been planning on moving to San Francisco, yet she put it off for a few months, to spend the summer and fall in Nashville with George. Her parents were skeptical, which made it all the more alluring. She sent postcards—dolled-up country-music stars with paint-white teeth—just to tweak them. They rented a small apartment, stuffed it with dishes and silverware and paintings from thrift stores. They slept on a mattress on the floor, in a bedroom conquered by George's guitars and amps. Pedals and amps were planted across the carpet like landmines. She put candles and plants in the windowsills, tending to each as if they were children. She learned to fall asleep even while he practiced, came to depend on it like a pill.

Later, when winter was just starting to strip away the hopeful Tennessee light, they moved to California, joining the hordes seduced by Internet jobs and shambling Victorian houses. George had agreed only after Natalie promised they could stop in Bakersfield—home of Buck Owens—on the way out. They had little trouble finding work: Natalie toiled for a software maker; George spent his days in a guitar store, where all of his coworkers had stardom on their minds and none would admit it. They thought fame and money were like a stain.

Sam Rhodes was an architect. His parents had sent him to all the right schools—East Coast and elite—and he had sailed through, branded along the way, by teachers and classmates alike, as "promising." It is a word, Sam realized later, that confers not only praise but carries responsibility, and the more "promising" people told him he was, the less capable he felt of delivering on their expectations.

Still, he managed to tamp down his anxiety for long enough to finish graduate school and land coveted apprentice jobs in New York and Los Angeles. There he watched buildings grow, jump from drafting tables to plywood-fenced construction zones to finished products. It was an amazing process, he thought, to see something transform from ink and sketch and blueprint to sidewalk and sky. Often he didn't entirely believe the buildings were real, and at the ribbon cuttings he would walk right up to one of the outside walls and thumb it, to make sure the steel skeleton was no mirage. Some of them sliced upward, sleek as blades; others sat long and squat, one or two stories.

The rhetoric he had grown so weary of in school—the poetics of space, deconstructive tendencies, wry commentaries, sly references—sounded far less hollow and tired in the architects' offices. This is where buildings originate, Sam thought, not a place where we are merely studying them. For a time he was reenergized, and he logged late nights in the office, him and the other young assistants, puzzling over heating ducts, oxidized aluminum flashing, roof slopes, and sandblasted glass. They lined up their empty Dr Pepper cans like bowling pins, toppling them with punted Styrofoam scraps.

It was tiring, satisfying work, and he would return home exhausted but invigorated. He was newly married, a year and a half, and his wife accepted the punishing hours partly because she sensed how excited he was. Jessica tolerated the schedule, too, because he assured her it would get better, that all new architects put in eighty-hour workweeks while they establish themselves and perfect their vision. "There's no other way," he said. "You just have to totally immerse yourself. It's like learning a foreign language."

She would sit with him late at night, at the kitchen table, while he ate microwaved leftovers. She drank wine, watched him bring his fork to his mouth, listened to the projects that had kept him away so long. It was sexy to her, seeing him so in the grip of something, looking at his eyes and imagining the brain behind them, electric and searching, the neurons firing nonstop. "When will you build me a house, Sam?" she asked, curling into his lap and pulling his silverware out of his hand so she could latch her fingers in his. "When?"

It was late at night when it happened—more morning, in fact, than night. Three, maybe four, one of the vague hours between nighttime and next day, hours most people never pay attention to unless they're forced. Natalie had been at a bar with friends, and they had ended up staying until last call, and then even later, courtesy of a bartender repaying them for a steady stream of tips and a pinball machine intent on volunteering free games even though they were nowhere near the high scores.

She had had an argument with George earlier in the evening, and he had stormed out of the bar, one of their favorite places, tucked between a seedy motel and a warehouse district. It was a throwaway fight—days later neither of them could remember the details—yet it turned, quickly, into something more dramatic. Even when you have nothing to fight about, you find something. It's like pricking yourself with a pin: proof that you are alive and can hurt. It's a way of confessing vulnerability.

After George had left the bar, one of Natalie's friends said, "I guess this is your final drink."

"Why?" Natalie said. "I'm staying. Fuck him."

She knew, the moment the words tumbled from her mouth, that she would forgive him, probably only hours later. The jukebox would tell her to, Cheap Trick, AC/DC, Charlie Rich; a drink would tell her, maybe nothing more than a boy sitting at a table in the back and the way the boy held his Budweiser, which was like the way George did, but not exactly. His forefinger was a little more pointed. He had the same boots, with a steel toe and pale yellow stitching. Some girl would find this boy, tonight or next week or next year, and figure out how much love he had to give. Natalie thought, in the energizing aftermath of a fight, how lucky she was to have someone to forgive. There were so many people who didn't.

Sam and Jessica soon had a baby, Sabrina, born healthy at Oakland Downtown Hospital. By this time they had moved north, to San Francisco, where Sam had decided to open his own practice, banking on a steady stream of newly minted computer-industry millionaires eager to cash in their stock options for a daring building. Sabrina was a difficult baby—colicky all the time, fussy, relentlessly demanding. She strained the marriage like nothing else had, and their near constant exhaustion left them ill-equipped to deal with the emotional tangles they soon faced. The stress of Sam running his own practice didn't help, either.

Sam began to feel, once more, as if he was always disappointing people: his clients, his wife, his daughter. When his parents called and asked when they would be able to see a building he had designed, he muttered, "Never," right before begging off the phone because Sabrina was screaming from her crib, having woken up prematurely from a nap. He went to the baby's room and picked her up from the foam mattress. He was always amazed at how small she was. So tiny and yet a complete human being. He hooked his hands under her arms and held her in front of him like a cross. She had his wife's pale blue eyes, and her hair was just beginning to thicken. She was dressed in one of the endless Baby Gap outfits that had begun to multiply in the house like some unstoppable bacteria. "Sabrina, honey, *shh, shh,*" he said. "Just wait, baby girl, you have the whole rest of your life to find things to cry about. Right now you have no idea."

What finally set him off was the alumni magazine. He arrived home one night, after a day in which he learned that a promising client had dropped him, and found his wife on the couch leafing through his architecture-school magazine. On the cover was one of his classmates, smiling, next to a blueprint for the new Portland Museum of Art in Maine. Sam snatched the magazine from Jessica's hands, in a movement so sudden it left her holding a single ripped page.

"What the hell," she said. "What are you doing?"

"I've had a crappy enough day already," he said, burying the magazine in the newspaper recycling pile. "I don't need to come home to my wife fawning over that frat-boy shithead Andy Dalton."

She sighed, put the lone remaining page on the coffee table. Something about the way she did it, carefully, so it wouldn't sail off, fanned his rage. He grabbed it from the glass surface, balled it up, and threw it in the trash.

"Jesus," she said. "Calm down."

"What if I don't want to?"

"You've been drinking, haven't you?"

He didn't answer her. Because he had. To blunt the disappointment of losing a client, he had poured himself whiskey from a bottle he kept at the office. He had bought it originally to celebrate his successes, though lately its main purpose was to soothe the sting of failure.

"So what if I have," he said. "I'm allowed. Wanna card me?"

"Keep your voice down," Jessica said. "You'll wake the baby."

"She'll go back to sleep."

"No," said Jessica, "she might not. Actually, odds are she won't."

Then there was a silence between them, tight and angry. It was the sound of something unresolved, many things unresolved.

Years earlier they would have choked this fight with a kiss, a finger trailing down a cheek. Some small essential physical gesture, assurance that the blowup wouldn't ruin them, leave them shipwrecked and alone. But this time it was different. Too much unsaid had passed between them in the preceding eight months. Sam had suffered a series of setbacks at work; Jessica was more and more frustrated and exhausted from taking care of Sabrina. They hadn't been close for a while, though neither of them wanted to talk about it, hoping that a single event—a major commission for Sam, Sabrina suddenly turning angelic—would change their course. Remake them into the couple they wanted to be.

The wealthy, open-minded clients never materialized. Sabrina grew, if anything, even fussier, more demanding. Their pediatrician assured them nothing was wrong. Some babies are just difficult, he said, not much you can do about it. He told them to be patient, and they nodded and forced smiles and thought, Fuck you, no one is this patient.

Sam's cocktail hour crept earlier, lasted longer, and within a year he had to shut down his practice because he lacked clients. He made several perfunctory inquiries about joining other firms, but an abundance of pride prevented him from seriously considering working for someone else. Jessica sensed his hesitation and said to him one day, "I don't see what the big deal is. You did it before, for years."

"Exactly," he said. "I'm past that."

"Well . . ." She didn't finish her sentence.

" 'Well' what, Jess?" He always shortened her name when he was angry with her. He knew she hated it.

"Nothing."

"Come on, Jess, say it. Tell me obviously I'm not past working for someone else. Tell me that if I were, then clearly I wouldn't be in this position. Tell me how much I suck."

She folded her arms in front of her chest. "I'm not talking to you when you're like this," she said.

"Good."

When she told him she was moving out, Sam wasn't surprised. He was almost relieved. Their small house had become a cold war, week after week of indicting, brittle tension. Ironically, just as they were reaching their unavoidable separation, Sabrina started behaving much better. She cried less, slept more. Her smiles were frequent, and she began learning how to play with her toys at a pace that was nearly alarming.

There were moments she forced Sam and Jessica together. A new physical coordination she mastered, a word she was circling ever closer to saying. They would gravitate toward each other, gazes focused on their child, sitting on the floor, perhaps unaware of the peacekeeper she had become. Occasionally they even touched, brushed shoulders, thighs, though nothing more.

And in the end those moments weren't enough. They were ephemeral, temporary as sirens and mist, little match for the loathing that blanketed Sam's body.

George had been over it so many times. The whys and wheres and whens and all the torturing, unanswerable questions, the cancer of what-ifs. If they hadn't gotten in a fight. If he had stayed at the bar. If she had left five minutes later, or ten minutes earlier. If they had moved to a different city. Even: if they had never met. If he hadn't kissed her that night in school, when neither of them knew what genuine violence was, the cloister of their verdant campus so lethally impenetrable. In its classrooms they had learned so much, and nothing that would save them. If they had never met, George reasoned, Natalie would never have been raped. She wouldn't have been in that bar with him, she would have spent her night elsewhere, surrounded by different people and different landmarks. He wouldn't have ruined her life.

Everyone—friends, family, shrinks, books and magazines—tried to assure him that it wasn't his fault. They said it over and over again, like a mantra, and sometimes the effect of so much repetition is that you doubt it even more. The truest things are things you don't need to keep telling yourself. They are things imbued in you like blood. He wanted to believe them, all of them, wanted to snap open his eyes one morning shaken by a realization: Yes, my girlfriend was raped; no, I didn't cause it. I had no control over it, nothing to do with it. Yet he never woke up like that, never went to sleep without revisiting that night and its unspooling, unstoppable horror. Him walking swiftly out of the bar, wanting to turn back and apologize but being too proud. Him leaving her alone and vulnerable. Giving her, handing her, to a monster.

Sam had checked into the motel because that is what he did every six months. He brought gin, sleeping pills, more. The desk clerk knew him because he had stayed there several times before, locking himself in a musty, $35-a-night room for three days of drinking and smoking and getting high and wondering if there was any mercy, some rest. Seventy-two hours of taking him away from the life he had fallen into and didn't know how to escape. When he was awake, he listened through the thin walls to the other guests coming and going. He heard fights, sex, mundane phone calls, sometimes just the buzz-saw snore of a trucker grabbing a few hours of rest.

He could replay the details, yet it hardly mattered. Failed marriage, a daughter he wasn't allowed to see, a slew of disappointments piled like bricks. Parents back East who told him he wasn't welcome to contact them until he had solved his problems. Small tangles with the police. Each one was so intractable; even if you fix one, there are ten others.

He had been arrested there before. A year ago, maybe two; once you are far enough gone, the months and years merge together. It was a fight with a family from Utah, maybe Idaho—one of those states that seems more land and mountains than people—and they were having an argument that kept ballooning. The last thing Sam remembered was telling the man, "Fuck you. Fuck you, fuck your screaming family, fuck your RV, and fuck Disneyland—or wherever the fuck you're headed to waste tons of money and wish you'd never gotten married or had kids in the first place. Fuck all of you." Then the police came and hauled him away.

Natalie knew better. The lessons had been drilled in since elementary school, first in static film strips and then from the mouths of stiff police officers visiting the auditorium: Don't walk home alone; don't stay out too late at night; don't talk to strangers. She knew better, and yet she didn't—or she thought it wouldn't hurt anyone if, just this once, she was a little reckless. She was smart, she knew how to handle herself.

She had wanted, in fact, to be alone. She thought the starry sky and chilly air might somehow scrub away the unpleasantness of earlier. The empty streets, the shuttered stores, the eighteen-wheelers with hulls outlined in white Christmas lights: There must be redemption and renewal somewhere. Small, unannounced things that rescue us. If she could find it, or if it could locate her, she would arrive home to George loving, with a sharp, deep wanting. Slip under the covers and next to him, trace the line of his spine, press her cheek against the back of his neck. You have to give up a little control, she had always thought, if you wanted to stumble into true happiness. Nothing calculated could ever make you feel good. She could kiss him into waking up, wrap her body in his, be grateful and quiet. Action, sounds, wordless. Moan, breathe, touch.

There was an old school bus. Sam remembered a rusting bus several blocks from the motel, tires melting into the pavement, hugging the curb by a warehouse. Half the windows were shattered, and the windshield wipers hung limply like crippled, useless arms. It seemed strange to him to see a school bus so late at night, idle, because they were vehicles for daytime. Beehives of swarming kids. In a few years Sabrina would be riding one, her face glued to the glass.

He had thought about sleeping there, wedging open the door and just lying down on one of the cracked vinyl seats. There would be faded graffiti, the gossip and boasts and slander of teenagers. He had been on those buses, years ago, one of a boisterous thousand who couldn't sit still, who liked to look down at the passing cars. The driver tried to quiet them with threats and rewards, but little worked. Not songs, not candy, not the dark cloud of a report to the principal. There was something inevitable and innocent about the chaos. It was just children spilling all their endless energy.

Beyond the school bus was an intersection, and the traffic lights had gone to flashing because it was so late. Yellow in one direction, red in the other. He stopped on that corner, too, let the pulses mesmerize him for a moment. Maybe you can see the blinking lights from the bus, he thought, maybe the city's electric heart will lull me to sleep. Maybe, Sam thought, the buildings and all their taunting will finally blacken.

Then he saw her. She was walking down the street cater-corner to him.

She spotted him, too, and she picked up her pace. She had the gait of someone buzzed, trying to make sure her steps were straight, knowing they probably weren't. Her knees came up higher than necessary on each stride. He followed her, and her strides got even quicker. She was wearing jeans, sneakers, a windbreaker that billowed with the breeze.

When they neared an alley, he grabbed her from behind. She yelped, but he managed to clamp his hand over her mouth to silence her. She struggled at first, until he punched her in the small of the back. She gasped and coughed and doubled over in pain, and her body tightened in shock. He yanked her back up and growled, in her ear, "Don't. I'll kill you if you fight." He could smell the perfume on her, mixed with the residue of the bar. "You're too pretty to fight, anyway."

He took her into an alley and pushed her up against a dumpster. As he unbuckled his belt, he said, "When I'm finished, you're going to face the brick wall and count to two hundred and don't turn around and don't start screaming for help." She didn't do anything, and he said, "Do you understand?"

She nodded.

"Good."

He started pulling down her pants. She wasn't struggling anymore, and her body was all slack, like a doll, only with human proportions. "Please," she managed, and the word was little more than a hiccup, far too flimsy for what was about to happen.

It was the only thing she would say. She was silent while he worked on her, his pants around his ankles. No cars drove by, no planes scored the sky above. The only mark of this wreckage was the ugly, rhythmic slap of flesh against flesh. "Please," she mumbled again, and the word sounded to him completely inappropriate, because there was nothing pleasing about this. It was all about silencing, and he was going to keep screwing her until he stopped hearing the truth.

At the hospital, after she had spoken with a doctor and the police, a rape counselor came into Natalie's room. She introduced herself and then turned, softly, to George, and said, "Sometimes this is easier if we're alone." George looked at Natalie. "It's okay," Natalie assured him. "Why don't you get a cup of coffee."

When George left the room, the counselor took the seat next to Natalie's bed. "Have you been treated well here?" she asked. "Is there anything I can bring you?"

Natalie shook her head.

"Mostly I just wanted to introduce myself," said the counselor. "Let you know that I'm here if you ever want to talk."

"I don't want to talk," Natalie said.

"That's okay. It's probably too soon now. But I'm going to leave you a card. When you're feeling up to it, maybe in a few weeks or a few months, you can give me a call and we can make an appointment. I can meet you anywhere you want. I'm available in the evening hours as well."

"I said I don't want to talk," said Natalie. "Not now and not in a few weeks. If you leave a card, it'll be a waste. Save it for someone who's interested."

The counselor opened her purse and started digging.

"I don't want to talk because I know what you're going to tell me: Rape is about power, not sex. It's a crime, a violation, right?" Natalie trailed a finger through her dirty hair. "I already know all that stuff, and it's totally fucking unhelpful. It didn't help five hours ago, it's not helping now, and it won't help in a few months. It's just words, some lame theory. It has nothing to do with the real world."

The counselor nodded, laying a card on the bedside table. "We don't have to talk about theories. We can talk about other things."

Natalie thumbed a bruise on her wrist. "Theories, non-theories, I don't want to talk about any of it. I just want to let this fade. I want... I want... I just want to go home." She looked at the counselor. "Can you get my boyfriend and ask him to come in here?"

A few minutes later, George returned to the room. Natalie was sitting on the edge of the bed and had her coat on already and was tying her shoes. She was having trouble tightening her right hand around the laces, so he crouched down to help her.

"Are you all done?" he asked, palming her calf and looking up.

She nodded.

He finished with the shoes and stood. "Was that woman helpful?"

"No."

"At all?"

"No."

He reached out his right hand to help her off the bed. She noticed his bloody knuckles and stared at them.

"Punched a wall," he explained.

"Before or after?"

"After. When you called from the hospital." He remembered her voice, so shaky it almost wasn't there. She took his hand, stood up, and they threaded their way out of the warrens of the emergency room, the sterile fluorescent light and efficient nurses making it impossible to hide anywhere.

After it happened, she didn't want to be touched and she didn't want George to not want to touch her. An impossible position to put him in, she knew, but she couldn't help it. There was something reflexive, almost automatic about it. When she sensed him reaching for her, she would shut her eyes and try to relax, let herself be held and wanted, but her body tensed up and there was no way she could pretend otherwise, no way she could veto the instinct. "Give me time," she kept saying, "it's bound to get easier." He looked at her with such deep sadness and patience she nearly cried. And she thought maybe his unmitigated kindness, his boundless generosity, might soldier them through. His guitar strumming and his Merle Haggard records, skips and pops and all. One night, lying next to him, she palmed his chest, on the left side, as if the rich blood surging through his heart might somehow make its way to her body, where it could transfuse her own, replace tarnished with clean, weak with strong. Attacked with unattacked.

Sometimes she feared that she might simply crumple and vanish. Walking down a crowded sidewalk, her body would implode, shrink into nothingness, and her clothes would fall to the concrete in an unruly pile, as if dumped from a hamper. Strangers might look at them, the unoccupied shirt and jeans and sneakers, might stoop down and finger them and wonder where they came from. Maybe someone would look up, as if the garments had been dropped magically from the sky, so absent would any evidence of her body be.

Most victims of violent crimes hated to be alone. She had read this in articles and books, many sent by friends who weren't sure what to say so they let printed words stand in. She didn't hate them for it; she understood it was a hard thing to talk about. But she actually craved time by herself, sought it out as much as possible. She avoided crowded parts of the city—Chinatown, the tourist-packed piers—and traveled instead to empty corners of Golden Gate Park. She gazed out at the bay and the bridge, tried to let the lilt of the water and the sinewy, muscular cables mold her back into what she used to be. During rush hour she let her vision blur, and the stream of cars became a string of pearls. All those white lights, gem after gem heading home. When it was raining, she didn't even have to let her vision unlock. The lights turned fuzzy and warm on their own.

George flew back to Nashville. He didn't want to do it in San Francisco, didn't want to stain the pavement of her city with his blood. If it happened there, he knew she would have to leave, even if it occurred on a street she never walked by. She was like that: she put a lot of stake in symbols. Stars, planets, the tops of trees—everything was metaphor and message. He had already taken so much from her; he didn't want to rob her of a home, too.

Nashville was where they were happiest. They were poor, but it didn't matter—they were intoxicated with hope, fueled with each other and the seamless dream your life becomes when you let yourself love. In their apartment, above a pawn shop, they wasted hours slouched on a Salvation Army couch, drinking, smoking, meandering effortlessly into sex. There was something almost painfully satisfying about the depth of their physical connection—he knew when she wanted to take it slow, he knew when she wanted him to grip her hips so hard she'd have bruises in the morning, soft amber and lavender reminders of lust and need. They were badges, something neither of them ever talked about. Sometimes, in the middle of the night, he would wake up to use the bathroom, and when he came back to bed, he would stand there, hover over her, and stare at her nearly motionless body, thinking, You're a gift, you're a gift. He shivered. *How did you get here?* It doesn't matter. The arrival, not the journey.

He could watch her for fifteen minutes, more. If the air conditioner was off, he heard the hiss of the neon signs in the windows below. He watched her softly rising and falling chest, or the involuntary flutters of her eyelids during REM sleep. What was she dreaming? He didn't care. He didn't quite believe where he was, in this apartment in Tennessee full of love and little else, and he thought it might be he himself who was asleep. Graceland, the Opry, Elvis could walk right in and rhinestones could splash the walls and he wouldn't notice. Fat, sad Elvis, or the Army-trim one. Play them a concert, sing "Kentucky Rain" and "In the Ghetto."

George occasionally worried, when he wasn't with her, that she would disappear. That she was too good, that the two of them fit too well, for it to be real and lasting. The world isn't generous like that, he thought, there is no way this can continue without the smack of some tragedy. Other times, like when he saw her round the corner, or enter the café where he was playing an open-mike night, he told himself he was being irrational, that he was going out of his way to find something to be anxious about. "They have medication for this kind of thinking," a friend of his told him one night when he confessed his anxiety. "My uncle's a shrink, maybe I could get some for you." Just then, Natalie walked into the bar, and George gestured at her coming toward them and said, "There's my pill."

No note. What could George possibly say? There is no rationale, finally, and to leave a few sentences, a few pages even, would only make the hurt hurt more. He would rather leave her with memories, indelible, times they were unmarred and didn't need anything like an explanation. They themselves were an explanation. There were a hundred, more, but here is one: They are in a bar in Nashville. His set is ten minutes away, and he is nervous, far more nervous than usual, and the shots aren't helping like they should. (Tequila, because that is what Gram Parsons drank: Souza, chilled.) She knows he's uneasy, because he can't maintain eye contact, and she pulls his stool close to her own. He is fingering a pick, passing it knuckle to knuckle in his right hand. She's hypnotized for a second, it looks like a Jacob's ladder. Their thighs are brushing. She beckons, with her hand, for him to lean in close. He does. She starts singing, quietly. She has a terrible voice for singing but it doesn't matter, it is so far from mattering, it can never matter. He is staring at the liquor bottles lined up flawlessly against the mirror behind the bar. Soldiers in formation. It's a Waylon Jennings song. "They ought to give me the Wurlitzer prize / All the silver I let slide down the slot / Playing those songs so blue / Help me remember you / I don't want to get over you / I don't want to get over you." The bartenders pass in and out of his sight. They are mannequins, and the other drinkers aren't real, either. The woman on stage is wax, her strumming arm bionic. The street outside is another planet. There is no way to get there, and no need to. All we need is an island. The candles flicker. Cigarettes glow orange. Smoke kisses the ceiling. "A fresh roll of quarters / Same old songs / Missin' you through and through." *I don't want to get over you, I don't want to get over you.*

Her life, she thought, had transformed into pure aftermath. Natalie remembered other times, precise events and people and places, but they didn't seem hers. She no longer felt like she owned them, as if they had happened to a different person. Why can't the rape be like that, she wondered, why is it that everything except the assault belongs to someone else? Why does violence tattoo you, and joy doesn't? Still, she knew it was early—only seven months—to expect to feel significantly better. She managed to hold on to her job and maintain at least semi-regular contact with friends and family. She knew that both of these things were important, and she tried to draw some consolation in them. She never phoned the counselor.

George. What frightened her most was that she would never again feel comfortable being touched by him. She tried, desperately, to recall him kissing her, the two of them entwined on a drowsy late morning, or at night, when they didn't need to talk, just needed each other—the imperative of desire. But she couldn't, and she was amazed at how quickly all the nights they had spent together were scrapped. She scoured her journals and piles of old snapshots, looking for some spark of memory, irrefutable indications of love and want and need and happiness.

For a few weeks she spent hours every day on the Internet, tracking down former classmates she barely knew, hoping the re-ignited contact would bring her old life streaming back. A random, unpredictable anecdote from college to catalyze a chain reaction. She found a few, e-mailed enthusiastically for several days, then let the contact dissolve. Because it wasn't working, and she felt slightly guilty: She didn't care where they were living, what impressive job titles they held, who their husbands were, whether they planned on being at the upcoming five-year reunion. She didn't care if they had dogs or children or both or neither. It wasn't their fault, but she wanted something they couldn't give her.

The detectives never found him. He never had a name. They interviewed Natalie three separate times, had her meet with a sketch artist, even though she saw his face only fleetingly. There were no witnesses, and the crime didn't match any recent sprees.

"These people tend to fade in and out of society. They're really fringe people," the detectives told her. "He'll probably surface again at some point and try something like this again, and that's when we'll get him. They're not brain surgeons, these people. They tend to be uneducated." This was supposed to reassure her. She sensed resignation in the detectives' voices, and she recalled a statistic she had read: If they're not caught within seventy-two hours of their crimes, most criminals are never arrested for what they did.

She didn't blame the police. She didn't blame anyone, except for her attacker. Maybe if they had apprehended him, she would have begun to feel better. But she doubted it. It wasn't fear that she felt most acutely, some panic that she would be a victim again; it was more a dull, persistent pain, along with the perpetual agony of both craving and refusing physical contact. What if her fate was to never be held again?

George was surprised how familiar Nashville seemed. It was a cloudy day when his plane touched down, and he spent most of it driving around their old street, past their apartment, the movie theater where they wasted rainy afternoons, the diners and bars they depended on. He walked by one of the cafés where he had played a few times, saw that they still had weekly open-mike nights. He peered in the plate-glass windows but didn't recognize any of the waitresses. They had become friends with one, Karen, and she let them stay long past closing time, joining them for drinks while the bartenders cashed out and the busboys mopped the floor.

He had expected to be flooded with doubt, hooks that would pull him back to the airport and back on to a plane. Not necessarily back to San Francisco but another city, any city, where there was light and air and no history. Taxis streamed by him, tour buses on their way to Music Row and megaphoned narration. The passengers were pressed to the windows, weighed down with cameras and guidebooks and bottled water.

He found the neighborhood: Buena Vista. It was the part of Nashville where you weren't supposed to go, the streets littered with abandoned houses and drug dens. It seemed like an entirely different city, immune to the charm and gleam of the country-music mecca just several miles away. On the corners stood liquor stores, cashiers shielded behind thick glass partitions. Many of the houses, the ones where people were still sentenced to live, had bars on the windows.

Once it was dark, George started his search in earnest, taking random turns, losing himself deeper and deeper in the labyrinthine blocks. He lingered by a playground, watching the remnants of a pickup basketball game, and an older man passed him and hissed, "You in the wrong neighborhood, son. Best be getting the fuck out." George shook his head, mostly to himself, and unthreaded his fingers from the fence he had been gazing through. He kept walking, slowly, scanning for people.

An hour later he knew it was about to happen. He had strolled by an all-night grocery store, where a pack of young men was smoking and drinking from liquor bottles sleeved in brown paper bags. Three of them started following him, and George led them down a quiet street with streetlights that buzzed but gave off no brightness—somewhere they were likely to think they wouldn't get caught.

When he heard the quickening of their steps behind him, he braced himself. One of them poked his shoulder and said, "Okay, man, gimme your wallet and your watch."

George turned around to face them. Two tall ones, and another a few inches shorter than him, flashing a gold tooth. He was the spokesman of the group. A tattoo of a snake curled up his forearm.

"No," said George.

"What?" said Gold Tooth, suddenly erasing the space between them.

"I said no," George repeated. "Something wrong with your hearing?"

Gold Tooth started laughing, a sinister, prescient laugh, and turned away from George to face his friends. "You believe this motherfucker?" Then he locked his hand around George's throat and dropped him to the ground in a single, crisp motion.

Gold Tooth leaned over him, his fingers still tight around his neck. "My hearing's fine. Now you gonna give it up?"

Twisting and gasping for air, George said, "Fuck you." The back of his head was already beginning to throb from where it had hit the pavement.

Laughter again. George realized why he was the leader of the group: There was genuine cruelty and sadism in him.

"Really?" he asked. "You sure that's the answer you want to be sticking with? You sure you don't want to choose answer B?"

George nodded.

"Answer B, man, that's usually the more popular answer. Nine times out of ten, skinny-ass white motherfuckers like yourself go with answer B. B—for bawling like a baby."

"Fuck you," George managed again.

"Okay," Gold Tooth said calmly. "Time to pay."

The two others rushed up and started rifling through his pockets, taking out his wallet and stray bills. Gold Tooth kept one hand clamped around his throat and ripped his watch off his wrist with the other.

Then they started kicking and punching him, burying their unlaced boots in his ribs and knees and hips. The blows came swift, one after another, and George heard his bones snap, felt the strange cool warmth of newly released blood. He knew it was flowing from his nose, around his eyes, other places as well. He heard them laughing, too, and he wondered if they had any idea they were giving him exactly what he deserved.

LAURA KASISCHKE

If a Stranger Approaches You about Carrying a Foreign Object with You onto the Plane...

Once there was a woman who was asked by a stranger to carry a foreign object with her onto a plane:

When the stranger approached her, the woman was sitting at the edge of her chair a few feet from the gate out of which her plane was scheduled to leave. Her legs were crossed. She was wearing a black turtleneck and slim black pants. Black boots. Pearl studs in her ears. She was swinging the loose leg, the one that was tossed over the knee of the other—swinging it slowly and rhythmically, like a pendulum, as she tried to drink her latte in burning sips.

By the time the stranger approached her and asked her to carry the foreign object with her onto the plane, the woman had already owned that latte for at least twenty minutes, but it hadn't cooled a single degree. It was as if there were a thermonuclear process at work inside her cup—the steamed milk and espresso somehow generating together their own heat—and the tip of her tongue had been stung numb from trying to drink it, and the plastic nipple of the cup's white lid was smeared with her lipstick.

Her name was Kathy Bliss. She was anxious. At home, her two-year-old was sick, but she'd had to go to Maine, anyway, because she'd been asked to speak on behalf of the nonprofit for which she worked, and possibly thousands upon thousands of dollars would be gifted to it by her hosts if she were able to conjure the right combination of passion and desperation with which she was sometimes able to speak on behalf of her nonprofit. She didn't much believe in what they were doing, which was, to her mind, mostly justifying the spending of their donations on computers and letterhead and lunches with donors, but she had her eye on another nonprofit, one devoted to curing a disease (or at least *publicizing* a disease) which no one knew about until it was contracted, at which time the body attacked itself, turning the skin into a suit of armor, petrifying the internal organs one by one.

The vice president of this nonprofit had his eye on the regional directorship of the American Cancer Society, she knew, and with some luck his position would be open, and she would be ready to move into it.

Still, she'd always understood that you have to put your energy into the place you are if you want to move on to another place; and, on occasion, she could be convincing—something about the podium, a bottle of water, a few notes, and all eyes on her—and there was clearly no one else at her nonprofit who could even remotely have been considered for this engagement. (Jen, with her multiple piercings? Rob, with his speech impediment?) She had to go.

The baby was sick, but the baby would be fine. Kathy Bliss had a husband, after all, who would take care of their baby. He was the baby's father, for God's sake. This wasn't 1952. The man had a Ph.D. in compassion; who was she to think the baby would be any better off with her there just because she was *of a certain gender*? And if she hadn't had to go to Maine, Garrett would have gone to work himself, which would have left only one parent at home, anyway, doing the same thing either way—cuddling, cleaning up puke, taking the temp, filling the sippy cup with cold water.

Still, Kathy Bliss felt a pain, which she knew, intellectually, was imaginary, but nonetheless was excruciating, hovering around a few inches above her breasts, as if only moments ago something adhesive—a bandage, duct tape, a baby—had been ripped away from her bare flesh and taken a top layer of cellular material with it.

The latte had scalded her tongue (just the tip) to the point that she could feel, when she moved it across the ridge behind teeth, the rough little bumps of it gone completely dead—just a prickling dullness. Without the taste buds to interfere, Kathy Bliss could really feel the ridge behind the back of her teeth, the place where the bone smoothed into flesh, the difference between what was there for now and what, when she was dead, would be left. She took another sip. Better. Maybe it had cooled down a bit, or maybe her tongue couldn't register the heat of it anymore. That was probably dangerous, she thought. The way people got scalded. Their nerve endings dulled, and they stepped into the tub without knowing it would cook them.

"Sorry," the stranger said after his pant leg brushed her knee, but she didn't really look at him, not yet. His tan belt was at eye level, nothing remarkable about it, and then he was gone.

As was always the case in airports, there was a small crowd of confused people (the elderly, the poor, some foreigners) standing patiently in a line they didn't need to stand in, and a woman behind a counter who was waving them away one by one as they approached her with their fully sufficient pieces of paper.

"We'll be boarding in forty minutes," the woman said over and over, refusing to smile, make eye contact, or answer questions. The woman had a spectacular hairpiece on top of her head. A kind of beehive with fronds. When she waved, the fronds shivered, caught the light, looking fountain-like, or like incandescent antennae. Although the woman had dark skin (tanning booth?), her real hair was a pale pink-blond beneath the hairpiece, which was the synthetic blond of a Barbie doll. What had the woman been thinking, Kathy Bliss wondered, that morning at the mirror, placing it atop her head. What had she believed she would look like with that thing on her head? Had she *wanted* to look the way she did—shocking, alien, a creature out of an illustrated Hans Christian Andersen?

Many years before, when Kathy Bliss was a college student, in an incident that had, she believed, changed and defined her forever, she'd come across a dead body in the Arboretum. A woman. Stabbed. Mostly bones and some scraps of clothing—and she (Kathy Bliss, not the dead woman) had run screaming.

It had been a very quick glimpse, so of course she hadn't known at the time that the body was that of a woman, or that the woman had been stabbed, knew nothing of the details until she was given them later by the police. Still, she knew that she must have stood there open-mouthed for at least a second or two (she had been running on a trail but gone off of it to pee) because she clearly saw, or *remembered* seeing, that there were bees in that dead woman's hair.

When a few people left the line, a few more entered it. All over the airport, there were such sad, small crowds. They hesitated together at every counter, not ready to believe that all was well, not able to so easily accept the assurance that they already had what they needed, that they had found their proper places so quickly and had only now to wait. Kathy Bliss herself had forced one such crowd to part for her when she entered the terminal, pulling her luggage on wheels behind her as she made her way to security. She could feel their eyes on her back as she passed, knew they were probably loathing and admiring in equal measure her swift professional purposefulness. *She* knew where she was going. *She'd* done this a million times.

But, to her ears, anyway, the wheels of her luggage made the sound of a spit turning quickly (but with some effort) over a burning pit, as she dragged it behind her. She had no idea why. They weren't rusty. It was a fairly new bag. It had never been left out in the rain or pulled through the mud. But there it was, the sound of a spit, turning. A pig on that spit. An apple in its mouth. That final humiliation: *We shall eat you, Pig.*

She couldn't believe it when, at the *SAVe a LIFe!* picnic that summer, that they'd actually *done* that, actually roasted a pig on a spit with an apple crammed into its mouth.

At first, she hadn't noticed it because she'd been busy meeting and greeting. ("Yes, yes, of course I remember. Nice to see you again. Thank you for coming.")

But after she'd filled her glass with punch and had just tipped the glass to her lips, she'd seen it out of the corner of her eye, taken one step toward it, seen it fully then, and reeled—literally reeled—and splashed pink punch onto her chest, where it trickled down in a sweet zigzagging rivulet between her breasts.

Luckily, she'd been wearing a low-cut dress, also pink.

"Whoa," the college president she'd been standing next to said when she reeled. "Friend of yours or something? Are you a vegetarian?"

"Jesus," she'd said, "I am now," turning her back to the spit, trying to smile. But there was a cool film of sweat all over her body, as if each pore had opened in a moment, coating her with dew. "What a spectacle."

"Isn't that the point?" the college president had said.

"Because of heightened security measures," the ceiling droned, *"we ask that you report any unattended luggage. If a stranger should approach you and ask you to carry a foreign object with you onto a plane, please contact a member of security personnel immediately."*

"Excuse me?" the stranger said, taking a seat beside her.

Kathy Bliss turned, swinging her leg off her knee, placing both black boots beside one another on the floor.

"Yes?"

The stranger was young and handsome. He had dark hair and tan skin and large brown eyes. Slender fingers. What appeared to be an actual gold Rolex on his wrist. He was wearing a white shirt with a red tie and a black leather jacket. An Arab, she thought right away, and then felt bad for thinking it. He had no accent; she could tell that already from the two words he'd spoken. He was an American, not an "Arab." He was probably more American than she was, her mother's parents having stumbled into this country from Liverpool, broke, in the twenties, her paternal grandparents having dashed across the Canadian border in the thirties in search of higher-paying employment with the US Postal Service.

Still, it must be awful, she thought, to *look* like an Arab in an airport these days. It must have felt, she supposed, like wearing a scarlet *A*. Everyone staring, either wondering suspiciously about you and feeling guilty about wondering, or feeling suspicious and self-righteous about staring and wondering. "I'm sorry to bother you," the stranger said. "Are you, by any chance, going to Portland?"

"Yes," Kathy Bliss said.

"Well—" he smiled, and then his breast pocket began to play the theme from *The Lone Ranger* loudly and digitally, and he reached into it and fumbled around for a moment until it stopped and he said, "Sorry," shaking his head. For a crazy second Kathy Bliss thought of asking him to check the caller ID, to make sure her husband wasn't trying to reach her with some news about the baby (she'd turned her own cell off to conserve the battery, and would check it just before she got on the plane)—but, of course, this stranger had nothing to do with her baby.

"Can I help you?" she asked.

The man had a tiny gold cross in his left earlobe. It was really very beautiful—and strange, too, how masculine that little earring made him look with the dark shadow of beard on his chiseled jawline, and how masculine he made that earring by wearing it in his ear, with its foiled brilliance. A small, bold statement. It might have been a religious statement or a fashion statement, what difference did it make?

"Yes, but please," he said, "if this sounds strange to you, just send me away."

"Okay?" she said. A question.

"Okay," he said. "I'm supposed to be going to Portland for my mother's seventieth birthday, but I just got a call from my girlfriend telling me"—he smiled ruefully, rolled his eyes to the ceiling—"I'm sorry, I should make something up here, but I'll just tell you the truth: she's pregnant. And she's flipping out. And I feel like"—he tossed some emptiness into the air with his palms, making a gesture she'd seen men make many times in response to women's emotional states—"honestly—I think I ought to go buy her an engagement ring *today*, and get my butt back to our apartment. I mean, this isn't a disaster. Or it doesn't *have* to be. We were getting married, anyway, and we knew we might get pregnant. We weren't even using any—" He shook his head. "I'm sorry, *really* sorry, to be filling you in on all these details. I'd made it through security, I was planning to just go and come back maybe even tonight, and then I realized—I just realized I shouldn't go at all. That I should go straight back to my girlfriend right now." He inhaled, looked at Kathy Bliss as if trying to gauge her reaction. "I'm sorry," he said, "to fill you, a complete stranger, in on these sordid details."

Kathy Bliss tried to laugh sympathetically. She shook her head a little. Shrugged. "It's okay," she said. "Been there, done that!"

The stranger laughed pretty hard at this. His teeth were very straight and white, although one of the front ones had what looked to be a hairline crack in it. A very thin gray crack. Her two-year-old, Connor, had just recently gotten so many new teeth that it surprised her every time he opened his mouth. The teeth were like little dabs of meringue. Clean and white and peaked. She liked to smell his breath. It was as if there were a pure little spring in there. His mouth smelled like mineral water.

"Well, there you have it," the stranger said. "I guess, if nothing else, we're all here because *somebody'd* been there and done that."

"That, too," Kathy Bliss said. "But, I mean, I have a child. It's a great thing."

"Yeah," he said. "I'm starting to forget, in all this hysteria, the great fact that I'm going to be a dad—"

"Well, congratulations from me," Kathy Bliss said. She felt the warm implication of tears starting somewhere around her sinuses, and swallowed. She changed her latte cup from her right hand to her left, reached over the metal armrest, and offered her hand to him. He shook it, smiling. Then he shook his own hand as if it had been burned. "Jeez," he said, "that's one burning handshake."

"My latte," she said. "It's like molten lava."

"I guess so," he said.

The stranger was wearing khaki pants with very precisely ironed creases. For a quick second Kathy Bliss wondered if his girlfriend was also an Arab, and then she remembered that she had no way of knowing that *he* was an Arab, and far more evidence, anyway, that he *wasn't*—and reminded herself that it didn't matter, anyway. So, maybe his parents had been born in Egypt, or Iran. The color of his skin was beautiful! A warm milky brown. She felt a pang of jealousy about the girlfriend, lying on their bed at home, not knowing that this beautiful stranger was making desperate plans to buy her a diamond that day. What a thing, this life. Love. God, when it worked, it really worked! She had, herself, fallen in love with her husband upon first sight. She'd been given his name as the best shrink in town for the kind of problem she was having—which was spending every minute of her day trying not to think about the dead body in the Arboretum for two solid years after she'd seen it—and she had no sooner settled herself in the chair across from his, and he'd crossed his legs, looking more anxious and frightened than she, herself, the *patient,* felt, that she knew she wanted to marry him. And he'd cured her, too. Without drugs. A few behavior modifications. A rubber band around her wrist, a mantra, a series of self-punishments and rewards.

"Well, to make a long story short," the stranger said, "my girlfriend's freaking out back at our apartment, and my mother's turning seventy in Portland, and I'm her only son, who's such a scoundrel and an ingrate, not to mention morally reprehensible for impregnating someone he's not married to, *yet,* that he's not even showing up for her party, so"—and here he shook his head and looked directly into Kathy Bliss's eyes—"I wonder if I, a stranger, could ask you, a passenger, to carry a foreign object with you onto the plane?"

"Oh my God," Kathy Bliss said. "All these years I was wondering if anyone was ever going to ask me that."

"I think," the stranger said, "now is the point at which you ought to contact security personnel—like, right away."

"Yes," she said, "I think I may have heard an announcement pertaining to that. And I've always wondered to myself what kind of idiot would actually do such a thing, like carry a foreign object onto a plane."

"Well," the stranger said, "here's the object you've been waiting your whole life to carry with you onto the plane."

Out of a pocket in the inner lining of his coat, the stranger produced a narrow rectangular box wrapped in gold paper. He sighed. "It's a gold necklace, and if you'd be so foolhardy as to carry it with you onto the plane, I'd call my brother and have him meet you at baggage claim and get it to the party this evening. *But*"—he waved his slender fingers around over the box—"I totally understand if you think that's nuts."

"I have no problem with it," she said. "Don't worry, I won't contact security personnel."

"Let me open it for you, at least," he said, "so you know you're not carrying a bomb—"

"If you managed to get a bomb in that little package," she said, "you deserve to have it carried by a passenger onto the plane."

She regretted the joke even as she said it, saw the Towers dissolving into dust on her television again. It had been on the floor because the entertainment center had not yet arrived (it was being custom-built somewhere in Illinois) and there was no table or counter big enough to put the television on. The baby was crying (eight weeks old), so she'd had to stand and pace with his hot little face leaking tears onto her shoulders as those Towers collapsed at her feet. The front door had been open, and it had smelled to her as if the stone-blue perfect sky out there were dissolving in talcumish particles of dried flowers—such a beautiful day it horrified her. An illusion dipped in blue. She could have walked with her baby straight out the front door or right into the big-screen TV of it, and they might have turned themselves into nothing but subatomic particles, blue light, perfume.

There was nothing funny about terrorism. Nothing even remotely funny about terrorism. Still, she was from the Midwest, and it seemed like a long time ago already. No more National Guard in the airport—those boys with their big weapons trying not to look bored and out of place around every corner. She had, herself, only been to New York a few times, and never to those Towers, having only glimpsed them from her plane as it banked into LaGuardia. From the plane, they'd looked like Legos, and no matter how real she knew it all was, on the television, on the floor, it had not looked real. And the least likely plane a terrorist would want to blow up or hijack was one traveling from Grand Rapids, Michigan, to Portland, Maine. Right? "Don't unwrap that," she said. "It's exquisite. I trust you."

"I insist," he said. "This is too weird and too much of a . . . cliché! I have my dignity!" He laughed. "And in any case, I will doubt your sanity if you don't let me open it. I can't have a crazy woman delivering my mother's birthday present—"

"No," Kathy Bliss said, snatching the little present off his lap. "You'll never get it wrapped like this again. It's like a little dream. I'd be insane if I thought you could get anything *but* a necklace in that box."

He made his mouth into a zero, and sighed, loosened his tie a little by inserting his index finger between the knot and his collar. From somewhere on the other side of the wall of screens that listed arrivals and departures, a baby began to cry, and the feeling came back to her—the ripping, intensely, as if yet another layer of skin, or whatever was underneath her skin, were being pulled off her torso in one quick yank. The stranger took the cellphone out of his pocket and said, "I'll call my brother. Can I tell him your name? I'll have him at baggage claim—I mean—" He interrupted himself here. "I'm assuming that's where you'll be going—" He looked at the black bag at her feet. "Did you check luggage?"

"Yes," she said. "I mean no, but I can go to baggage claim, no problem. Tell him—"

"I'll have him carry a sign, with your name on it, okay?"

"Yes. Kathy Bliss."

"Bliss?" He smiled. "Like, 'bliss'?"

"Yes," she said. "Like the Joseph Campbell thing. 'Follow your bliss.' "

He smiled, but she could tell he hadn't heard of Joseph Campbell, or the advice of Joseph Campbell. She had, herself, been in graduate school when the PBS series with Bill Moyers had aired, and gotten together every Tuesday night with a group of women from her Mind, Brain, and Violence Seminar to watch it. A lot of joking about Bliss, and following it, had been made. When she'd get up to go to the bathroom or to get a beer out of the refrigerator, someone always pretended to follow her.

"We would like to begin boarding passengers on Flight 5236 to Portland, Maine. Passengers traveling with small children or needing special assistance..."

"That's me," she said.

"Yes," he said. "Of course. I'll make the call after you board. But let me tell you, my brother—he's twenty-two, but he looks a lot like me. I haven't seen him in a year, and sometimes he has long hair and sometimes he shaves his head, so"—he shrugged—"who knows. But he's about five-nine, one hundred sixty pounds—"

Kathy Bliss slipped the gold-wrapped box into her black bag carefully, so he could see that he could trust her with it. "Well," she said, "he'll have my name on a piece of paper, right? It'll be simple."

"Am I right, the plane's supposed to land at 12:51?" the stranger asked, peeking into the inner lining of his suit coat again, as if to look at his own unnecessary itinerary.

"Yep," she said. "12:51, assuming we're on time."

"Here," he said, hurrying with a piece of paper and a pen he'd taken from the pocket of his suit coat, "my brother's name is Mack Kaloustian. He'll be there. Or I'll kill him, and he knows it."

Kaloustian. Armenian. Kathy Bliss blinked and saw a spray of bullets raking through a family in a stand of trees on a mountaintop, a mother shielding her child, collapsing onto him: That child might have been this stranger's grandmother. And then they were boarding her row—12. Kathy Bliss stood up and extended her hand to the stranger. "Good luck to you," she said with all the warmth she could generate with only four words. The second word, *luck,* caught in her throat—a little emotional fishhook made out of consonants—because it was all so lovely, and simple, and lucky. Nothing but goodness in it for anyone. And her part in this sweet small drama moved her deeply, too—this gesture she was making of pure human camaraderie, this nonprofit venture, this small recognition of the cliché *We're all in this together.* That it mattered. Love. Family. The stranger. The favor. The bond of trust between them. He knew she wouldn't disappear into Portland with his gold necklace. She knew he wouldn't—what? Send her onto a plane with an explosive? He shook her hand so warmly it was like a hug. He said, "I can't tell you how much I appreciate this," and she said, "Of course. I'm happy to be able to help," and then she walked backwards so she could extend the moment of their smiling and parting, and then turned, inhaling, and began the dull and claustrophobic process of boarding her plane.

Kathy Bliss had been born and raised in a little stone house at the edge of a deep forest. "Honest to God," she always had to say after giving someone this piece of information about herself for the first time. "But it was nothing like you're imagining."

Her father had worked for a minimum-security prison, and the prison had been the thing her bedroom window faced, its high cyclone fencing topped by hundreds of yards of coiled barbed wire. In the summer, the sun rising in the east over the prison turned that barbed wire into a blinding fretwork, all spun-sugar and baroque and glitter, as if the air had been embroidered with silver thread by a gifted witch. She'd squint at it pretending that what her bedroom faced was an enchanted castle, as if the little stone house at the edge of the dark forest really were something from a fairy tale. But it was a sedentary childhood. Her parents wouldn't let her play in the yard or wait outside for the bus because, if there were an escape, she would make too good a hostage, being the prison director's daughter. For this reason, Kathy Bliss rarely had the chance to see the prisoners milling around behind that barbed wire, wearing their orange jumpsuits, and was able, therefore, to imagine them handsome and gallant as knights.

She and her mother had moved, when Kathy was nine, after her father died from an illness that announced itself first as bleeding gums, and then paralysis, and then he was just gone. She was thinking about this blip in her first years—the stone house, the barbed-wire castle—and watching the other passengers struggle onto the plane, shoving their heavy luggage into overhead compartments, the fat ones sweating, the thin ones trembling, the mothers with babies and little children looking blissfully burdened, when a voice came over the plane's intercom and said, "If there is a Katherine Bliss onboard, could she please press the flight attendant call button now?"

"Oh my God," Kathy Bliss said so loudly that an old woman standing in the aisle next to her whirled around and hit the call button for her. "Is that you?" the old woman said, as if she knew what they were calling Kathy Bliss about, as if everyone knew. "Yes," she said. "I forgot to check my messages." "Oh dear," the old woman said. The skin hung off her face in gray rags, and yet she'd made herself up carefully that morning, with tastefully understated foundation and blush, the kind of replica of life that would cause all gathered around her casket to say, "She just looks as if she's sleeping." There began a cold trickling at the tip of Kathy Bliss's spine, and then it turned into a fine mist, coating every inch of her. She could not close her mouth. She tried to stand, but there were so many people in the aisle she couldn't get out of her seat, although the old woman had turned to face the strangers surging forward and put a bony arm in front of her as if to try to block their passage. "Ma'am," a flight attendant said from ten feet behind that line, looking at the old woman. "Are you Mrs. Bliss?"

"No," the old woman said, and pointed to Kathy. "This is Mrs. Bliss."

"We have a message for you, Mrs. Bliss," the flight attendant called over the shoulders of the passengers in the aisle. She was a huge blond beauty, a Norse goddess. Someone who might stand on a mountain peak with a bolt of lightning in her fist. The crowd in the aisle dissolved to make way for her, and she pressed a folded piece of paper into Kathy Bliss's shaking hand: *Baby in hospital. Call home now. Husband.*

It was a week later—after the long pale nights at his crib-side in the hospital, taking turns pretending to sleep as the other paced, the tests, and the antibiotics, and the failure of the first ones to fight off the infection, and the terrifying night when the baby didn't wake during his injection, and they could clearly see the residency doctor's hand shaking as he punched the emergency button. It was after they'd begun a whole new life on the children's floor. *Sesame Street* in the lounge all day, as if the world were being run by benevolent toys, and then CNN scrolling its silent, redundant messages to them all night below images of the cynical and maimed. After they'd gotten to know the nurses. It was after Kathy Bliss had fallen in love, madly, with one doctor after another—not a sexual love, but a deep wild worship of the archetype, a reverent adulation of the Healer—and then grown to despise them one by one, and then to see them merely as human beings. It was after she'd spent some self-conscious moments on her knees in the hospital chapel, which turned into deep semi-conscious communions with the Almighty as the hospital intercom called out its mundane codes and locations in the hallway behind her—and the baby was taking fluids, and then solids, and then given a signature of release, and the nurses hugged Kathy Bliss and her husband, and let their hands wave magically, baptismally, over the head of the baby, who laughed, sputtered, still a little weak, scarlet-cheeked, but very much of this world, and cured for the next leg of the journey into the future, when they packed up the stuffed animals and picture books and headed for home—it was after all these events had come to an end that Kathy Bliss remembered the foreign object, given to her by the stranger, which had stayed where she'd tucked it into her carry-on luggage, where she'd left it in the hallway of her house, tossed under a table, in a panic, on her brief stop there between the airport and the hospital.

Garrett had gone to work, and the baby was napping in a patch of sunlight that poured green and gold through the front door onto the living room floor. It was a warm late-summer day. The phone had been unplugged the night before, and stayed that way. She hadn't turned the television on once since they'd come home. The silence swelled and receded in a manner that would have been imperceivable to her only two weeks before, but which now seemed sacred, full of implication, a kind of immaculate tableau rolled out over the neighborhood in the middle of the day when no one was anywhere, and only the cats crossed the streets, padding in considerate quiet on their starry little paws. She glanced at the black bag.

She got down on her knees and pulled the bag to her, and removed the umbrella, and the pink makeup bag, and the folded black sweater, the brother's name, *Mack Kaloustian* (but hadn't the stranger said he was his mother's only son?), and saw it there, the box, in its gold paper, and recognized it only vaguely, as neither a gift nor a recrimination, a threat, or a blessing.

She didn't open it, but imagined herself opening it. Imagined herself as a passenger on that plane, unable to resist it. Holding it to her ear. Shaking it, maybe. Lifting the edge of the gold paper, tearing it away from the box. And then, the certain, brilliant cataclysm that would follow. The lurching of unsteady weight in the sky, and then the inertia, followed by tumbling. The numbing sensation of great speed and realization in your face. She'd been a fool to take it with her onto the plane. It could have killed them all.

Or, the simple gold braid of it.

Tasteful. Elegant. A thoughtful gift chosen by a devoted son for his beloved mother. And she imagined taking the necklace out of the box, holding it up to her own neck at the mirror, admiring the glint of it around her neck—this bit of love and brevity snatched from the throat of a stranger—wearing it with an evening gown, passing it down as an heirloom to her children:

Who was to say, she thought to herself as she began to peel the gold paper away, that something stolen, without malice or intent, is any less yours than something you've been given?

LILY KING

Five Tuesdays in Winter

Mitchell's daughter, who was twelve, accused him of loving his books but hating his customers. He didn't *hate* them. He just didn't like having to chat with them, or lead them to very clearly marked sections (if they couldn't read signs, why were they buying books?) while they complained that nothing was arranged by title. He would have liked to have a bouncer at the door, a man with a rippled neck who would turn people away or quietly remove them when they revealed too much ignorance.

His daughter loved the customers. She sat behind the counter at the cash drawer every Saturday, writing up receipts in an illegible imitation of his own microscopic hand and chatting like an innkeeper. She was too tall and too sophisticated for a Maine preteen. She made him uneasy. She had recently learned the word "reticent" and used it on him constantly.

"Isn't he the most reticent person you've ever met?" she asked Kate, his only other employee.

"Maybe not the very most," Kate said, not looking up from her pricing.

"But he's—"

"That's enough, Paula," he said, then, feeling an unexpected pulse of blood to his cheeks, fled to the stockroom in back.

Mitchell had good ears, and just before he shut the door behind him, he heard Kate's gentle reprimand: "I think as a rule people don't like being spoken of in the third person."

He'd hired Kate three months ago. She'd recently moved to Portland from San Francisco for a man named Lincoln. They lived in a small apartment in the East End. On their machine, Lincoln sounded high-strung and full of anticipation, as if he only ever expected good news after the beep. Despite her strong résumé, Kate had unexpected gaps in her knowledge of books. She had never read *The Leopard* or *Independent People.* She had never even heard of Thomas Bernhard. Once he overheard a customer ask how many lines were in a sestina, and she didn't know.

She was a reader (she borrowed and returned as many as ten books a week) but not a speller. On the dupe sheet, she wrote J. Austin and F. Dostoyevski. At the end of the day, when she stapled the credit card receipts to the ticker tape totals, she didn't always align the edges evenly. She let the pencils run out of lead. She had thin, sometimes dry lips which she picked at when she was thinking deeply and which he would have liked to kiss.

Wanting to kiss Kate was like wanting a larger savings account for Paula's college education or one of those infallible computerized postal scales for mail orders. It was a persistent, irritating, useless desire. He had been on two dates since Paula's mother left. The first one, over five years ago now, had been a setup, a friend of a friend. They'd gone to an Italian restaurant for pasta puttanesca. She'd picked out all of her capers and left them on the lip of her bowl, explaining that she was allergic to shellfish. Then she'd wanted to talk about his wife's departure. The story—his college buddy Brad coming to visit from Australia and leaving a week later with a box of live lobsters and Mitchell's wife—seemed to arouse her. He couldn't bear to take her out again and lost the mutual friend as a result. Thankfully, others had left him alone.

He hadn't been devastated when his wife walked out. People vanished. It had been happening all his life. His mother died when he was six, his father nine years later. His best friend from childhood, Aaron, had found a lump on his back—Mitchell himself had spotted it first on the beach—and he was dead by Labor Day. Even his favorite customer, Mrs. White, had died within a few years of the shop's opening.

Mitchell stood at the stockroom's one window and watched three gulls flap restlessly above the harbor. Thick broken slabs of ice, the size of mattresses, had been pushed to the shore by the tide. Out farther, beyond the frozen crust, the open water shimmered a luminous summer blue. In these kinds of cold spells everything seemed confused. Even the gulls overhead seemed lost.

Later that afternoon, Paula said, "Kate speaks Spanish." Kate demurred from where she was shelving, but Paula overrode her. "She does. Did you know that, Dad?"

"Mmm-hmmm." He was going through a mildewed carton a student had just brought in. They were good books, without writing or highlighting on any page, but the bottom edge of nearly every one had a pen and ink drawing of a hairy testicle.

"That's my icon, in my frat," the student said. "It's a—"

"I *know* what it is." Mitchell was sharp, even for Mitchell.

Paula glowered. She was trying to train him to be more forgiving of his patrons. That was her campaign, ever since she'd grown tall, learned words like reticent, and found him flawed.

After the frat boy had gone, Paula said, "I was thinking. Kate could help with my Spanish conversation."

Kate approached the counter as if she were a customer. "I'm not a teacher. I just lived in Peru for a couple of years."

"Are you fluent?"

He could see from her face that it was a rigid question. "By the time I left I could say pretty much anything I wanted. But it's been six years now."

She would have been living in Peru when his wife left. He hoped, with an uncomfortable swell of feeling, that she had been happy there, that if his and Paula's life had been redirected, like the course of a river, she had been the recipient of those higher waters. Full of this fervent thought, he headed, for a reason he'd forgotten, to anthropology.

Paula found him there, staring blankly at the spines on the shelf. "She said she could come on Tuesday evenings. Can she?"

"If you think it will help."

"I've *told* you Mr. Camargo never lets us speak."

He did not say that she'd never mentioned this before.

To the store, Kate wore faded, untucked shirts and jeans slashed at the knee. He was often tempted to tease her, tell her that just because she sold used books she didn't have to wear used clothes, but he thought she might snap back with a crack about the pittance he paid her, so he refrained. To the first Spanish lesson, however, Kate walked up the path to his door in wool pants the color of cranberries. Tuesday was her day off. Perhaps she'd had a late lunch date downtown with Lincoln. Worse, she might have had a job interview. It was an easy thing to find out. She was the type who could not take a compliment. If he told her she looked nice, she'd give the reason instead of saying thank you. But he was the type who could not give a compliment, so he just said hello and let her in.

Paula called from her room, and he directed Kate down the hallway. The door clicked shut, and he heard no Spanish, just peals of laughter, for the next half-hour.

He'd planned to do some paperwork before starting dinner, but when he sat down at his desk, he pulled out Kate's application instead. 2/14/68. Just as he'd remembered. She was well into her thirties, plenty old enough to be Paula's mother. So what was she doing in there, giggling like a seventh-grader? Her birthday was coming up. On Valentine's Day, no less. Maybe she'd quit before then. She might expect a gift, or he might want to give her a little something and she'd take it the wrong way. Or Lincoln would.

They emerged from Paula's bedroom rosy-cheeked and watery-eyed, speaking gibberish. He quickly slipped the application back in its file.

"*Entonces, nos vemos el sábado, ¿no?*" Kate said.

"*¿Sábado? Sí.*"

They passed his desk without noticing him.

"*Bueno. Hasta luego, Paula.*" She added an extra half-syllable to his daughter's name.

"*Adiós, Caterina.*"

They kissed on both cheeks, as if in Paris.

He waved from his chair, not wanting to break the flow with the clunk of English.

When she came to their house the next Tuesday, she wrote down on a slip of paper (a bank receipt, he saw later, that stated she had $57.37 in her account) from her coat pocket her new address and phone number. She was moving closer to the store.

"With Lincoln?" Paula asked, and Mitchell for once was grateful for her prying.

"No," Kate said, as if she might say more, then didn't.

"Why not? He has such perfect teeth."

Paula read the question on Mitchell's face and said, "She showed me a picture of him."

Long after she'd gone, he got up from his reading to start supper and realized the slip of paper was still crushed in his hand.

The second and last date Mitchell had had since his wife left was with a woman who worked in the insurance office next to his store. Sometimes she'd come in when she got off work, and even though she talked too much and only looked at the oversized books with photos in any given section, he agreed to go to the movies with her when she got up the nerve to ask him. They chose a comedy, but she kept whispering in his ear right before every joke, so that everyone in the audience was always laughing except them. He'd come out of the theater excruciatingly unsatisfied, far more unsatisfied than a movie whose jokes he'd missed should have left him. He felt abstracted and disjointed, and it occurred to him that the sensation was only a slight magnification of what he felt all the time. He couldn't wait to get back to his car in the store parking lot and drive away. But she was in an entirely different mood. She nearly twirled down the street, swayed not too subtly against him, and asked if he'd like to get a coffee. He said no, without excuse.

The next day while he was unpacking a shipment of remainders in the stockroom, he heard her through the wall. She was on the phone with a friend. "No," she said, "it wasn't that bad. It was fun, actually... Yeah, he is, but I kind of like that..." (Huge hoot of laughter.) "I *do*... All right, details. Let's see... The high point? Oh God. Let's see..." Mitchell left the box half full and went back to the front of the store. That day he didn't stay till closing but left at quarter of five. He did this for a week straight until one evening when his former employee, the employee before Kate, had a dentist's appointment and he'd had to stay. She didn't come in. She never came in again. He saw her crossing the street once, and another time she was behind him at Westy's, the takeout place up the block, but they didn't speak. He couldn't say when he stopped seeing her altogether, when she must have left the insurance company, over a year ago, maybe two.

He listened to Kate's new message: *Hi. I'm not here. Say something funny, and I'll get back to you.* But her voice was not hopeful. It was the voice of someone stuck in Maine for no good reason.

The only time he ever got any information about her was on Tuesdays and Saturdays. The rest of the week, without Paula, they worked together in the uninterrupted professionalism he'd established the first week of her employment. It was as if she'd never stood in his living room or giggled in Spanish with his daughter. He often hoped that Paula would bring up Kate's name in the evenings, let something slip about her he didn't know, but she never did. She spoke instead of teachers, friends, projects, a concert she wanted to go to. In history she was studying Watergate, and she wanted to know what he knew about it. His friend Aaron had been an intern in DC that summer of the hearings, the summer before Mitchell saw the hard knot on his spine. He and Aaron had talked on the phone a lot, sometimes until two or three in the morning, passionate talk about the implications of impeachment and then, that hot August, the resignations. Paula waited for Mitchell's version of the events, but what he remembered most now about Watergate was the feeling of being nineteen in a one-room apartment, and the sound, though it had been silent for so many years now, of Aaron's hyena laugh. Finally, when he began to describe the break-in, Paula said she already knew all that, and when he said that it was the end of an era, the government's undeniable breach of faith with its people, she said her teacher explained that, too. So he told her about his one-room apartment and how Aaron's laugh nearly broke his eardrums, and she was inexplicably satisfied.

On the third Tuesday, as Kate was leaving, the phone rang. Paula ran to answer it. It was for her, of course, so Mitchell walked their guest to the door alone. She was dressed up again; she had put her coat on carefully so as not to wrinkle her soft ivory shirt. She had thin, straight hair that she'd probably complained about (as Paula had about hers) all her life, but which was clean and shiny and soft-looking. Again he wanted to say how nice she looked but instead said that he hoped she was keeping careful record of her tutoring hours. She nodded that she was and told him he didn't have to keep reminding her. He was embarrassed she remembered he'd said this before. It was his default line; it came out of his mouth when he wanted to say other things to her.

He watched her walk to her car, which, during the lesson, had received a light coating of snow. He wondered if she'd brush off all the windows, or just the front and back. She didn't do any of them. She just got into the car, put on the wipers, and, without looking sideways to see him standing unconcealed at the window of his brightly lit living room, drove away.

"Kate has a date," Paula said, catching him in the act of watching her car disappear around the corner.

"Lincoln?" he asked hopefully, more comfortable with an old rival than a new one.

"They're over. With some guy she met at the store."

"My store?"

"She just said *tienda,* but I think so."

"She told you this in Spanish?"

"That's why she's here, isn't it?"

"Sí," Mitchell ventured uneasily.

The next day he told Kate she'd have to start addressing fliers for the sale he had every April.

"I don't mind at all, but you do know it's only the first of February."

He remembered her approaching birthday and the dilemma about Valentine's, and said, "There are over a thousand to send out, so we should get started on it."

He set her up in his office in the back, and waited on the thin stream of customers himself.

"Call if you need help," she'd said before he shut her in.

"I will." But he knew even if there was a line ten deep he wouldn't call.

Around two, a young man in a dark green parka came up to the counter. Mitchell knew he was going to ask for Kate, and when he did, he explained that she was busy at the moment. He was careful not to indicate in which direction she was so busy. Unperturbed, the man asked where the art section was, then slowly made his way towards it, lingering at the new arrival bin, the poetry shelves, mythology, psychology, before arriving at art. If he pulled out a book, he replaced it exactly as it had been, flush with the other spines and the edge of its shelf, just as Mitchell liked them. But he had bad posture, which made the bottom of the coat hang away from his body.

He could see Kate looking at her watch as she came out of his office. He couldn't think of any way to keep her from coming forward.

She looked down all the aisles until she found him.

"Hey," Mitchell heard her say.

"How're you doing?"

"A little disoriented." She flexed her hand, the one that had been addressing fliers for the past five hours. Her friend didn't ask why, and Mitchell was pleased that he shared this information with Kate alone. "Let's go," she said. Mitchell's spirits plummeted.

She hadn't mentioned leaving early. She had to stay until six. She came around the counter to get her coat and scarf. "I'm going to grab something at Westy's. Want anything?"

He'd forgotten all about lunch. "No," he said, even though he was suddenly starving. "Only mushroom soup."

It was a very small joke they had. Once, about four years ago, Westy's had served, for one day, the most delicious mushroom soup he'd ever tasted. They'd never offered it again, but he'd never stopped looking on the specials board for it, every time he went in. Occasionally he put in a request, but the teenager at the register clearly had no say over soups.

Commercial Street was covered in a thick, lumpy layer of ice, and they crossed it slowly without touching. But they were talking a lot. Blue puffs came out of their mouths at the same time. They opened the door to Westy's and disappeared. They'd probably eat at one of the booths. He couldn't very well complain if once in the three months she'd been working there she ate her lunch there instead of bringing it back.

There was a couple in the far room whispering in fiction. He'd been pricing a stack of books he'd just bought from a composer, but now that Kate was gone he'd lost his concentration. He went down the aisle her friend had chosen, and pulled out, one by one, the books he'd looked at. Each one was a decent book in a sea, he acknowledged with familiar shame, of mediocre books. He would have liked to have an intensely intellectual selection—no confessional poetry, no mass market psychology, no coffee table crap. But as it was, business was precarious. Most intellectuals were like the composer: selling, not buying. A few days ago, a woman had come in with swatches of fabric and asked him to find books only in those colors. Last week a man had been looking for *War and Peace,* and when Mitchell explained that he was temporarily out of anything by Tolstoy, the man asked if he had it by anyone else. It was a terrible time for books.

"Hey, where are you?" She pulled on his sleeve. "I got it! Mushroom soup!" She held up two containers. She was smiling as wide as he'd ever seen. Her nose was red and dripping and beautiful. "It better be as good as you promised."

Hadn't she already eaten? Where was the guy in the green coat? How much did he owe her? Questions swarmed but stayed behind the tight knot in his mouth.

There was always one stool behind the counter and another that he used to prop open the door in summer, which now stood by the coat rack nobody ever used. He'd once wanted the store to be a homey place, the sort of place where you come in and hang up your coat and stay awhile, but it never had been. He'd never given any customer the impression that he wanted them to stay awhile. Kate found this other stool and dragged it around back, so that the two stools were now side by side, with a bowl of mushroom soup on the counter in front of each one.

He felt as if he would burst. He'd read about this feeling in novels, but he was sure he'd never experienced it. Meeting his wife had brought him pleasure, or a sort of relief, the mystery of whom to spend his life with solved—or so he'd thought. But he'd actually been fairly content before he met her, talking on the phone with Aaron, eating tuna in his little room, reading from the stacks of books borrowed from the store he now owned.

They took a long lunch. Customers, as always, were irritating and disruptive. They were worse in this kind of weather. There was a focus that went out of people's eyes. They often forgot what they were looking for and lingered absent-mindedly in the aisles. When an elderly woman finally made it out the door, Kate grunted, imitating the way he had responded to her gratitude for finding her a book.

"It was *Middlemarch*," he explained.

"Which is a great book."

"I *know* it's a great book." He was aware of how much like Paula he sounded when he whined. "But shouldn't she have read it by now? She's only a hundred and thirty-seven years old."

"She could be reading it for the hundred and thirty-seventh time. Or she could be giving it to her granddaughter. Or great-granddaughter." She seemed amused, entirely uninterested in changing him. He knew it was like that at first, with anyone. He also knew it might mean that she didn't care about him at all.

He tried to think of what it really was that had bothered him about the old woman. For once in his life, the thought turned instantly to speech, before he could stop it. "I miss Mrs. White."

"What?"

"An old woman who used to come in here."

"What was she like?"

Mitchell hadn't thought about the actual Mrs. White in a long time. When he thought about her now it was just a feeling, not a person, just a deep longing. He hadn't known her very well. She used to sit on the hard pink chair in science, reading Stephen Jay Gould. They'd shared a laugh once, when a girl a few years older than Paula moved swiftly through the store to the picture of Thomas Pynchon which hung on the back wall, and burst into tears. It was the only picture of Pynchon available then, and not many people had ever seen even that, a reproduction of his high school yearbook photo, teeth like a donkey's. "The only person who should cry over that picture is his mother," Mrs. White had said.

Kate allowed him his silence. She didn't try to reframe the question or ask another. Mrs. White would have done the same thing. *What was she like?* She was like you, he realized, watching Kate bend to take a sip of her soup.

"She was like you," he said, incredulous.

The following day he couldn't bear her to be so far from him, and told her, at the risk of her finding more dates, that she didn't have to spend more than an hour a day addressing fliers. He stayed at the counter with her, but they spoke very little. He pored through the boxes of books people lugged in from their cars, she took money from the customers, and in between they priced in silence. He wanted to ask her if she was planning to move back to San Francisco, or somewhere else, but every time he rehearsed it in his head, it sounded like a boss's question and not a friend's. Just before closing a customer came up to the counter and asked if they were related. "You two have the exact same kind of eyes," he told them. He was drunk, and the comment was preposterous. Kate had warm thick-lidded brown eyes, and his were a narrow, suspicious green. The man didn't have a coat, and they watched him lurch away into the frozen air. They were careful not to look at each other's eyes. It was only yesterday, the day of the mushroom soup, but it was already far away.

Mitchell comforted himself with the thought of Saturday, the day after next, when Paula would be there with them. But that night she told him she had play practice in the morning—she'd been cast as Uncle Max in *The Sound of Music*—and that her friend Holly had invited her over afterwards.

Once he recovered from that blow, he saw on his calendar that the fourteenth of February fell on a Tuesday, the fifth Tuesday of Spanish lessons.

Saturday then Tuesday came and went, eventless. On Wednesday and on Friday it snowed. He woke up in the middle of the night thinking about snow clinging to the ends of Kate's hair and the slope of her back when she sat on the stool, then scolded himself until dawn. He tried to think of how to mention, offhand, to Paula that Kate's birthday was approaching. But, as usual, she was three steps ahead of him. "I completely forgot to tell you," she said at dinner. "I asked Kate to stay for dinner next Tuesday. It's her *cumpleaños*."

"Her birthday?" He feigned uncertainty.

"Have you been listening at the door, Dad?"

He wished he had the nerve.

"What should we get her?" Paula asked.

"How about a brooch?" he suggested.

"A brooch? What's that?"

"You know, a sparkly," he put his fingers on his chest, "pin thing."

"Oh my God. You are not serious."

"Then make her something."

"Like what?"

"I don't know. A drawing. A necklace. Or, what about doing what you used to do to the gravel?"

"Dad!"

Mitchell, remembering the hours Paula spent with her rock polisher, lamented the loss of the driveway as a primary source of entertainment and gifts. He knew he'd have to drive Paula to the mall.

They saw Kate there that Sunday in the food court. She was eating a burrito, alone. Both he and Paula had the same irrational impulse to conceal themselves for fear that she would guess their purpose, and shadow her through the shops in order to discover her preferences. After lunch, she went to the perfume counters in Filene's. A saleslady offered her some powder on a brush, but Kate shook her head and said something that made the woman laugh. Mitchell's chest contracted slightly at being denied the words. Then they watched her weave through the smaller stores and their red streamers and glittering hearts and loud reminders with the words *Sweetheart* and *Someone Special.*

"She seems sad," Paula said.

Mitchell was relieved she'd noticed. He thought it was just his own wishful thinking.

Kate didn't buy anything. They watched her leave the mall, scan the parking lot for her car, then head toward it. There was nothing outside—not above or below or in the woods beyond the mall—that wasn't some shade of gray. The cold had eased, and everything that had been solid was now a thick, filthy sludge.

"It's an awful time of year to have a birthday."

Paula agreed. They stood at the door Kate had walked through. She unlocked her car, lifted her long coat in behind her, shut the door, and sat for at least a minute before starting the engine. She'd been born in Swanton, Ohio. She'd had her appendix removed. She didn't like green peppers or people in costumes or Henry James. She had a mole on her head, just where her part began. With only this handful of facts, he admitted to himself, as Paula drew hearts in the clouds she breathed on the plate glass, he'd begun to truly care for her.

They bought her a brooch and went home.

His wife had left because she claimed he was locked shut. She said the most emotion he'd ever shown her had been during a heated debate about her use of a comma in a note she'd left him about grocery shopping.

There was no reason why anything would be different, why he would be able to make anyone happier now. He was the same person. He'd always been the same person. He marveled how in books people looked back fondly to remembered selves as if they were lost acquaintances. But he'd never been anything but this one self. Perhaps it was because physically there'd been little change; he'd lost no hair, gained no weight, grown no beard. He'd read a great deal in the past twenty years, but nothing that threatened his view of the world or his own minuscule place within it.

Still, on the fifth Tuesday, as Mitchell made dinner during the lesson, the lasagna noodles quivered in his hands as he placed them in the pan. He was as nervous as a schoolgirl. He wondered where that expression came from, for he had never seen Paula ever behave this way. Nervous as a forty-seven-year-old bookseller was how the saying should go.

Kate had arrived with a small heart-shaped box of chocolates, which he'd set on a table in the living room. He'd been so startled by the gift he hadn't taken in the rest of her, and now he couldn't picture her in Paula's room, sitting at the foot of the bed where they always sat (he'd often seen the indentation after she'd gone). Every now and then, as he went about preparing dinner, Mitchell glanced through the open doorway at the box of chocolates.

He was just putting the lasagna in the oven when Kate flew past.

"Where're you going?" he said, unable to conceal his horror as she flung her coat over her shoulders without bothering to fit her arms in the sleeves, and reached for the door.

"I'll be right back." The door slammed shut, and he heard her holler from the walkway, "She'll be fine."

He went to his daughter's room. The door was open, but she wasn't in it. On her quilt on the bed was a dark red stain and a few pale streaks. Her bathroom door was shut. He stood in silence before it.

"I'm okay, Dad." She sounded like she was hanging upside down.

"You sure?" He couldn't control the wobble in his voice.

"Kate's gone to get some stuff."

He actually already had "stuff" in his bathroom; he'd bought it for her years ago, just in case. "That's good," he said.

He felt pleased that he was not overreacting, that he knew right away what had happened and hadn't called an ambulance. And then he looked down and saw the blood up close. He was holding the quilt in his arms. He didn't remember taking it off the bed. It was a quilt his mother had made and he had slept beneath as a child. The mottled stains seemed like warnings. Soon Paula would begin complaining that he didn't understand her, didn't appreciate her, didn't love her enough, when in fact he loved her so much his heart often felt shredded by it. But people always wanted words for all that roiled inside you.

"How do you feel?" he ventured.

"All right. Kinda weird."

"Your mother used to get terrible cramps." He waited for the clutch that came with talking about her, like someone had grabbed him by the chest hair. "She got headaches sometimes, too. She took extra iron. We probably still have some. They're green, in a white bottle." He waited, but the clutching feeling never came. "And she had a bullet birth when you were born, you know. Thirty-five minutes, I think. We barely made it to the hospital. Not that you want to be thinking of that right now." Sweat prickled his scalp. Shut up, he told himself. "One time she was wearing these white pants and—"

"Do you miss her, Dad?"

"No." He was astonished by the truth of it.

"I don't, either, anymore. I feel like I *should* miss her. All I really remember is her walking me to school and holding my hand and giving me big hugs at the door. But I always knew the minute she turned her back I was out of her mind completely. She wasn't like you. I knew you were thinking about me always."

She was revising now, creating new memories out of what she was left with, but his eyes stung, anyway.

When Kate came back from the pharmacy, he retreated to the kitchen. He could hear her coaching Paula, first in the bathroom and then through the door. At times her voice was serious and precise; other times they were both laughing. After a long while, she came in the kitchen. She caught him standing there in the middle of the room, doing nothing. She touched the quilt in his arms. "If I run cold water on it now, it won't stain."

"I'll do it." He went down the narrow back hallway to the laundry room with the big basin, and she followed. He never expected her to follow.

He turned on the faucet. "You may have to undo some stuff I told her while you were gone. I babbled on about iron and pregnancy and probably scared the lights out of her."

"You babbled? I thought you were the most reticent man in the world."

"Every forty-seven years or so I babble."

She still had her coat on. It must have started snowing again. Melted flakes glinted like stars all over her.

They had to do the quilt bit by bit, wringing out one part before starting on another. He wished, as in a fairy tale, the cloth would never end, and they could spend the rest of their lives washing and wringing.

He heard the timer buzz, then the oven door squeak open.

They hung the quilt on the fishing line he'd strung up years ago. When they were done he could do nothing but look at her. She looked carefully back. Paula called them to dinner, but they made no move toward the kitchen.

"Why do you think," he asked her, "that man said we had the same eyes?"

"Maybe he saw something similar in them."

"Like what?"

"Fear." She looked away. He'd forgotten how disappointing these conversations could be.

"Desire," she added quietly.

Love, he thought. It would come out soon enough. Words and feelings were all churned up together inside him, finding each other like lost parts of an atom. He didn't try to push them apart or away. He let them float in the new fullness in his chest.

She brought her hand to his face. It wasn't the face other women had touched. The skin wasn't the same. His nerve endings had multiplied. He could feel each one of her fingers, their different sizes and temperatures. His stomach made a long slow twist in anticipation of all that his lips would feel.

He pulled Kate close, but Paula came around the corner then, and they jumped back. His daughter took them each by the arm and led them to dinner. She'd lit a candle and poured apple juice into wineglasses. She'd put the heart of chocolates by his place. Lasagna sizzled in the center of the small table, and Kate was smiling. Mitchell felt that a long conversation was just beginning, and, if only for this moment in his kitchen, if only for this one winter evening, he had a lot to say.

KATHLEEN LEE

The Shadow of Love

Olivia Alcuaz set down platters of spaghetti, tortillas, tomato and cucumber salad. She sat, lifted her chest as if she were in posture class, and launched into a tale about her cousin Enrique. Enrique had been driving down from Mexico when there were reports of a terrible crash involving a white car. Enrique's car was white, so Olivia and her son, Fritz, drove out to the accident site. They battled their way to the front, through a mess of traffic and hysteria, shouting, We are relatives of people in the accident. When they arrived at the scene, there was Enrique, stuck on the other side of a barrier, peacefully eating an apple. "Aiee! Enrique!" said Olivia.

The next story was about a woman whose two children died within a year of each other; the daughter in a car accident on a road in the mountains, the son murdered in the capital city. The silence at the table was reverential, the air slightly electric, as in a flirtation. Olivia addressed Ellen, her large, coy eyes limpid with emotion. Although Olivia's Spanish was clear and measured, Ellen relied on her capacity to guess and surmise meaning from a tangle of language. Ellen listened without contributing to the conversation—ever since the day when she thought she'd said she liked sausages, but instead had said that she liked tits. Silence was a virtue; those who listened had power. At least they weren't likely to commit acts of self-humiliation.

I've become a part of this family, Ellen imagined telling Charlie. The meals resemble episodes of an American talk show in which being a victim is an exalted condition, approaching sainthood. Tears for anointing the sacred, sorrow for entering heaven. Except, she was not, in fact, a member of Olivia's family. And she couldn't tell Charlie.

Jesus and the Apostles looked down from the wall. The dining room was long and narrow, with glass doors leading to a courtyard. Ellen imagined that each dining room in this Central American town was guarded by identical prints of the Last Supper, illustrating a final feeding of the body. Carmencita, la abuelita, obsessively arranged and rearranged the table setting, moving a bowl a half an inch, straightening a napkin, counting spoons. She smiled at Ellen, but avoided speaking to her. Thin and stooped, her temples were sunken, making her forehead bulge. Her soft frizz of gray hair formed a vaguely saint-like halo.

Fritz knocked over a pitcher of water as he sat, then apologized to Don Pablo for drenching him. Don Pablo peered up through the thick, distorting lenses of his eyeglasses and smiled, as if he'd been baptized afresh. Ellen was fond of Don Pablo, who occupied the head of the table like a mushroom. His shrunken figure was barely visible, his chin exactly at the level of the table, so that he shoveled food in a straight line from plate to mouth. Deaf to conversation, he never looked up. Instead he mumbled to himself, his rosy, sagging cheeks jiggling as he chewed. Olivia said he was rich, a former chemistry professor and politician. She said his daughter, who lived in Washington, DC, refused to speak to him; his granddaughter regularly flew him to Boston, but he always returned after a week because he missed his horse—just as decrepit and aged as he was. Olivia gave him bus fare to come in and out of town because he never seemed to have cash, and she reported on his status to his nephew in the capital, who sighed and said, "I am helpless." Don Pablo refused to keep a muchacha to cook and clean for him in the fancy house on his finca, so he ate at Olivia's. Olivia, una matriarca grande, welcomed strays at her table. Every day Don Pablo said he was bringing a squash from his garden for her, but he never did.

Fritz was tall with a heavy, hooked nose, hair hanging in his face, and bloodshot, puffy eyes. He winked at Ellen as he helped himself to spaghetti. He whispered, "Last night, you leave too early. Crazy." Ellen had gone out with Fritz and one of his friends the night before, except she'd only stayed for one drink. Olivia tilted her head and sniffed, then she looked at Ellen in a soft, pained way, her mouth bent. As the only man in the house, Olivia's son, Fritz, was adored. Even though he was twenty-six, everything was provided for him: food, clean clothes, spending money. Ellen poured herself coffee, feeling guilty, as if by going out for a drink with Fritz she'd betrayed Olivia, who hated Fritz's drinking. But, anyway, Ellen was a paying guest, a boarder; loyalty should not be expected of her.

Olivia told more stories: about bus robberies, children bought and sold for their parts, four men murdered the previous week in a nearby town. Each detail, factual or otherwise, was noted with ecstatic lushness. Ellen didn't have to gird herself against sorrow. She didn't feel like crying. She twirled spaghetti onto a fork and leaned over her plate to avoid splashing sauce on one of her two T-shirts. She felt a coolness inside, like opening a refrigerator.

Don Pablo wrapped tortillas and a pile of wet spaghetti into a napkin, then slipped them into his coat pocket, smiling beatifically into the air above the table.

Weekdays, after classes and lunch, Ellen studied on the third floor of the school. There was a roof and two walls to stop the worst of the afternoon winds. The two open sides looked over rooftops to steep hills and the volcano that rose above the town, austere and poised. It had last erupted forty years ago, according to a geologist studying Spanish at the school. Forty years in geological time, he said, was equivalent to less than thirty seconds. Ellen would turn forty in a few months. If she thought of her life, so far, as a thirty-second flash, it shrunk any sense of importance she might mistakenly have.

She memorized and conjugated verbs, and wrote short essays. She was a diligent student, but not a great speaker of Spanish. Ellen wanted to have a clear accent and to learn effortlessly, but in conversation she stopped to think and correct herself, and her American twang flattened Spanish vowels, her tongue stiff and unable to roll the *r*. It reassured her to recall that Charlie, who sang and danced with flair, who cooked divine meals, who could tear apart a car engine, then put it back together, had been terrible at learning foreign languages. Ellen needed to speak Spanish to the employees of her landscaping company, so this was her life for three months: language instruction five hours a day, and residence in Olivia's house.

Alone on the third floor, she watched the thin veils of steam unfurling from vents in the mountain. Her notebook was open, her homemade flashcards stacked before her while her mind lay down like a dog in the street, indifferent to the fact that anybody might see the pale tenderness of its exposed belly.

Tomorrow, it would be a year since Charlie had disappeared while on a climbing trip in Pakistan. He wasn't her husband—he was somebody else's husband. Someone he'd left but hadn't yet divorced. Her sister had said, "Make him tell her he's involved with someone else. It's unfair to her and to you. It's dishonest." But if Ellen told him what to do, how would she know his feelings were genuine? When he disappeared she felt abruptly rendered invisible. Well, perhaps that was a bit dramatic. Still, what kind of karma was it, to meet someone you really liked, only to have him disappear and then have to pretend as if you hadn't ever massaged his shoulders, bit his earlobe, smelled his warm neck?

"Hola, Elena, qué tal?" Fernando snuck up on her beneath the noise of palms flailing the wind, pulled a chair close, took out his guitar, and fixed Ellen with that desirous, mournful look of his. The beautiful Fernando. He appeared every afternoon, even, she imagined, when she wasn't there.

He strummed a few chords, tuned the guitar, and launched into a song. Before becoming a Spanish instructor to foreigners, he'd been a professional musician, so these impromptu performances were no sloppy sing-alongs. His voice was deep and thrilling, lifting and meeting the wind. The only word she understood was amore, love. His eyes, tidy black seeds, settled on her. His expression was solemn, as if he were working.

Where was she supposed to look during these serenades? She shifted her gaze from the volcano to his face, to his hands on the guitar, to her notebook, and then around again.

He stopped playing. "Comprendes?"

She shook her head. She hadn't even been trying to understand, wondering instead if she appeared to him as the clod she felt herself to be—a giant American woman, stumbling through a graceful language, crashing around a country of petite people. Ellen was what was politely called lanky. She was tall and thin, with kneecaps that looked like buried baseballs. But her eyes, gray as cloudy weather, were soft and expressive, and her pale skin, she'd been told, was exquisite to touch. She wore her thick, straight hair cut short so that in her own mind, she was a pin—thin and straight with a little hard head at the top.

He explained, in rapid, liquid Spanish, that the song was about two lovers (what a surprise!) who could not be together—was it illness, or her parents wouldn't allow it, or what? Anyway, some reason. A sad song, Fernando admitted. All love songs are sad, she said. Was that true? Silence. They stared at each other.

There was nothing hidden or subtle about Fernando and his intentions. You never wondered, Is he attracted to me? Carnivorous, Ellen thought. Lust was carnivorous. She couldn't insinuate the word *love* into whatever inappropriate thing was going on. For one thing, he was an instructor at the school—not her instructor, but still. And his hands were smaller than hers; she stared at them picking at the guitar strings. His feet were like a boy's, his waist like a girl's. He was perfectly proportioned with graceful features and deep eyes: a small thing of beauty.

"Demasiado trágico," Fernando said. "Como, ahhh." His breath exhaled in a fluttering sigh.

What would she possibly do with him? She smiled.

"Why are you smiling?"

"I was thinking of my sister." Of how they loved to add the phrase "in bed" onto Chinese fortune cookies. You are lucky to have many friends; in bed. When winter comes, heaven will rain fortune on you; in bed. Be on the alert for new opportunity; in bed. But she didn't tell Fernando this.

"Is your sister like you?"

"Better. Smarter, prettier, shorter, more responsible, married with children." Silence, made loud by the wind threshing the palms against the sky. Her mind was blank, separated from her body, one knee touching his.

"Why aren't you married," he said.

"I've told you already, I like solitude." She was in never-never land; never married, never had children. Maybe she would have married Charlie, maybe she would have been happy with him. She would never know. Never know, never yes, never no. "Why do you keep asking?" The hormonal bubble burst, she was herself again. "You've already got your foreign girlfriend. Besides, I'm ten years older than you." Two of the many reasons why she shouldn't grant this flirtation her attention.

He looked away. "You are so frank." Then he laughed. "I like foreign women. And I like older women." Softly, he rubbed his knee against hers. "Older women have more to give."

A baldly selfish sentiment. She fidgeted in her chair, taking her knee out of his reach. Give what? Not for her this abundance of giving; she felt crêpey and dry inside.

"A mí no me gusta la soledad." He didn't like to be alone.

Another way in which we're different, she said. Generally Ellen had flings, not relationships. She and Charlie had been together for nine months, a long haul. Of her nearly forty years, Ellen had spent perhaps three with steady boyfriends. Not an impressive record.

"Como, ahhh," Fernando sighed. "Demasiado trágico."

Bastante, suficiente, demasiado: enough, sufficient, excessive.

The director of the school appeared at the top of the stairs. She told Ellen there was a fax for her, but she looked at Fernando. A look full of remonstrance. Fernando pushed out his chest and said, "Meet me at the Shanghai, at eight?" He addressed Ellen, but watched the director. What was going on? A question she asked herself a hundred times a day.

They hadn't yet met outside the school. Inside her head she chanted no, no, no, while she nodded in agreement. Why not, after all. He was leaving soon, and so was she. She stubbed her broken pencil like a cigarette into her notebook.

The fax was from Cruz, her foreman. It was in Spanish and English and full of misspellings. He reported that they'd finished servicing all the machines; what next? When was she coming home? In nine days; she counted them on the calendar in her notebook.

At the house on Calle Querido, Olivia was frying plátanos in the kitchen, standing back from the pan to prevent grease from spattering her silky blouse. She was in her sixties, and she was careful about her appearance: a touch of mascara and liner, makeup to smooth her complexion, lipstick before she went out shopping or to mass. Ellen thought how Charlie would have loved plátanos fixed this way, how he would have been amused by Olivia's fondness for familial dramas.

Olivia was upset because Fritz refused to speak with Claudia, his brother's wife, not even buenas tardes, he hated her so much, and now Claudia's father had had a stroke. At least, this was what Ellen guessed from the torrent of language. So many relatives and friends came through Olivia's house and were featured in her conversation that Ellen couldn't keep relationships straight. Olivia was tenacious in her preoccupation with the troubles of others. But what of her own disasters? Olivia's husband was absent. He was either in Germany or in the capital or in some other Central American country. He had either been kicked out by Olivia, or he had abandoned her. Ellen never knew if something was genuinely obscure, or if the obscurity was due to her bad Spanish. She wondered what tore Olivia's heart into pieces, what made opening her eyes in the morning an act of desolation, what made her soul lie awake at night, chewing itself into bits?

Putting beans into a bowl, Olivia launched into an account of the collapse of some bleachers at a soccer game in the capital in which twenty people had died. She had heard from a friend that someone she knew—a friend of a distant cousin, or something like that—had lost five sons in the tragedy. Ellen felt like Olivia's confessor. She listened carefully, sympathetically; she gave herself headaches trying to make connections and understand.

Dinner—black beans, plátanos, white cheese, and tortillas—was a somber affair, with only women present. Fritz was out, as usual, and Don Pablo was presumably in his expansive, empty house eating leftover spaghetti, or perhaps he fed that to his chickens and ate nothing. Marisol, daughter of a friend, arrived. She was in her twenties with thick, soft lips reddened with lipstick, sultry eyes, and a pillowy chest. She lifted her fork the way she would remove her blouse, and she chewed as if she were kissing. Ellen imagined her lying down on a bed, opening her legs, taking a bath in some man's desire. With Marisol at dinner, the room became warm and languid.

Olivia tried once again to theorize why four men had been killed by a mob in a small town in the mountains several weeks earlier, as if that might give her some purchase on the soccer stadium deaths, which seemed to be too fresh and tender for direct analysis and discussion. Then she turned to the topic of Pedro, a young man in the neighborhood who had cerebral palsy. The doctors had told his mother, Sophia, that he'd contracted the disease because she had refused to have a C-section and the baby became infected with fluid. Sophia had had a difficult life. Oh, such a lovely woman, muy amable, gentile, linda. Sophia's aunt had been an intellectual, a professor of political science married to a decorated WWII soldier from France. The aunt was thought to be a communist, and when the guerilla war started, masked government soldiers gunned her down outside the Institute of Women where she worked. Except she didn't die. On her third day in the hospital, her niece Sophia there to spend the night with her, the soldiers entered and shot the aunt dead. Olivia's face was shining with sorrow and grace, and Ellen felt a rush of admiration and affection for her, for her capacity to excavate suffering so thoroughly and regularly, two meals a day. Carmencita smiled, deaf to the tragic. And Marisol was damp with sympathy. There was a long moment of respectful silence before Olivia sighed and said, Oh, the soccer stadium deaths.

Fernando and Ellen sat in a red naugahyde booth in the Shanghai, the town's Chinese restaurant, a blond plastic table between them. Fernando ordered fries, and they split a beer. He and Ellen traded Spanish and English. It was this talk that thrilled her, the way her lips moved, the way her tongue lifted and fluttered, and the obscurity of meaning all made her heart beat hard. The feel of unfamiliar words in her mouth was like a stranger's tongue. She sounded simple-minded in Spanish, each sentence constructed from basic words, in the wrong order or form. When she switched to English it was a blessing of fluency, and she fired off sentences, giddy with the effortlessness of it, pleased by her cleverness, her wit, her virtuosity. In English, Fernando was vulnerable and exposed, mispronouncing words and delivering sentences without verbs. They traded their incompetence back and forth, as if they were undressing, then dressing up, then stripping again. The waitresses turned off all the lights in the restaurant except for the one over their table. Fernando asked for five more minutes, and one of the women shook her head, no. An ugly pale dog with pink eyes began to run around the restaurant, barking, toenails clicking on the linoleum. Fernando was going to the capital in a day or two and then flying to Switzerland to meet his girlfriend.

He insisted on walking her home. The streets were dark and empty. Their shoulders touched as they tried to fit side-by-side on the narrow sidewalk.

"You have a boyfriend, right?" Fernando asked, drawing his shoulder free of hers.

"If I had a boyfriend, I wouldn't be flirting with you." My boyfriend is dead. Maybe.

"Como, ahhh. You are so frank." He looked exasperated. "But that is unusual. Women are not loyal. Do you think I'm faithful?"

"No."

"It's difficult, eh? Sometimes you just meet someone you really like." He stopped and took her hand, laced his fingers through hers. The international signal of impending intimacy. She rolled her eyes. They were on a dark street corner, near the Blue Angel café, which was closed. Dogs barked.

"I want to have some memory of you," he said.

"Yeah, well." Ellen felt brisk, resistant to the mush of love, the press of lust. She had a sudden resentment against romance; so much trouble, so little payoff. Or, the results could be huge, painfully so.

He pushed up against her and licked her throat with the strong point of his tongue. He maneuvered her into a corner, and she felt the cobbled stones of the street beneath her feet. A dog barked from behind a wall, and a large speckled one ran past. "No olvidas los perros," he said, against her mouth.

"No. Not like a couple of adolescents." She grabbed his hand, held it still.

"Sí. Necesitamos una cama." What about your room? he wanted to know.

Absolutely not. Ellen's room abutted onto Olivia's—the door between telegraphing phone conversations and television shows.

"Nothing is going to happen," she said. They kept kissing. She forgot how small he was, and she had a sudden, inappropriate desire to laugh. How inglorious: groping in a back street that smelled of rotting fruit and dog shit. Romance.

They went through the discussion about her room once again; he showed her a condom he had in his pocket, full of hope. He pinched her left nipple. "It's going to end like this. Como, ahhh, nada, al final."

They stood in silence, his fingers strumming her ribs.

Outside the house on Calle Querido, he kissed her mouth and both cheeks. She thought for a moment that he might be the love of her life about to disappear forever. Everyone was dipped in a yearning for romance. He turned to look at her three times before blending into the darkness. She stood outside the door until he was gone from sight, not because she loved him, but because it took her that long to feel the black moonless night pressing against her, like a cool hand stroking her forehead.

When Ellen closed the front door, it was midnight, and the house was in an uproar. Fritz had just called from a disco to say he was going to be late. Olivia was certain that he and his friend, who had a car, were drunk and would get in an accident. Once, in church, she'd been praying to a shrine, which spoke and informed her that Fritz was in danger. Three days later, Fritz broke his arm and nose and something else Ellen didn't understand; he was in the hospital for weeks.

Olivia called a taxi. Before the hallway mirror, she applied fresh lipstick and tied a turquoise scarf around her neck. Fetch the boy home. The plan was to tell Fritz that Carmencita, his abuelita, was ill. At first, Olivia wanted Ellen to stay home and take charge of Carmencita, but what was Ellen to do with an eighty-year-old who could hardly hear, much less understand Ellen's flawed Spanish? Ellen didn't approve of the panicked launching of this expedition. Fritz was an adult, let him encounter his own fate. She didn't approve of lying, or of using the old and infirm to lure the young and risk-hungry. But it was clear that Olivia considered Ellen's participation important. Olivia, Ellen, and Marisol, who was staying over, loaded into the taxi and drove into the night.

The walls and floor of the disco vibrated with the pulse of salsa, making Ellen, posted by the exit, move her hips. Charlie had loved to dance. She stripped down to her T-shirt. Couples matched forward and backward movements, and Ellen felt the stroking, grinding rhythm. Olivia, like an evangelist knocking at the doors of strangers, prowled the dance floor. Marisol sank into the scene, and Ellen watched as a man wrapped an arm around her waist and pulled her tight against him. Marisol seemed to forget the task at hand, submitting dreamily to a session of dry-humping, leaning her head against the stranger's shoulder while he squeezed her ass. Desire was so uncomplicated for some people. Ellen sighed. They weren't going to find Fritz. It didn't matter if she never saw Fernando again, if she never spoke beautiful Spanish, if love was not the answer to anything. She stood against the wall, and nobody touched her, nobody even brushed against her by accident. She allowed herself the dark, secret pleasure of anonymity. She was nowhere; she was no one.

They gave up and returned home to find Carmencita sitting in the bed she shared with Olivia, late-night TV blaring, all the lights on, looking more fit and cheerful than usual. Olivia bugged her eyes out at her mother, snapped the bedroom light off, and hissed that she was supposed to be sick.

In her dream Ellen was trying to remember the future form of salir—to leave. I will leave. He is going to leave. The sounds of traffic and the smell of exhaust creeping from the street into her room woke her up. Her nose, the only exposed part of herself, was cold. She looked at the painting of Jesus on the wall of her room. Each thorn of his crown created a prick in the skin, shown by a line or dot of red paint. Catholicism used such brutal imagery, you'd think it would be adequate preparation for life on earth. Yet everyone was unprepared. On the opposite wall hung a doll by its neck. It looked desolate and suicidal. She dressed quickly and snuck out of the house before breakfast.

On her way to the bus stop, she stepped around drunks passed out on the narrow sidewalks. This morning there was one on the street that smelled of piss with a trickle of blood from where his forehead had hit the concrete. She stared at the line of red against the pale gray of the sidewalk.

She took a bus and then hiked up La Muela, a petite, inactive volcano at the edge of town. Everyone had told her it was dangerous to hike alone, but she had to be outdoors. The country was open, fields of wheat and onions, rolling foothills, views across the valley. The trail passed through cedars, oak, a kind of manzanita, and bushes of yellow daisies, up into tumbled black lava rocks. She glanced around and scanned the trees, wary. Each of Olivia's stories ran through her head.

As she climbed higher, it appeared as if the clouds were drifting below her, as if she had risen above them. Or perhaps the clouds were closer to earth in this country. It didn't take long to arrive at the crater, which had a couple of renegade pines growing from the middle of it. She could hear, in the distance, the thud of blade against wood—someone was cutting down a tree. Clouds drifted past. Her mind was empty for a few minutes, and she simply listened to her breath moving in and out of her lungs. Why had Charlie disappeared? Like a cramp, she felt the intensity of her desire that he not be gone. She bent over. *Please, please.* An ant labored across the sharp lava. It slid down a sheer bit, then turned and went off to the side, black as the rock, petite and dogged.

Charlie had been trekking to the base camp of K2 with two friends, who saw him one minute, looked back for him another minute, and he was gone. Was it an accident, suicide, murder? Was he dead or was he living a new life elsewhere—in Auckland, maybe, or Madagascar? A search and investigation were conducted. Charlie's wife flew to Pakistan, and Ellen fretted at home in Santa Fe. Charlie's friends told her what was happening and kept her existence a secret from Charlie's wife. It was November, and the landscaping season was at an ebb. She planted tulip and daffodil bulbs, her fingers kneading the cold earth. Nothing was discovered, no body, no bit of clothing, no knapsack or water bottle, no witnesses. How do you grieve for someone who isn't definitely dead, isn't definitely yours to mourn? What had she lost?

Although Ellen didn't believe in the rebirthing-past-life-regression approach to life prevalent in Santa Fe, she went to see Rosa, the psychic, who told her that she and Charlie had been brother and sister in their previous lives and the spirits felt it wasn't right for them to be intimate in this lifetime. Maybe he'd stepped off a cliff to avoid a relationship with his former sister. It sounded like complete nonsense, but Ellen felt terrible, nonetheless, which lent a new focus to her misery. This was what the New Age could do for you: implicate you in your own troubles.

She took out a photo of Charlie, in baseball cap and sunglasses, standing at the open door of her work truck. She knew the way his eyes looked behind the sunglasses, warm, affectionate. She had a sudden memory of him pinning her to a bed with his weight, how her rib cage would sag in an accommodating way, how her thinness could tolerate the heft of him. She folded the photo into a clumsy airplane and launched it into the crater. It lifted for half a second in the wind, then plunged into the rocks in a nosedive. If it were a real plane and Charlie were on it, he'd be dead.

She descended the path quickly, stumbling over rocks, as if her luck were on a timer and it might run out. White vapor emerged from two holes at the base. Maybe the volcano was only pretending to be inactive. Then there was a man. Legs spread, he held a machete point down against his left thigh, standing in the middle of the path. She stopped, her heart pounding into her shoulders. He walked towards her, and she looked for signs of evil intent, but all she noticed was how short he was, much shorter than she, and then how beautiful, with a compact, strong body and face like a Mayan god. Was he a bad person?

He lifted her right hand with the point of his machete and waved his left at her. He wanted her? He wanted her things? She took off her watch, not a very good watch, fumbling with the strap. Her movements felt slow and thick. He looked her over, but she didn't wear jewelry, not even earrings. She unslung her knapsack and opened it, showing him her notebook, reading glasses, water bottle, wallet. She gave him all the cash in the wallet, maybe five dollars' worth of currency. She didn't carry her passport, only a copy of it. He folded the bills into his pants pocket, staring into her knapsack sternly. Addressing the practical aspects of handing over her possessions soothed her, but she was aware of their measly nature. He wasn't getting much of a haul. He lifted the edge of her skirt above her knees with the machete, and she felt embarrassed for her bony kneecaps. She was wearing a long skirt and a long-sleeved T-shirt, her sweater wrapped around her waist. He raised the machete. She held her breath and saw, as if from a distance, her head cleaved from her body. Furious, relieved, stomach roiling, body frozen and immobile, she felt hot and cold at once. And if she died now, who would know how? Who would know why? But he only brought the flat side gently down onto her head, pressing her so that she bent over, as if to permit her to throw up. Then he flipped the machete and tapped her under the chin, lifting her slightly. She felt the touch of metal, glimpsed its dull sheen, the sharpness of its edge. She was bent horizontal, and he stepped closer so she had a view of his wide, bare feet; they looked like farm implements. What was he doing? Could she run from a man with a machete? She was in a position of supplication, her hands resting lightly on her knees. She might be bowing or praying. The inside of her head felt enormous, a vacant plain filled with undulant light. How still she felt, as if becalmed. Stalled in a world gone windless. The dirt was soft here; it was a Saturday. He was not a bad person, perhaps, just curious. She tried to sense him, this man looming above her, out of her line of sight.

He stepped back, lifted her a bit more with the machete beneath her chin, then pulled the top of her T-shirt out with the point. Oh, he was trying to see her breasts, but they were small and unimpressive, hidden in a close-fitting, elastic bra. She felt herself flush with a sudden impulse to swat at him. Who was he to take this . . . this look? After all, a mere look. Then, he moved away, quick and silent, his feet—feet of a thief, a potential rapist, a silent man whose language she did not share—disappearing from view.

She walked back to town because she had no money for the bus. Adrenaline ran through her like fresh water. How strange that a small man with a fierce beak of a nose had made her bow, had taken five dollars from her, and looked down her shirt. It was as if he'd be-knighted her. She did not feel violated. This was the oddity of aborted danger; it left you feeling blessed. And merely because you'd looked down the throat of pain and suffering and death, you felt deserving of the bit of life left to you. On her right, the hillside was planted with ragged cornstalks in steep patches. Why didn't they terrace their fields? Everything felt mysterious, strangely wonderful and wonderfully strange. The air smelled dry and sharp, like geraniums, with the slightly burnt scent of coffee.

Olivia brought coffee, pineapple, and a scrambled egg into the dining room. No sign of Fritz, she said and wiped at the dark circles beneath her eyes. Ellen couldn't look at her fallen face. She bent to her plate and concentrated on the radio's stream of prayer. The Virgin del Rosario's mysteries were being detailed each morning. What good did this do anyone? Its chanting repetition made her feel sarcastic. Olivia turned her large, suffering eyes to Ellen. Would she come to mass with her? Ellen glanced at the painting of the Last Supper, then leaned over to retie her shoes. If this were her real family, she would say no without hesitation. You could deny anything to the people you loved, but you were obligated to strangers.

Leaving the dishes in the stone sink, Olivia put on pink lipstick and arranged a rose-patterned scarf over her shoulders, and she and Ellen went to mass.

Inside the church, in the empty space behind the pews, hundreds of people knelt on the cold, stone floor. Olivia chose a pew, greeting a few people. She whispered to Ellen that it was the month of the Festival of the Virgin del Rosario. Her breath feathered at Ellen's ear, evoking a memory from childhood of whispering in church with her sister for the sake of the sensual tickle of breath against the tender skin of an ear. She thought about Charlie, then Fernando, then the man with the machete. The priest droned, and the people responded, as if from one throat. Ellen didn't feel religious. Her back ached terribly, her knees hurt, her hands and her neck were cold. The smell of candle wax and incense plagued the headache she always seemed to have.

She looked around. She was surrounded by several hundred unsmiling people on their knees in a building made entirely of gray stone, praying in unison. Hoping for simplicity, craving relief from their mistakes. The sound filled the frigid air around her, pressing against her chest: the noises whales made, the rumbling of a volcano, song of prayer. Olivia's head was bowed in prayer, or defeat. Fritz would be fine, or not. It was out of Olivia's hands. Ellen remembered the feel of Fernando's delicate body against her own. She looked up at the Virgin, who gazed down the length of the transept with an expression of such depression and desolation you wanted to offer her a vodka tonic, some Prozac, a piece of fruit, anything. She held a chubby, golden-shoed baby with an adult face and head, wearing a crown and clutching a dove. His head was dropped back as if in ecstasy, or maybe his neck was broken. An old woman in front of Ellen began to cough in convulsive spasms, as if she were trying to throw a knot of air from inside her. Ellen stared at the sorrowful Virgin absently cradling her malformed child. And all the stories of death and disaster filled her head, trickled down into her heart. Her heart was filling and filling with water. Her throat turned into a rock, her eyes burned. She concentrated on the dry, twisting cough of the old woman. She thought of the battles in *The Iliad,* the gruesomeness of human affliction and destruction. Remembering how eyes were stabbed and guts pushed out, the graphic quality of the mayhem calmed her a little. Human beings were destined for messy endings. Still, she might weep in the midst of this orderly mass.

Ellen fled. She stumbled over knees in the aisle, half-ran toward the doors, then walked the streets without thought, grateful for the secular beat of idling cars and the perfume of diesel. And there was Don Pablo on a corner, hands in his pockets, smiling at nothing. She shouted buenas at him, and he gazed at her as if he might know her, or perhaps he imagined she was someone else entirely, someone he'd once known. Seeing him in public, it was obvious how derelict he was: a man who hadn't showered in weeks, never combed his hair, or rinsed his glasses, or changed his pants. A parked bus beside him had an ornately decorative sign on its forehead: La Sombra del Amor Sufre al Verme. The shadow, she translated. Of love... Then she hesitated, looking over her shoulder as if for someone to confirm her translation, or correct her. There was no one. She read the sign again, wondering what it was doing there, on a bus, in Spanish, in a Central American town, this message: The shadow of love suffers to see me.

ABOUT ANTONYA NELSON

A Profile by Merrill Feitell

Ask most writers about their craft, and they'll likely talk about character, setting, and narrative arc—the simple rise and fall of dramatic action. Ask Antonya Nelson, and she'll surprise you with the structures and schematics she refers to as *shape.*

Her story "Loaded Gun," for instance, tells of a teenager's mounting frustration with her family life, but Nelson explains that it's actually written in the *shape* of a gun. "Each little secret, of which there are six," she says, "is being loaded into the chamber of a teenage girl's barrel or mind, until she's ready to discharge—at her mother."

Or consider her current project, a novel about a woman's search for solitude, which Nelson says takes the shape of a word game she likes to play with her son. The object of the game is to change one word into another by adjusting only one letter at a time, morphing, for example, "call" into "home" in the fewest moves. The impact of this shape on her fiction? "It's really become a story of acquisition. Each scene introduces another character, rendering this woman a step further from solitude every time."

Forget Nabokov. Such playfully intricate operating systems recall the sharp-minded antics of Hollywood's most enchanting serial killers. But these so-called shapes are primarily clues for Nelson and her writing process, not for her readers. In fact, she prefers that the reader not detect them at all. "I like stories best when I can't discern the shape in the first reading—but I can feel its effects working on me." To her credit, one could read "Loaded Gun" a hundred times without ever detecting the six-shooter design. Yet even though this structure is invisible, one can't help but feel the inherent mounting tension, the accumulation of ammunition and power. Both the explicit work of the narrative and the implicit structure conspire to make the story resonate in ways the conscious mind can't even understand. With her piercing insights, dogged characters, and sinewy prose—and the oddly affecting suggestions of shape—Nelson's fiction both engages and haunts.

For this work, among many other honors, she has been awarded a Guggenheim fellowship, a National Endowment for the Arts grant, and a Rea Award for the Short Story, and was named by *The New Yorker* as one of the "twenty young fiction writers for the new millennium" and by *Granta* as among the "best of the young American novelists."

Nelson was born in 1961 in Wichita, Kansas, and grew up there as the middle child of five siblings in an intellectually stimulating household. Both her parents were English professors, her mother also a writer, and family lore has it that Allen Ginsberg, in one of his poems, refers to a young Antonya sitting on his lap during a visit to her family's house.

Nelson was always a bookworm. Even in her earliest writing, she found she had a good phonic sense, and postulates that if someone had steered her toward poetry, she probably would have gone there. Instead, she found herself in a fiction writing workshop at the University of Kansas and realized that "this was where I feel the most comfortable, working with the malleable text, shaping it rather than criticizing it."

After earning her M.F.A. from the University of Arizona in 1986, her story "The Expendables" was selected by Raymond Carver as a first-prize winner for the journal *American Fiction* in 1988. A collection by the same title won the Flannery O'Connor Award and was published in 1990, followed by two more story collections, *In the Land of Men* (1992) and *Family Terrorists* (1994), the title story of which was a novella, paving her way to the longer form. She then published three novels, *Talking in Bed* (1996), *Nobody's Girl* (1998), and *Living to Tell* (2000), and returned to stories with *Female Trouble* (2002).

Despite the success and acclaim of all three novels, Nelson still feels most at home in the short story form. "The novel is daunting to me still. I still feel very much a beginner at it. I don't want to write a slack novel," she says. She finds validation in the fact that all three of her novels began as short stories—and resisted—proving that the scope of their content simply couldn't conform or be contained.

Since her publishing debut, there has been a steady drive forward, Nelson producing a new book nearly every two years. "I don't tolerate boredom well," Nelson says. "I have to constantly

Jack Parsons

change things up—buy a new pet, repaint. I am always busy doing shit." In addition, Nelson owns up to a competitive streak—not against anyone in particular insomuch as she is challenged by a potential project itself. "I was a drag as a child, too critical, too perfectionist. It made me want to try to do things—and try to do them better."

In addition to writing, Nelson also teaches, dividing her time between New Mexico State University and the University of Houston, where she shares a chair with her husband, the writer Robert Boswell. She gets immense pleasure from teaching because, she says, it keeps her engaged with questions of writing and because she likes being around students. "They're funny and lively, and generally at a point of transition."

Her latest offering, *Some Fun,* is a collection of stories forthcoming in March 2006. The title refers to both a line from the John Prine song "Illegal Smile" and one at the end of the Flannery O'Connor story "A Good Man Is Hard to Find," ironically layering the former's wry nothing-to-lose optimism with the latter's deranged and inevitable defeat—yet another instance of Nelson's harrowing wit and attentive brand of play.

Clearly, there is very little lost on Nelson; her attentiveness is palpable just being in her presence. She is nimble with chitchat and pop culture (as often evidenced in her comic dialogue), a good drinker and laugher, and you can feel her ease with the momentum of hanging out and storytelling with a group. Yet even in the throes of such social exuberance, her writerly eye is still at work. To view a group telling jokes through the lens of her keen psychological awareness is like watching stories almost write themselves. She says, "A lot of inspiration comes from noting the gesture or expression that's most often missed. The one that doesn't quite line up with what's happening in the moment. Often there is a story there."

More often than not, Nelson writes about families—big Midwestern families similar to the one in which she was raised, and similar to that which she heads up with Boswell (they have two children, Jade and Noah). Some of her stories grow out of fictional projections of actual dynamics—which makes having another writer in the family a relief. "Robert understands what fiction is and what it does to facts, so we have developed a certain necessary immunity." But Nelson can find inspiration for her stories and novels anywhere. She can recite details of the most tawdry tabloid dramas from memory, puzzling over the fictive shape a given salacious conflict could take—and searching for the place it intersects with her life. "I just have to find something—the smallest or largest aspect of the dilemma—that has to do with me."

In the stories from the forthcoming *Some Fun,* Nelson forges a rugged and acute exploration across a wide terrain of family, adultery, and unhinged youth. Whatever the particular contours she had in mind while writing, these stories seem to spread out from their central protagonists, the impact of any given action echoing to the very edges of a group, lending an empathic omniscience to even a third-person limited narrative, and most often rendering these complex characters as forgivable as they are forgiving. In "Dick," a woman ponders if her decision to move her family from Los Angeles is ultimately responsible for the disappearance of her young son's friend: "She feared that [her son] would utter her own suspicion, that it had been their departure that set events in motion. That in some skewed way she, Ann, was directly responsible for the boy's sorrow, for the reverberating despair of everyone who knew him."

While Nelson might claim that the short form engages with an individual while novels take on a community, in these stories she often manages to wrestle with and illuminate both at once. With her savvy, her prose, and her abundant empathy, there is surely no individual Nelson couldn't capture. Yet the effects one feels of these stories go beyond the individual, as if, in the writing, Nelson is moving outward from each character in concentric circles, mindful of that individual's bliss and torment—and of everything left in its wake.

Perhaps it's such an obsession with this scope that inspired her to take on the writing of another novel. Or perhaps she's just demonstrating that in the right hands, with the right shape in mind, what can be done with the two forms is not so very different after all.

Merrill Feitell is the author of the story collection Here Beneath Low-Flying Planes, *which won the 2004 Iowa Short Fiction Award. Her stories have appeared in* Glimmer Train, Best New American Voices, The Virginia Quarterly Review, *and elsewhere. She is currently at work on a novel and a screenplay. Visit www.merrillfeitell.com.*

POSTSCRIPTS

Miscellaneous Notes · Fall 2005

COHEN AWARDS Each year, we honor the best poem and short story published in *Ploughshares* with the Cohen Awards, which are wholly sponsored by our longtime patrons Denise and Mel Cohen. Finalists are nominated by staff editors, and the winners—each of whom receives a cash prize of $600—are selected by our advisory editors. The 2005 Cohen Awards for work published in *Ploughshares* in 2004, Volume 30, go to Daisy Fried and Xu Xi. (All of the works mentioned here are accessible on our website at www.pshares.org.)

DAISY FRIED *for her poem "Shooting Kinesha" in Spring 2004, edited by Campbell McGrath.*

Daisy Fried was born in Ithaca, New York, in 1967. The daughter of a wildlife biologist and an early childhood education teacher—both of them also writers—she grew up in Albany, New York, and graduated with a B.A. in English from Swarthmore College in 1989. After a series of post-college slacker-type jobs in Philadelphia, she worked in the mid-nineties as a staff writer for alternative weekly newspapers, first *Philadelphia Weekly*, then *Philadelphia City Paper*. The discipline of a weekly deadline leaked into her occasional poetry writing, and poetry writing took over. Though she still occasionally freelances, she has supported herself since 1998 with a combination of poetry fellowships, grants, and part-time teaching.

She is the author of two books of poetry, *My Brother Is Getting Arrested Again* (forthcoming from the University of Pittsburgh Press in 2006) and *She Didn't Mean to Do It* (Pittsburgh, 2000), which won the Agnes Lynch Starrett Prize. She was a 2004–05 Hodder Fellow at Princeton University, a 2002 Bread Loaf Fellow, and a 1998 Pew Fellow in poetry. The recipient of the 2001 Leeway Award for Excellence in poetry, she has taught creative writing in Warren Wilson College's low-residency M.F.A. program, at Haverford College, University of Pennsylvania, and Rutgers–New Brunswick. She is currently the Grace Hazard Conkling Writer-in-Residence at Smith College. She lives in Northampton, Massachusetts, and Philadelphia with her husband, the writer Jim Quinn, and their cat, Mister Buster. They travel as much as they can, mostly renting tiny cheap apartments in European capitals for a month or two at a time. She is working on her third book of poetry.

About "Shooting Kinesha," Fried writes: "My poems, particularly the longer narratives, accrue over time through a process of adding and sloughing, cutting and pasting, mixing together true stories and fiction, various things I'm thinking about, till all the parts seem necessary. I believe 'Shooting Kinesha' started when I was sitting with my husband at my favorite Philadelphia bar, the Standard Tap, drinking my favorite Philadelphia beer, Yards Love Stout, telling Jim something someone said to me that I thought was funny, and he said, 'That sounds like a poem.' Then all kinds of other things got in there and patterns began to emerge. I'm thirty-seven and have been to/heard about/been in a lot of weddings over the last ten years or so. People write a lot of epithalamiums, but I like the moment after the ceremony, when no one's sure what to do next, and everyone's life is pretty much going on the same, but you've still got the party to go to—which can be fun, but also means you've got a few more hours in your painful shoes.

Pierce Backes

"I like to see how much simultaneous humor and seriousness I can get into my work. I like specific settings and people having conversations inside quotation marks. I like at least a couple of other people besides my narrator in my poems. I like a poem that goes here and there but eventually finds its way, and which (maybe) enacts the process of realizing what it's about before the reader's eyes. And I'm interested in tones that don't often get into poetry, like querulousness and anxiety. Affirmation, consolation, and healing are, to me, pretty uninteresting."

XU XI *for her story "Famine" in Winter 2004–05, edited by Joy Harjo.*

Xu Xi was born in 1954 and raised in Hong Kong. An Indonesian citizen of Chinese ancestry, she spoke English and Cantonese as native languages, though neither was her parents' mother tongue. Her father was an international trader of manganese ore, her mother a pharmacist. Xu Xi started writing and publishing stories in English as a child and never stopped.

After getting her undergraduate degree in the US at the State University of New York at Plattsburgh, she went home and worked in international marketing for seven years. Her city inspired fiction, but offered little space for a writer in English. She left and flitted around Europe for a year, ending up at the University of Massachusetts, Amherst, where she got her M.F.A. Marketing jobs followed in Cincinnati, then New York, where she became a US citizen. After eleven years in the US, she found a job that returned her to Hong Kong. The greatest influence on her writing, she says, has been Hong Kong itself, "with its hybrid national and international culture, and linguistic mix." In 1998, she left corporate life forever, and now splits her time between New York, Hong Kong, and New Zealand. She teaches fiction in Vermont College's M.F.A. program.

Fellow Mui

Her books include three novels, *Chinese Walls, Hong Kong Rose,* and *The Unwalled City;* two fiction collections, *Daughters of Hui,* named an *Asiaweek* best book, and *History's Fiction;* one mixed-genre volume, *Overleaf Hong Kong;* and two companion anthologies of Hong Kong literature in English that she co-edited, *City Voices* and *City Stage.* Her honors include a New York Arts Foundation fiction fellowship, a State University of New York distinguished alumni award, and residencies at Chateau de Lavigny, Kulturhuset USF, the Jack Kerouac Project, and the Anderson Center. She is currently writing an essay collection, *Evanescent Isle: Glimpses of Hong Kong, My City Village,* and a novel inspired by Sino-US relations and Bugs Bunny. For more information, visit www.xuxiwriter.com.

About "Famine," Xu Xi writes: "The story was born of an old obsession, of existence comprising an above life and under life, something that became my mantra when I first started writing fiction as a child. I wanted to merge the faces we wear in public with private longings, and push this idea to its outer limits. My longtime friend, an English teacher, was taking early retirement. She and I always met over leisurely, cuisine-centered dinners, and her anecdotes about teaching in Hong Kong schools informed my protagonist. The Plaza Hotel intruded because a traveler must arrive somewhere. And famine was China's horror under Mao, a historical truth worth remembering."

MORE AWARDS Our congratulations to the following writers, whose work has been selected for these anthologies:

BEST POETRY Beth Ann Fennelly's poem "I Need to Be More French. Or Japanese.," from the Spring 2004 issue edited by Campbell McGrath, will appear in *The Best American Poetry 2005* this September from Scribner, with Paul Muldoon as the guest editor and David Lehman as the series editor.

PUSHCART Daisy Fried's poem "Shooting Kinesha" and Cynthia Weiner's story "Boyfriends," from the Spring 2004 issue, have been selected for *The Pushcart Prize XXX: Best of the Small Presses,* which will be published by Bill Henderson's Pushcart Press this fall.

O. HENRY Xu Xi's "Famine" has been chosen for *The O. Henry Prize Stories 2006* by editor Laura Furman. The anthology will be published next May by Anchor Books.

BOOKSHELF

Books Recommended by Our Staff Editors

Mother of Sorrows, *stories by Richard McCann* (Pantheon): The pieces in this debut book are so tightly interwoven that the whole is novelistic, and they have a ring of truth to them so profound that the effect is practically memoiristic (indeed, one story was reprinted in an anthology of memoirs). The overall effect of the "sunstruck" suburban world of mourning and resurrection, evoked by the sole survivor of a family of four stricken by sudden death, addiction, and disease, is both luminous and surprisingly witty. "Our Mother of the Mixed Messages; Our Mother of Sudden Attentiveness; Our Mother of Sudden Anger; Our Mother of Apology," the narrator incants about his mom, in a moment that manifests the prose's capacity for capturing and evoking the contradictions within these complex characters. McCann is a clear-eyed poet who knows what sorrow is, and isn't afraid to give it to us in its kaleidoscope of grief and humor, fact and fiction. *—Fred Leebron*

The Maverick Room, *poems by Thomas Sayers Ellis* (Graywolf): In this marvelous and accomplished volume of poems, Ellis works the page the way his musical subjects (crooners, masters of funk, DC-based Go-Go bands) work a room: with rhythm, sass, and self-deprecating wit. The sonic effects of these poems duplicate the experience of listening to live music; as Ellis observes in his poem "Sticks": "[W]ords are part of speech / with breaths and beats of their own. / Interjections like flams. Wham! Bam!" Demonstrating an immense range in subject matter and formal invention, this collection serves up an education in the cultural appreciation of a history that is at once personal, collective, and necessarily political. These are gregarious poems, always socially conscious, that never shortchange the intelligence of the reader as they dissect, intersect, embrace, and reject traditional tropes of African American literature. The linguistic swerve of this book, rooted in the poetics of Gertrude Stein, elevates the pun; weaving and reweaving repetition, Ellis insists on having *fun* with his reader, in all the many senses of the word. *—Cate Marvin*

I Got Somebody in Staunton, *stories by William Henry Lewis* (Amistad): In his second collection, Lewis sketches out a complicated and often mesmerizing view of black America with lyrical, sensual language. Traveling up and down the paths of the Great Migration, from South to North, from small towns in Tennessee to Bed-Stuy, these ten stories brim with the sounds of chickadees and wrens, the smell of honeysuckle and kudzu. They trace abandonment and betrayal, love and lust, and, always, they remember history. The title story has a young professor agreeing to give a ride to a white woman he meets in a bar, but as they drive through the countryside, her brazen behavior—attracting the attention of some local rednecks—makes him recall his uncle's lectures about lynchings. Yet to conclude that Lewis's stories are grim would be wrong. His work conveys a crackling sense of humor and a seductive nostalgia: "The heat of the day had long given up, and the air was sweet, the way it is at four in the morning, when only drunks and lovers take notice." *—Don Lee*

Any Holy City, *poems by Mark Conway* (Silverfish): Conway's debut book, *Any Holy City,* maps a rich and mysterious landscape haunted by ghosts—ghosts of the dead and the living, of addiction, sacrifice, of loss and love. This place, however, is very much alive with a poet fully engaged in the natural and not-so-natural world around him: "We coast on an unlimited sequence / of yes and not-yes which gets us / where we're going. The darkness / deepens as we travel the electric divine." The result is a book buzzing with life; in fact, the background voices—a kind of primeval susurrus of mosquitoes, bees, gnats, and of all those ghosts—threaten to overwhelm the voice, or the present life, of the poet, but they don't; rather, all become part of a holy, human, witty, and very moving chorus: "*Stick it up your ass,* I sing, / and kick around my yard. Everything's / fine..." —*David Daniel*

EDITORS' SHELF

Books Recommended by Our Advisory Editors

Madeline DeFrees recommends *Cain's Daughters,* poems by Phyllis Collier: "From the Dust Bowl of Oklahoma to the labor camps of California, Collier follows the migration and celebrates the hard lives of pioneering women. *Cain's Daughters* is a singular example of the way art transcends and transforms the world of fact." (Blue Unicorn)

Philip Levine recommends *Nobody's Baby,* stories by Leo Litwak: "Leo Litwak, the author of the finest memoir of WWII combat I have read by an American, *The Medic,* again demonstrates his superb gift for narrative in this astonishing collection of short stories, *Nobody's Baby.* His insights into the complex motives of human behavior and the effects we have on each other feel utterly true. In these largely urban stories, Litwak presents us with a fascinating collection of characters, people largely under stress, people with the ordinary daily courage to endure because they must. He can be outrageously comic in stories that finally make you weep. The prose moves with that necessity we associate with true poetry. It is so rare to encounter such mastery and such humility in the same book." (El León Literary Arts)

Margot Livesey recommends *Tenney's Landing,* stories by Catherine Tudish: "I don't know quite how Catherine Tudish does it, but somehow in this remarkable collection of linked stories she evokes the people and places of Tenney's Landing so vividly and completely that every reader will surely want to take up residence in this small Pennsylvania river town." (Scribner)

Al Young recommends *White Lipstick,* poems by Geri Digiorno: "With these pages—sparsely worded, richly lived—Geri Digiorno reminds us how entangled the delicate roots and tendrils of family and 'individual' identity can become. Her lovingly subjective subjects include kin and neighborhood, coming of age, friendship, betrayal, initiation, baptism, masquerade, transformation, sexual discovery and conquest, marriage and parenthood. Sketching poetically, Digiorno—at heart a realist unafraid to risk sentimentality—relives a working-class life begun in San Francisco's Noe Valley. In clipped, lowercase memoir-vernacular, she tells all. In so doing, she serves up clues to the meaning of life worldwide." (Red Hen)

EDITORS' CORNER

New Books by Our Advisory Editors

Ann Beattie, *Follies,* stories: In nine scintillating stories and a novella, Beattie—with her keen, morbid wit—looks at baby boomers, aging parents, and the chance encounters that irrevocably alter lives. (Scribner)

Frank Bidart, *Star Dust,* poems: Finishing the sequence that began with his chapbook *Music Like Dirt,* Bidart illustrates with unforgettable passion that the dream beyond desire is rooted in the drive to create. (FSG)

Donald Hall, *The Best Day the Worst Day,* a memoir: This beautiful book's account of Hall's life with his late wife, the poet Jane Kenyon, is joyful, intimate, heartbreaking, and generous. (Houghton Mifflin)

Joyce Peseroff, *Simply Lasting: Writers on Jane Kenyon,* essays: Peseroff gathers personal and critical essays, letters, poems, and memoirs that piercingly celebrate Kenyon's spirit and charm. (Graywolf)

CONTRIBUTORS' NOTES

Fall 2005

BETH ALVARADO's story "Just Family" is from her collection, *Not a Matter of Love,* which won the MVP award from New Rivers Press and will be published in fall 2006. Her fiction and creative nonfiction have appeared in *Calyx, Northwest Review, Spork,* and *Cue,* a journal of prose poetry. She is a lecturer at the University of Arizona in Tucson.

GEOFFREY BECKER is the author of a collection of stories, *Dangerous Men,* and a novel, *Bluestown.* A past winner of the Drue Heinz Literature Prize, the Nelson Algren Award, and an NEA fellowship, his work has recently appeared in *The Antioch Review, Prairie Schooner,* and *The Best American Short Stories.* He lives in Baltimore, Maryland, and teaches at Towson University.

KATHERINE BELL is a graduate of the Iowa Writers' Workshop and the managing editor of *Harvard Review.* She lives in Somerville, Massachusetts, where she is writing her first novel. Her work has appeared previously in this magazine.

JON BILLMAN is the author of the story collection *When We Were Wolves.* He lives with his family in southern New Mexico.

FREDERICK BUSCH's new novel is *North,* published in May 2005 by W.W. Norton.

MAYSEY CRADDOCK was born in Memphis, Tennessee, and graduated from Tulane University and Maine College of Art. Her work has appeared in group and solo exhibitions, mostly in the southern United States, since the mid-nineties. She is represented by the Francine Seders Gallery in Seattle, David Lusk Gallery in Memphis, and PanAmerican Gallery in Dallas. She is currently living in Munich, Germany.

LESLEY DORMEN's short stories have appeared or are forthcoming in *The Atlantic Monthly, Five Points, Open City, Glimmer Train,* and the anthology *20/40* (Mississippi). She is the recipient of fellowships from the MacDowell Colony and Yaddo, and teaches at The Writers Studio in New York City. She is completing a collection of short stories that includes "Curvy."

PETER GORDON's fiction has appeared in *The New Yorker, The Yale Review, Glimmer Train, The Carolina Quarterly, The Gettysburg Review, The North American Review, The Antioch Review,* and elsewhere. He is at work on a collection of stories. A Pushcart Prize winner, he lives in Framingham, Massachusetts, with his wife and two children.

CASEY GRAY was born and raised in southern Indiana. His piece in this issue is an excerpt from his first novel, *If There's a Hell I Hope You Burn There with the*

Others, which is being represented by Inkwell Management. This is his first published work.

ETHAN HAUSER's short stories have appeared in *Esquire, Playboy, Witness, The Antioch Review,* and *New Stories from the South: The Year's Best, 2005.* He lives in Brooklyn.

LAURA KASISCHKE's most recent novel is *The Life Before Her Eyes* (Harcourt, 2002). A new novel entitled *Boy Heaven* is forthcoming. She has also published six collections of poetry, and this year received an NEA fellowship. Her writing has appeared in *Harper's, The New Republic, The Iowa Review,* and elsewhere. She teaches in the M.F.A. program and the Residential College at the University of Michigan, and lives in Chelsea, Michigan.

LILY KING is the author of two novels, *The Pleasing Hour* (1999) and *The English Teacher* (2005), both with Grove/Atlantic. This is her second story to appear in *Ploughshares.* She is the recipient of the Barnes & Noble Discovery Prize and a Whiting Writer's Award. She lives in Maine with her husband and their two daughters.

KATHLEEN LEE is the author of *Travel Among Men,* a collection of stories. She is the recipient of a 1999 Rona Jaffe Writing Award. Sometimes she writes for *Condé Nast Traveler* magazine, and her travel essays appear in *Best American Travel Writing 2001* and *2002.*

~

GUEST EDITOR POLICY *Ploughshares* is published three times a year: mixed issues of poetry and fiction in the Spring and Winter and a fiction issue in the Fall, with each guest-edited by a different writer of prominence, usually one whose early work was published in the journal. Guest editors are invited to solicit up to half of their issues, with the other half selected from unsolicited manuscripts screened for them by staff editors. This guest editor policy is designed to introduce readers to different literary circles and tastes, and to offer a fuller representation of the range and diversity of contemporary letters than would be possible with a single editorship. Yet, at the same time, we expect every issue to reflect our overall standards of literary excellence. We liken *Ploughshares* to a theater company: each issue might have a different guest editor and different writers—just as a play will have a different director, playwright, and cast—but subscribers can count on a governing aesthetic, a consistency in literary values and quality, that is uniquely our own.

~

SUBMISSION POLICIES We welcome unsolicited manuscripts from August 1 to March 31 (postmark dates). All submissions sent from April to July are returned unread. In the past, guest editors often announced specific themes for issues, but we have revised our editorial policies and no longer restrict submissions to thematic topics. Submit your work at any time during our reading period; if a manuscript is not timely for one issue, it will be considered for another. We do not recommend trying to target specific guest editors. Our backlog is unpredictable, and staff editors ultimately have the responsibility of determining for which editor a work is most appropriate. Mail one prose piece or one to three poems. No e-mail submissions. Poems should be individually typed either single- or double-spaced on one side of the page. Prose should be typed double-spaced on one side and be no longer than thirty pages. Although we look primarily for short stories, we occasionally publish personal essays/memoirs. Novel excerpts are acceptable if self-contained. Unsolicited book reviews and criticism are not considered. Please do not send multiple submissions of the same genre, and do not send another manuscript until you hear about the first. *No more than a total of two submissions per reading period.* Additional submissions will be returned unread. Mail your manuscript in a page-size manila envelope, your full name and address written on the outside. In general, address submissions to the "Fiction Editor," "Poetry Editor," or "Nonfiction Editor," not to the guest or staff editors by name, unless you have a legitimate association with them or have been previously published in the magazine. Unsolicited work sent directly to a guest editor's home or office will be ignored and discarded; guest editors are formally instructed not to read such work. *All manuscripts and correspondence regarding submissions should be accompanied by a business-size, self-addressed, stamped envelope (S.A.S.E.) for a response only. Manuscript copies will be recycled, not returned.* No replies will be given by e-mail or postcard. Expect three to five months for a decision. We now receive well over a thousand manuscripts a month. Do not query us until five months have passed, and if you do, please write to us, including an S.A.S.E. and indicating the postmark date of submission, instead of calling or e-mailing. Simultaneous submissions are amenable as long as they are indicated as such and we are notified immediately upon acceptance elsewhere. We cannot accommodate revisions, changes of return address, or forgotten S.A.S.E.'s after the fact. We do not reprint previously published work. Translations are welcome if permission has been granted. We cannot be responsible for delay, loss, or damage. Payment is upon publication: $25/printed page, $50 minimum and $250 maximum per author, with two copies of the issue and a one-year subscription.